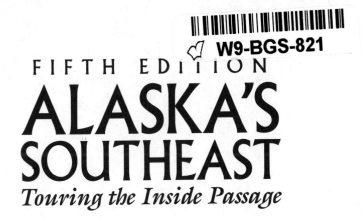
FIFTH EDITION
ALASKA'S
SOUTHEAST
Touring the Inside Passage

Sarah Eppenbach

A Voyager Book

The
Globe
Pequot
press

Old Saybrook, Connecticut

LIBRARY OF CONGRESS CATALOGING-IN-PUBLICATION DATA

Eppenbach, Sarah.
    Alaska's southeast : touring the Inside Passage / Sarah Eppenbach.
— 5th ed.
        p.   cm.
    "A Voyager book."
    Includes bibliographical references and index.
    ISBN 1-56440-363-7
    1. Alaska—Guidebooks. 2. Inside Passage—Guidebooks. I. Title.
F902.3.E66 1994
917.98'045—dc20   93-37920
                                                              CIP

Illustrations by Connie Hameedi.
Photographs by Larry Eppenbach unless noted otherwise.

Manufactured in the United States of America
Fifth Edition/Second Printing

Contents

List of Maps

Preface to the
Fifth Edition

My husband and I made our initial trip to Southeast Alaska in September of 1969. We sailed from Prince Rupert (where we saw the northern lights for the first time) on the Alaska ferry *Taku,* in the days when passengers on Alaska ferries were served by white-jacketed waiters in luxurious dining rooms. Alas, more practical heads have prevailed and the Alaska ferries have acquired a utilitarian image more in keeping with government service.

Nevertheless, in 1969 the ferries were close kin to cruise ships and we were enthralled with the blue and white vessels that transported Alaska's citizens "Outside" and home again with such style and grace. It is many years ago now, but I remember the sensation of steaming steadily northward, the pace never slackening or hastening, past vast island wildernesses and forested inlets, past corrugated glaciers and rocky beaches, as we made our way from one isolated settlement to the next along the Inside Passage.

That first trip to Alaska was to get acquainted. When we reached Juneau we jumped on a plane and toured the rest of the state: north to Point Barrow, west to Nome, then down to Fairbanks, Anchorage, and the Kenai Peninsula. Every place we went we saw spectacular mountain and water views, but our hearts went out to the gray-green landscape of Southeast Alaska, with the great cloaking forests and endlessly branching waterways. We determined to come back one day and stay.

We moved to Southeast in 1971, in winter, with no idea what our future would be. In the days that followed, we moved from the best hotel in Juneau to the better and the not-so-good before my husband was offered a job as a research analyst with the treasury division of the Alaska Department of Revenue. Those were memorable times for anyone in the field of economics and investment theory. Alaska was already launched down the path to immense oil revenues, and treasury was just about the most exciting place in the world to be employed.

Some things have changed in the more than twenty years since we moved to Southeast Alaska. Clear-cuts now dot the Tongass National Forest—logging roads have scissored open the cloaking swaths of green. Towns have sprouted taller buildings, wider sidewalks, flower boxes. Today we have more traffic lights, and more petty crime. When we first came to Alaska, people routinely left their car keys in the vehicle and couldn't remember where they'd last seen the house keys. That's changed, in Juneau at least. (Now we know where the house keys are; we just don't always lock the door.) The gap between the Lower 48 and Alaska has narrowed. We have McDonalds and Burger King. There's not a major town in Southeast where you can't start your day with a latte.

But many more important things have stayed the same. Southeast Alaska is still a watercolor study of cool grays and greens and glacial blues. The passage north from Bellingham or Prince Rupert remains one of the fine experiences in life. Crossing that broad boundary of Dixon Entrance that separates Alaska from the world "down there," the mountains grow perceptibly taller, the landscape distinctly wilder. The people who live in this vast land continue to be the most energetic, personable, and generous of any I know. Alaskans will open their homes to you, lend you their cars, give you their time on the strength of a smile.

Certainly they have been generous to me. As I have returned time after time to the communities of Southeast Alaska, I have never encountered a single person who was not willing to help. I am especially grateful to those staffing the visitor information centers who have given me such assistance throughout the years. In this same vein I offer my thanks to the dozens of employees in state and federal agencies (most particularly, the Alaska departments of Fish and Game, Commerce and Economic Development, Community and Regional Affairs, and Transportation and Public Facilities; and the USDA Forest Service, National Park Service, and U.S. Coast Guard) who interrupted their duties to answer my questions. I appreciate as well the financial assistance provided by a Juneau Arts and Humanities Council Individual Artists Assistance Grant, which partially funded computer equipment for this project; the transportation assistance afforded by the Alaska Marine Highway System; and the many other courtesies extended to me during my travels.

And so to you, fellow traveler: Whether your interests lie in fishing, camping, kayaking, hiking, walking on glaciers, photographing wildlife, viewing totem poles, or simply sampling life in Southeast's towns and villages, may your journey through the Inside Passage be as filled with wonder and adventure as ours was that first time, and may you return again and again to savor Alaska's Southeast.

Wherever you go and whatever you do in the outdoors, move at Nature's pace, seeking not to impose yourself but to lose yourself. If you must leave footprints, make them not with blindness but with care and awareness of the delicate balance around you. And if you must take souvenirs, take them not in your pockets but in your mind and spirit. In preservation lies the promise of renewal.

PART I:
Getting Acquainted with Alaska's Southeast

SOUTHEAST ALASKA

ALEXANDER ARCHIPELAGO

Chapter 1
Southeast Traveler Basics

There are ten million acres of forest in Southeast Alaska; 1,000 islands, 10,000 miles of shoreline, 50 to 70 major glaciers, 25,000
brown bears, 15,000 bald eagles, and 70,000 people. The people
have caused a blight here or there upon the land, but on the whole
have had little visible effect. When you visit this land of cascading
glaciers and forested islands, you will look upon a part of the
earth that has changed remarkably little in the past one thousand
years. The deep green fjords that you travel by cruise ship or ferry
appeared largely the same to the Tlingit and Haida Indians who
plied these shores in their cedar canoes. Now, as then, stands of
giant spruce and hemlock reach toward the mountain peaks,
while thickets of wild berries run rampant over the land.

We of the twentieth century, contemplating matters from the
womb-like comfort of our heated living rooms, think of Southeast
Alaska as prohibitively cool and wet for aboriginal dwellers, but
the early Native residents knew it for what it truly is: a hospitable
land. The climate was temperate—yes, *temperate*. The rain forest
provided an environment that was pleasantly cool most of the
time and seldom so cold, even in winter, that a fire and some animal skins could not provide adequate warmth within the walls of
a planked enclosure.

The forest and the sea provided all the food that could be
wanted, and it was easily gathered. The Tlingit and Haida Indians
did not need to range far to feed their people: they went down to the
mouth of the salmon stream and harvested the required amount
of fish. For a change of pace, they sent a line down to the bottom
and brought up a halibut. Or a snapper. Or a crab. Salmonberries,
blueberries, nagoonberries, crowberries, cloudberries, thimbleberries, cranberries, currants, and more grew in profusion.

The land provided food, shelter, fuel, and transportation.
There were no lions, tigers, or crocodiles to prey on helpless humans, not a single poisonous snake or insect. There was only the
occasional grizzly or the icy water that could snatch a precious life
in moments.

Southeast Alaska is still a hospitable land. Those of us lucky

enough to live along this forested coast know that the land continues to provide food, fuel, shelter, and spiritual solace in generous
portions. The cold, clear waterways—so beautiful to gaze upon—
still provide the only certain link between communities. Water is
our lifeline.

The waterfront atmosphere enjoyed by all Inside Passage
towns is a unique aspect of Southeast Alaska. There are few
places in the world where the toot of a ferryboat heralds an important event, but in Southeast Alaska an entire population relies
upon this gentle means of transport for supplies and transportation. An automobile takes you only about 30 miles in most Southeast communities. Only one road south of Haines or Skagway
connects with the outside world, at Hyder, a community of 100
people at the head of the Portland Canal. The water is our highway. You will find the true Southeast Alaska down at the docks,
where fishing boats are unloading salmon, freighters are onload-
ing lumber, ferries and cruise ships are off-loading passengers,
and tugs and barges are delivering appliances and automobiles to
a grateful population.

WHEN TO GO

No matter what month of the year you make your trip, you
probably will not be able to escape some of the soggy weather that
keeps Southeast Alaska so deliciously green. There is no dry season in Southeast. Statistically speaking, May and June are the
sunniest months of the year and October the wettest, but picking
the right time to travel in Southeast is a little like betting on
horses—you can study the racing forms all you like, but you still
need a measure of luck. Traveling in May gives you the added advantage of beating the crowds, but temperatures can be in the
fifties and below. Many areas will be recently emerged from the
winter snow cover, and the scenery may not be at its prime. For
most people, June is the best choice, followed by July and August.

More and more visitors are venturing into Southeast in winter
for a less conventional view of the country. Besides the weather,
the obvious disadvantage to winter travel is that many exhibits,
shows, and excursions (including Glacier Bay) will be unavailable.
Cruise ships do not travel the Inside Passage in winter, so you
must fly or take the Alaska state ferry. Winter sports enthusiasts,
however, find Southeast at its best in this season, when the snow
transforms alpine meadows and open muskegs into vast, spark-

Eaglecrest ski area near Juneau offers downhill and cross-country skiing without lengthy lift lines. (Mark Kelley)

ling playgrounds for snowshoes and cross-country skis. Eaglecrest ski area in Juneau provides downhill skiing for all skill levels. Winter is also the time to view the world's largest gathering of bald eagles at the Chilkat Bald Eagle Preserve near Haines, to see the various Southeast communities in their everyday dress, and to take advantage of lower fares and guaranteed staterooms on Alaska state ferries.

WHAT TO BRING AND WEAR

Southeast Alaska is a casual place, where formal dress has little practicality. The most important factor for residents and visitors alike is comfort, which means dressing to stay warm and dry. Southeast Alaska can be wet and cool—with temperatures in the fifties even in summer—and wet plus cold makes an unpleasant and even dangerous combination. You will not enjoy walking around to see the sights unless you are adequately dressed.

Alaskans find that dressing in layers offers the optimum protection against the elements. Whatever time of year you visit, your most important article of clothing will be something to keep you warm. For example, wear a wool or fiberfill coat over a layer of moderate weight, such as a cotton turtleneck and sweater. Or, choose a warm underlayer—a heavy wool sweater, polyester fleece pullover, down or fiberfill vest—and top with a lighter jacket or windbreaker. Your outermost layer should be water-repellent. If your jacket or coat does not offer sufficient protection, bring a fold-up poncho or raincoat for rainy days. If you will be traveling in the shoulder seasons, equip yourself with a set of ultra-lightweight long underwear (such as silk), in case you need an extra layer.

Footgear should be comfortable for walking in wet conditions. Good choices include rubber, or crepe-soled walking shoes, athletic shoes, lightweight day-hikers, and rubber-soled moccasins. Rubber rain boots are always in fashion in Southeast Alaska. Bring a rain hat and also a warm hat and gloves for shipboard and for sightseeing around glaciers, even in summer.

Other items to consider bringing include a folding umbrella, insect repellent, and sunscreen. Also try to tuck in some good binoculars. Cruising along the quiet waterways of the Inside Passage, you will want to look closely at eagles, whales, glaciers, fishing boats—so many things.

USING THE ALASKA STATE FERRIES

The Alaska Marine Highway System has been in official service since 1963 when the motor vessels *Malaspina, Taku,* and *Matanuska* came on line—the first of the popular state ferries. Each of the blue-hulled ships was outfitted to carry 108 cars and 500 passengers on the regular service between Prince Rupert (British Columbia) and Haines. Today the Southeast fleet has expanded to four main-line ferries (the three mentioned previously plus the flagship *Columbia*) and two smaller ferries (the *Aurora* and *LeConte*). A new 380-foot vessel is planned to be on line for 1996.

THE SOUTHEAST FLEET

NAME OF VESSEL	CRUISING SPEED	LENGTH	PASSENGERS*	VEHICLES*	STATEROOMS
Columbia	17.3 knots	418 feet	625	158	91
Malaspina	16.5 knots	408 feet	500	107	84
Matanuska	16.5 knots	408 feet	500	108	108
Taku	16.5 knots	352 feet	475	83	44
Aurora	14.5 knots	235 feet	250	44	—
LeConte	14.5 knots	235 feet	250	44	—

*functional booking capacity

Southeastern ferry travelers rush to the solarium deck when the sun comes out. Sleeping bags top the lounge chairs at night.

The main-line service operates year-round, connecting the major communities of Southeast Alaska with each other and with the Lower 48 and Canada. There are two different routes to the system. One operates between Bellingham, Washington (85 miles north of Seattle) and Skagway, Alaska; the other between Prince Rupert, British Columbia (linking with the provincial ferry system) and Skagway. All the major Inside Passage towns, including Ketchikan, Wrangell, Petersburg, Sitka, Juneau, Haines, and Skagway, are served on both the Bellingham and Prince Rupert routes. The smaller vessels fill in the gaps with short-distance hauls to the smaller communities of Metlakatla, Hollis, Kake, Angoon, Hoonah, Tenakee Springs, Pelican, and Stewart/Hyder (summer only) off the main route. All of the vessels carry automobiles (including campers and trailers) as well as passengers.

The main-line vessels operate just like regular passenger ships except that transportation, and not luxury, is their aim. They feature functional staterooms, deck chairs, movies, video games, observation lounges, cocktail bars and dining rooms. There is elevator and wheelchair access to cabins.

If you do not want to pay for a stateroom, you can doze in a reclining chair or spread your sleeping bag on the floor. (You cannot sleep in your vehicle as the car deck is off limits between ports.)

All ships are equipped with a heated, glassed-in solarium on the top deck, an ideal spot for sleeping out-of-doors without getting wet. Coin lockers and public shower rooms are available, too, and you can rent a towel, pillow, or blanket on the four larger vessels. Neither of the two smaller ferries has staterooms. Overnight passengers stretch out in the lounge chairs in the solarium, or on the floor.

The meals aboard the ferries are self-service (the *Columbia* offers both restaurant service and cafeteria meals). In general, the self-service fare tends to be plain but adequate, ranging from sandwiches, salads, fresh fruit, and yogurt to hot entrees such as pasta and seafood, as well as the standard burger and fries. Travelers from the Lower 48, especially families with children, will probably find the meals expensive. It will help to carry aboard your own supply of fresh fruit, snacks, and sandwich makings. (Passengers are welcome to bring food aboard any of the Alaska state ferries, but cooking is not permitted.)

In summer, U.S. Forest Service interpreters are on board the main-line ferries to point out sights along the route, answer questions, and enhance your enjoyment of Alaska's scenic wilderness. Musicians, storytellers, or other artists from the Pacific Northwest might also be aboard to inform and entertain passengers as part of the Alaska Marine Highway's Arts-on-Board program.

Fares are charged from the port of embarkation to the port of debarkation. There is no additional charge for stopovers if they are reserved at the same time as the rest of the itinerary. If added later, they will be charged at the port-to-port rate, which may be slightly higher. Passenger and vehicle fares are reduced during the off-season, October 1 through April 30. Depending on the season, discounted rates may also be available to senior citizens and to passengers with disabilities.

You can design your whole trip around the state ferry system if you are willing to plan in advance. You can leave for Alaska from either Bellingham or Prince Rupert and stop at any port along the way to Skagway, and back. Get off and spend a few days in each town, then resume your trek on another ferry—providing you have made reservations if you have a vehicle or want a stateroom. With judicious planning, however, you can schedule your travels so that you make virtually every leg of the trip in the daytime and do not need a stateroom at all. In this case, foot passengers will need reservations for passage only if traveling during a heavy traffic period such as the weekend of the Southeast State Fair in Haines in August, or the Little Norway Festival in Petersburg in May.

Ferries link towns along the Inside Passage. Smaller vessels like the Aurora *serve communities off the main line.*

You can use the small vessels to make side trips from the major communities and investigate what most tourists miss. You can take the *Aurora* from Ketchikan to Prince of Wales Island, for example, and explore for days. There are several hotels and lodges where you can stay on the island. Take a day trip to Metlakatla; you can go over and back from Ketchikan in one day. Go to Tenakee Springs and spend a few restful hours in the hot sulfur baths, or go to Angoon on Admiralty Island and watch the tide boil through the narrow entrance of Kootznahoo Inlet. (See "Off the Main Line," page 277, for additional information.)

You can take your car or camper on the ferry, but should you? I would recommend against it, unless you particularly want to camp out, or unless you intend to get off at Skagway or Haines to connect up with the Alaska Highway for the trip to Interior Alaska or down to the Lower 48. Once arrived in each town, you will probably want to do most of your exploring on foot. If you decide to do some sightseeing outside of the city center, you can always rent a car or hire a taxi. It is decidedly more expensive to take a car, and you will spend precious time waiting in ferry lines—especially if you plan to get off and on at several communities.

APPROXIMATE MILEAGE AND SAILING TIME
BETWEEN PORTS ON THE
ALASKA MARINE HIGHWAY SYSTEM

PORTS	SAILING TIME	STATUTE MILES
Bellingham to Ketchikan	36 hours	595
Prince Rupert to Ketchikan	6 hours	91
Ketchikan to Wrangell	6 hours	89
Wrangell to Petersburg	3 hours	41
Petersburg to Juneau	7 hours, 30 minutes	123
Juneau to Haines	4 hours, 30 minutes	68
Haines to Skagway	1 hour	13
Petersburg to Sitka	10 hours	156
Sitka to Juneau	8 hours, 45 minutes	132

Reservations for peak season travel present something of a Catch-22. Summer sailings from Bellingham are so popular that you need to reserve early, but the summer sailing schedule does not come out until mid-November, with bookings typically opening on December 1. The Alaska Marine Highway reservations office accepts written requests for reservations at any time, but since the schedule will not be available yet, you will have to give the approximate dates you want to travel. Telephone requests are accepted as of the first working day in December. On that date, written and telephone requests are processed simultaneously, written ones in the order received. Because telephone lines are usually jammed, your best chance is to send in your written request well before the first of December.

Ideally, you should begin planning your trip a year in advance by writing for current schedule and tariff information. Even though the schedule will be out of date for your trip, you can get an idea of the itinerary you want to work out. Then, as far in advance as possible, put in your written request for reservations. Keep in mind that ships departing from Prince Rupert are usually less booked than those leaving from Bellingham, and southward bound ferries are usually less booked than those heading north. Try to be flexible in your planning and provide the reservations office with several alternative dates. For current schedules and reservations write *Alaska Marine Highway, P.O. Box 25535, Juneau, Alaska 99802-5535;* telephone *(907) 465–3941* or toll free *(800) 642–0066 (800–665–6414 from Canada).* If you are unable to get through on these central reservation/information lines, try telephoning one or more of the Alaska Marine Highway terminals (see Information

Sources, page 335, for telephone numbers). Any of the ferry terminals can handle reservations and information requests; however,
they usually are staffed only during ferry arrivals and departures.
Ellen Searby, a former Marine Highway employee, details the
workings of the Alaska ferry system in her book, *Alaska's Inside
Passage Traveler* (see Suggested Reading, page 337).

You may be able to save on ferry travel by purchasing a multiday *AlaskaPass*. Similar to European rail passes, the *AlaskaPass*
entitles you to unlimited passage on Alaska and British Columbia
ferries as well as rail and motorcoach services in Alaska and
Canada. The program offers several options, including family and
senior citizen rates. Write *AlaskaPass, P.O. Box 351, Vashon, Washington 98070-0351;* telephone *(800) 248–7598* or *(206) 463–6550.*

TRAVELING BY CRUISE SHIP

The number of ships cruising the Inside Passage during the
mid-May through September cruise season increases every year.
In 1993, the roster included twelve cruise lines and twenty-six
ships (see table). Most of the ships embark from Vancouver and
follow one of two basic itineraries: a seven-day round-trip cruise
through the Inside Passage, or a ten-day or longer cruise that
takes in the Inside Passage and then crosses the Gulf of Alaska to
Southcentral Alaska ports. A few sailings leave from Seattle or
other West Coast ports.

While itineraries differ, the typical Inside Passage journey includes stops at Ketchikan, Juneau, Skagway, and Sitka in addition to cruising Glacier Bay. You often have the option of cruising
in one direction and connecting with a land tour and/or flying in
the other. Ships stay in port for several hours to all day; you can
disembark and sightsee on your own or purchase shore excursions
from the ship (more expensive in most cases).

The ships cruising Alaska come in virtually every size and
style, from the most sumptuous vessel with all-outside staterooms
and private balconies to a serviceable "university at sea." The
trend in recent years has been to the two extremes. At one end of
the spectrum, increasingly larger ships (carrying 1,200 to 1,600
passengers) resemble floating resorts. They emphasize the luxury
cruise experience of fine dining, shipboard activities, and Las
Vegas-style nightclubs. At the other end of the spectrum, the
small ships (200 passengers or fewer) trade glamour for flexibility
and focus on the locale. They visit smaller, more out-of-the-way

ports and travel some of the more picturesque waterways of the Inside Passage. Holland America Westours and Princess Cruises are the giants of the luxury cruise industry, while Alaska Sightseeing dominates the small-ship scene.

In addition to ships cruising the Inside Passage from Vancouver, Seattle, or other southern ports, a number of small vessels make overnight or day cruises within Alaska to such scenic locales as Glacier Bay and Tracy Arm Fjord. You'll find many of these cruise opportunities mentioned later in chapter 8, "Main-Line Ports of the Inside Passage."

CRUISE SHIPS TRAVELING ALASKA'S INSIDE PASSAGE - 1993

Cruise Line	Ship	Passengers	Length
Alaska Sightseeing	Sheltered Seas*	90	90
	Spirit of Alaska	82	143
	Spirit of Discovery	84	166
	Spirit of Glacier Bay*	58	125
	Spirit of '98	101	192
Clipper Cruise Line	Yorktown Clipper	138	257
Costa Cruises	Costa Riviera	984	701
Cunard Line	Sagafjord	505	620
Holland America	Nieuw Amsterdam	1,214	704
Westours	Noordam	1,214	704
	Rotterdam	1,140	748
	Westerdam	1,500	800
Princess Cruises	Crown Princess	1,590	811
	Fair Princess	926	608
	Golden Princess	846	676
	Regal Princess	1,590	811
	Sky Princess	1200	789
	Star Princess	1,470	801
Regency Cruises	Regent Sea	756	631
	Regent Star	950	642
Royal Caribbean Cruise Line	Nordic Prince	1,012	637
Royal Cruise Line	Golden Odyssey	460	427
Special Expeditions	Sea Bird*	70	152
	Sea Lion*	70	152
World Explorer Cruises	Universe	550	564
Yacht Ship Cruise Lines	Executive Explorer*	49	104

Note: The cruise picture changes every season in Alaska. Check with your travel agent for current information regarding specific cruise lines, itineraries, and schedules.

*Cruises within Alaska only

BEFORE YOU GO

As a useful first step in planning your trip, write for the *Official State Guide and Vacation Planner* from the Alaska Division of Tourism/Tourism Marketing Council. This free color publication introduces all the regions of Alaska and includes more than 1,100 listings for hotels, campgrounds, sightseeing opportunities, charter companies, and other services, as well as local chambers of commerce and visitors' centers, state and national parks, and other government offices. Write *Alaska Tourism Marketing Council, Dept. 201, P.O. Box 110801, Juneau, Alaska 99811-0801.* You can obtain another excellent planning guide, *Alaska's Inside Passage*, free from the *Southeast Alaska Tourism Council, P.O. Box 20710, Juneau, Alaska 99802-0710.* See "Information Sources," page 335, for other useful addresses.

IF YOU WANT TO HUNT OR FISH

If you plan to hunt or fish, you should consult directly with the Alaska Department of Fish and Game for regulations concerning the particular quarry you have in mind. Write *Public Communications Section, Alaska Department of Fish and Game, P.O. Box 25526, Juneau, Alaska 99802-5526.* Several types of fishing, hunting, and trapping licenses are available. In general, a fishing license is required for anyone sixteen years or older fishing in fresh or salt water. For nonresidents of Alaska, four types of license are available: a one-year license ($50), fourteen-day license ($30), three-day license ($15), and one-day license ($10). Licenses are available at most sporting-goods stores in Alaska. You must also purchase a king salmon stamp if you intend to fish for kings (chinook).

Hunting licenses and appropriate tags are required for nonresidents of any age. Fees are $85 for a one-year license, or $135 for a one-year combination hunting and sport-fishing license. Tag fees, seasons, and bag limits vary with the species, so check with the Fish and Game Department in advance. Those wishing to hunt brown bear, mountain goat, or Dall sheep must be accompanied by either a registered guide or a relative within the second degree of kindred who is an Alaska resident and over age nineteen. ("Within the second degree of kindred" means blood relatives who are parents, grandparents, sisters, brothers, children, or grandchildren.) This rule is strictly interpreted and enforced. Visitors from other countries should check with the Fish and Game Department for special regulations pertaining to them. A list of registered guides is available for $5.00 from the *Alaska Department of Commerce and Economic Development, Division of Occupational Licensing, P.O. Box 110806, Juneau, Alaska 99811-0806.*

The Department of Fish and Game publishes free sport-fishing guides for various locales, and a fishing atlas of Southeast Alaska, *Salmon Holes and Halibut Hills,* printed on weather-resistant paper, that sells for $12.

IF YOU WANT TO CAMP

There are federal, state, or city campgrounds in all the major Inside Passage communities. Consult the *Alaska Vacation Planner* for specific sites, or write the appropriate chamber of commerce or visitors' bureau. In addition, you can camp almost anywhere in the Tongass National Forest (which encompasses much of Southeast Alaska). Exceptions include sensitive areas such as archaeological sites. No permit is necessary to camp or to build a fire, but you should be cautious about fires even in the rain forest. Many serious fires have been caused by campers who mistakenly thought the rain would put out their campfires for them. Not so: Use the same precautions you would camping anyplace else. Also be extremely wary of bear anywhere in the Tongass. Do not camp on known bear paths and do not leave food in or near your tent. Write the U.S. Forest Service or Alaska Department of Fish and Game for advice about camping and hiking in bear country.

There is a U.S. Forest Service office in almost every community along the Inside Passage. Staff members are glad to recommend places to camp, hike, or otherwise enjoy the national forest. Before striking out into the wilderness, it is a good idea to call or visit the local Forest Service office to ask their advice and let them know your plans.

For a wilderness adventure at a bargain price, consider renting a U.S. Forest Service recreational cabin. There are more than 170 from which to choose in the Tongass. Most are situated in remote locales: along saltwater inlets or freshwater lakes, accessible only by floatplane or boat. A couple are wheelchair-accessible. All cabins have a wood-burning or diesel stove, wooden bunks, and a table. Firewood is provided but not stove oil. Lakeside cabins are supposed to be equipped with a skiff and oars, but you should not depend upon either. For other equipment and food, you are on your own. In fact you are on your own, period, once the floatplane leaves, so plan accordingly. The cost is only $25 per night for your entire party, but you can spend $200–$300 for your round-trip

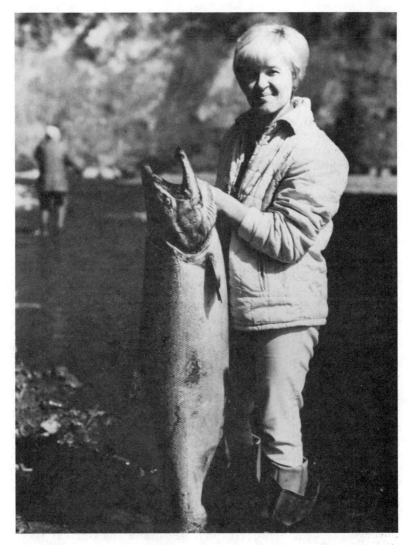

The king salmon lures many an angler to Southeast Alaska. (Alaska Department of Fish and Game)

transportation from the nearest town. Cabins can be reserved up to 180 days in advance for a maximum stay of seven nights (in summer). For a map of cabin locations and other information write *U.S. Forest Service, Centennial Hall, 101 Egan Drive, Juneau, Alaska 99801;* telephone *(907) 586–8751.*

VIEWING WILDLIFE

The Inside Passage abounds with wildlife: humpback and orca whales, bears, eagles, otter, deer, and more. The glossy brochures marketing Alaska destinations imply that you will see these creatures, up close and personal, practically at every turn. The truth is that you may see some spectacular wildlife displays, but you will probably not see as much wildlife as you would like, or as close as you would like, unless you travel into the more remote areas of Southeast. If you cruise the Inside Passage by tour ship or ferry, you will certainly see bald eagles—more, in fact, than you can imagine—and plenty of other birds. You will very likely see humpback whales, orca, and porpoise, although they may be in the distance. If you are very lucky, you may see a bear or black-tailed deer feeding on shore.

If wildlife viewing is a priority, you need to consider travel options that take you away from urban centers and heavily traveled waterways to places where wildlife congregates. This doesn't mean you have to go it alone in the wilderness. Wilderness lodges, simply as a function of their isolation, generally offer excellent wildlife viewing opportunities, as do smaller cruise ships and excursion vessels that travel the lonelier inlets and fjords. These include day trips to such locales as Tracy Arm near Juneau, overnight excursions into Glacier Bay or around Admiralty Island, and longer Inside Passage cruises. Finally, guided wilderness or nature trips offered by reputable companies such as Alaska Discovery take you safely into the wild country to observe the Southeast Alaska habitat and the creatures that live there.

There are three major designated wildlife viewing sites in Southeast Alaska, where animals can be observed in their natural habitat under conditions that optimize safety for both animals and humans. They are the Stan Price Bear Sanctuary at Pack Creek on Admiralty Island (see page 241), the Anan Creek Bear Observatory near Wrangell (page 190), and the Chilkat Bald Eagle Preserve near Haines (page 257).

Chapter 2
The Lay of the Land

If you look at a map of Alaska, you will see that the Southeast region consists of a narrow strip of coast wedged between the Pacific Ocean and the Canadian border and a multitude of sizable islands that lie offshore. The rest of Alaska is positioned far to the north in a distinctly separate chunk. The awkward shape of the state has been likened to that of a frying pan, which is why Southeast Alaska is frequently called the Panhandle.

Most of Southeast Alaska, whether island or mainland coast, is covered with either permanent snow and ice (10 percent) or with dense rain forest of spruce and hemlock (45 percent). The only exceptions are the alpine zones above tree level that are snow-free in summer, the marshy estuaries, and the river valleys that cut through the mountains to the sea.

THE PANHANDLE

The Panhandle extends from Dixon Entrance, which separates the Queen Charlotte Islands that lie in Canadian territory from their Alaska counterparts, to Icy Cape, on the western edge of Malaspina Glacier—a distance of some 600 miles. The mainland strip averages 120 miles across and is bounded by the Coast Mountains and the border between the United States and Canada that follows the line of the mountain peaks. These Coast Mountains are actually part of the Pacific Mountain System that continues along the coast to the north to take in the Saint Elias Mountains near Yakutat, the Chugach Mountains that border Prince William Sound, the Kenai Mountains that extend southward from Anchorage, the Kodiak Mountains on Kodiak Island, and the Aleutian Range. In total, this mountain system wraps 1,000 miles around the Pacific Coast. In Southeast, the most rugged of the Coast Mountains are those of the Fairweather Range, which forms the western edge of Glacier Bay, separating the national park and preserve from the Pacific Ocean. Mount

Glaciers flow out of ice fields high in the Coast Mountains.
(Tourism Collection, Alaska Historical Library)

Fairweather rises to 15,300 feet, the highest mountain in Southeast Alaska.

The coastal mountains extend into the Pacific Ocean to form a complex arrangement of mountainous islands called the Alexander Archipelago. Close to 1,000 in number, these islands constitute a major portion of the land mass of Southeast Alaska and contain four of the major communities in the area (Ketchikan, Wrangell, Petersburg, and Sitka) and most of the smaller ones as well. Several of the islands are more than 1,000 square miles in area. The largest is Prince of Wales Island, across Clarence Strait from Ketchikan, with 2,770 square miles.

Separating the islands from the mainland and one another is a veinlike system of waterways that has come to be known as the Inside Passage. Many of the waterways are fjords—narrow, deep sheer-sided troughs that were scraped out by advancing glaciers thousands of years ago and subsequently flooded by the sea. Some, such as Chatham Strait and Lynn Canal, follow faults that formed millions of years ago. The Inside Passage has served as a transportation and communication network since human beings first settled in Southeast Alaska. Even today, there is no road system to connect the communities along the Panhandle, and the waterways have taken the place of highways.

The rugged face of Southeast Alaska was carved during the Great Ice Age one million years ago. During this era, the Pleistocene, thick plates of ice covered all of the Panhandle except the very tops of the highest mountains and extended miles into the Pacific Ocean. Glaciers flowed down the natural drainage courses in the Coast Mountains, scouring the trenches into deep, narrow channels as they moved. When the Ice Age ended some 10,000 to 15,000 years ago, Southeast was frozen in place. As the climate warmed, the ice receded and ocean water flooded into the glacial trenches to form the fjords we see today. There followed other periods of cooler climate when the glaciers surged forward once again. The most recent was the Little Ice Age that culminated in the seventeenth and eighteenth centuries. Today, all but a few of the glaciers continue to retreat.

GLACIER FACTS

A glacier is an accumulation of snow and ice that continually flows from a mountain ice field toward sea level. Glaciers are formed when successive snowfalls pile up, creating pressure on the bottom layers. Gradually, the pressure causes the snow on the bottom to undergo a structural change into an extremely dense form of ice called glacier ice, a process that may take several years. Once the ice begins to accumulate, gravity causes the mass to move downhill. Glaciers usually take the path of least resistance, following stream beds or other natural channels down the mountain. As they move, they scrape the surface of the earth, picking up rocks and other sediment on the way. The ice and the debris carve a deep U-shaped valley as they proceed down the mountain. If they advance far enough, they will eventually reach the sea and become tidewater glaciers that break off, or calve, directly into salt water. Southeast Alaska is one of only three places in the world where tidewater glaciers exist. (Scandinavia and Chile are the others.) Other glaciers, called hanging glaciers, spill out of icy basins high up on valley walls and tumble toward the valley floor.

Glaciers are in a constant state of flux because of increases or decreases in precipitation and temperature. Minor changes can cause significant buildup or reduction in the accumulation of snow on the glacier. When the buildup of glacier ice is greater than the amount lost to melting or calving at the terminus, the glacier will gain ground and is said to advance. If the reverse is true and the ice melts faster than new ice accumulates, the glacier will lose ground and is said to retreat. Some glaciers are simply in a state of equilibrium, the new accumulation roughly equaling the degree of loss. Glaciers can stay in a state of equilibrium for years. Regardless of whether a particular glacier is advancing, retreating, or in a state of equilibrium, the ice continues to flow down the mountain at a measurable rate. Only the total length of the glacier is affected.

The surface of a glacier is interrupted by fissures that develop as the mass moves downhill. It also accumulates a dark layer of dirt and rocks and other debris that falls from the valley walls. This sediment, called a lateral moraine, usually occurs in two distinct dark stripes, one on each side of the glacier. When two valley glaciers meet and merge into one, the inner lateral moraines merge into a single medial moraine that can be seen in the middle of the new super-glacier. The moraines of some glaciers are so prominent that they look like asphalt highways from the air.

Glaciers are not blue, although they certainly look blue, especially where a new wedge of ice has just calved from the face. The blue appearance is attributable to a trick of light: The molecules of ice absorb all the colors of the spectrum except blue, which is reflected outward. The blue color is more noticeable on overcast days.

Glaciers exist only in areas that provide the heavy snowfall needed to accumulate into glacier ice. Most of the glaciers in Southeast Alaska are born out of two massive ice fields in the Coast Mountains: the Stikine Ice Field and the Juneau Ice Field. The Stikine Ice Field, which starts in the mountains north of Wrangell, has spawned at least a dozen sizable glaciers, many of which can be seen from the water. The best known is the Le Conte Glacier that empties into salt water at the head of Le Conte Bay, between Wrangell and Petersburg. The Le Conte is the southernmost tidewater glacier in North America. Although the glacier has been in a state of equilibrium since the sixties, it, like all glaciers, continues to flow downward into the sea and discharges icebergs into the bay.

The Juneau Ice Field consists of approximately 1,500 square miles of ice and snow sprawling back of Juneau, over the border into Canada, and north nearly to Skagway. The ice field has pro-

Icebergs from the Le Conte Glacier wash up near the Stikine River. (John Matthews)

duced more than thirty glaciers, including the famous Mendenhall. The Mendenhall Glacier measures approximately 12 miles long, and 1½ miles wide, and 50 to 100 feet high at the face and terminates in a deep lake. The glacier is retreating at the rate of 50 to 70 feet per year.

Reached by highway north of Juneau, the Mendenhall is one of Alaska's most accessible glaciers. A splendid view can be had even from the parking lot. The U.S. Forest Service operates a visitors' center and maintains trails to the flanks of the glacier; a self-guided nature walk illustrates features of the glacier-carved terrain.

Other glaciers visible from either the highway north of Juneau or from the water include Lemon Creek Glacier, Herbert Glacier, and Eagle Glacier. None of these glaciers descends to tidewater. Although these and the other glaciers from the Juneau Ice Field are retreating, the Taku Glacier, on the north side of Taku Inlet (south of Juneau) has been advancing steadily. Presently reaching thirty miles in length, this glacier is the largest from the Juneau Ice Field.

The sixteen tidewater glaciers of Glacier Bay National Park and Preserve course out of the massive Saint Elias Mountains. As recently as 200 years ago, when Captain George Vancouver charted the Southeast Alaska coast for England, glaciers completely filled the area now known as Glacier Bay. The various glaciers that flow into the bay have retreated to the point that the bay presently measures 60 miles long. Today, the Johns Hopkins and Grand Pacific glaciers on the west arm of the bay are slowly advancing; the others in the area are stabilized or retreating.

Traveling up Glacier Bay is like taking a trip back in time: the farther you proceed toward the active glaciers at the head of the bay, the more primitive the plant forms become. A retreating glacier leaves behind a deposit of rock and other sediment that was scraped along its advancing path. This deposit, called glacial till, is composed chiefly of ground-up rock with little or no organic content—only limited organisms such as lichens and mosses are able to establish themselves. With time, however, such low-growing pioneer plants as dwarf fireweed and dryas gain a foothold and begin improving the soil for other species. Next come low shrubs and broadleaf trees such as willow and alder, which improve the soil still further. Finally, evergreens take root and develop into the common spruce and hemlock forest of Southeast Alaska. At present established forest exists only at the entrance to Glacier Bay where the land has been ice-free the longest.

Despite the barren environment left in the wake of receding glaciers, a surprising number of organisms exist on or near the ice. Scientists report more than seventy species of wildflowers growing in the vicinity of the Juneau Ice Field. A variety of insects thrive there too, among them the snow flea, a species seemingly impervious to heat, cold, and moisture. Small black glacier worms, called ice worms, live off the algae that grows on glacier ice, or on other organic matter that falls onto the ice. First noted in Alaska on the Muir Glacier in 1887, the ice worm is the only species of earthworm known to inhabit snow and ice.

THE WEATHER FORECAST

Contrary to popular belief, Southeast Alaska enjoys a mild climate: cool in summer and moderate in winter (the average winter temperature is 33 degrees Fahrenheit). The sea provides a warming influence in winter when the water is warmer than the air, and a cooling influence in summer when the air is warmer than the water.

In every season, the ocean pumps quantities of moisture into the air. The moisture is gathered by storm clouds borne across the Pacific on the jet stream and released as rain and snow when they contact the steeply rising slopes of the Coast Mountains. In winter, the dense cloud cover over coastal Alaska also acts as a layer of insulation to retain the heat generated by the land and water. In summer the effect is reversed, and the clouds insulate the cool landmass from the sun's rays.

The temperature varies little from one Southeast community to another. The average year-round temperature is 40 degrees Fahrenheit, with the coldest weather usually in January and the warmest in July. Besides being moderate, the temperature is also quite constant in Southeast, normally varying fewer than ten degrees in the course of the day. In winter, temperatures usually range from the high teens to the low forties. In summer, the midfifties to the midsixties is the norm, although the thermometer can soar to the eighties on a sunny day.

Extreme temperatures can occur in winter, too. For example, in Juneau, the winds usually blow out of the southeast. But occasionally they blow across the ice fields of the Coast Mountains and rush down the glacier valleys in gusts of over one hundred miles per hour. This bitter wind, known as the Taku, occurs in clear, cold conditions, and sends the windchill factor plummeting.

While temperatures vary little from place to place, precipitation varies quite a lot. Southeast Alaska is basically a rain forest, averaging more than 100 inches of rain and snow a year (as a rule of thumb, 1 inch of snow is the equivalent of 10 inches of rain). But the southern third of the Panhandle is rainier than the rest. Ketchikan usually takes credit for being the "liquid sunshine" capital of the state with an average yearly precipitation of 152 inches, but the record is actually held by Little Port Walter near the southeast tip of Baranof Island at 221 inches of precipitation a year. Things become drier as you move north: 106 inches in Petersburg, 70 in Juneau, and only 26 in Skagway. In winter, most of this precipitation falls as snow. In the northern part of the Panhandle, much of the snow stays on the ground and accumulates, even at sea level. In the mountains, Southeast is able to produce more than 200 inches of snow a year, which is what fuels the pretty glaciers.

Southeastern residents, then, experience a predominance of

cool, moist days with overcast skies. June is usually the driest month and October the wettest. Winters, not at all unpleasant, produce moderate temperatures and lots of snow for skiing and sledding. Snow typically begins falling in late October. Heavy snowfalls can accumulate as late as April.

What drives southeasterners "Outside" for periodic respites is the gray cloud that seems to hang overhead for weeks at a time. When the cloud moves on, however, and the sun reappears, the beauty of the lush, green forests and the snowcapped mountains blots out all memories of overcast skies and winters that endure through spring.

THE WATERS

Alaska is a land of enormous tides and Southeast is no exception. The height of the tide increases as it moves over the continental shelf and squeezes up the narrow passages of the Alexander Archipelago. At maximum high, the tide reaches 20.9 feet in Skagway at the far northern limit of Lynn Canal, and falls to a maximum low of –4.0. In Juneau, the range is from a maximum high of 20.6 feet to a low of –4.0. At Sitka the tidal range is more moderate, from 12.5 feet to –2.6. There are two high tides and two low tides within every twenty-four-hour period.

The large tides cause powerful currents as the water ebbs and flows through the tight waterways. In Wrangell Narrows south of Petersburg and Sergius Narrows en route to Sitka—two of the most scenic stretches of water along the Inside Passage—the current has been clocked at more than 8 miles an hour. If you are traveling by canoe or kayak, the tidal currents can prove dangerous. Always check the tide table before starting through a narrow channel and talk with local residents about the conditions. Make the passage when the tide is slack—either high or low—and not on the change, and don't camp too near the waterline. Tide tables are available at most sporting-goods shops in Southeast.

The temperature of the water kills. Though warmed by the Japanese current that keeps Southeast ports ice-free in winter, the coastal water is too cold to support human life for more than a few minutes. The surface temperature of the water varies from place to place but the range is typically as follows: winter, 42.5 to 45 degrees; spring, 45 to 47 degrees; summer, 55 to 57 degrees; fall, 45 to 47 degrees.

When a human being is immersed in such waters, body heat is

lost into the water, causing hypothermia, or subnormal body temperature. If the body temperature drops far enough, the victim becomes unconscious and death will follow. Survival time in the water varies according to the size, shape, physical condition, and mental attitude of the victim, but the table in this section shows the approximate survival time of a human being immersed in the ocean.

In sum, the cool climate of Southeast Alaska can turn a normal situation into a dangerous situation in a hurry. Be cautious whenever you are facing the elements, whether boating, hiking, skiing, fishing, or simply walking around on the docks.

SURVIVAL TIME

WATER TEMPERATURE (FAHRENHEIT)	EXHAUSTION OR UNCONSCIOUSNESS	EXPECTED TIME OF SURVIVAL
32.5 degrees	15 minutes	15 to 45 minutes
32.5 to 40 degrees	15 to 30 minutes	30 to 90 minutes
40 to 50 degrees	30 to 60 minutes	1 to 3 hours
50 to 60 degrees	1 to 2 hours	1 to 6 hours
60 to 70 degrees	2 to 7 hours	2 to 40 hours
70 to 80 degrees	3 to 12 hours	3 hours plus (indefinite)

EVERLASTING DAYS AND NIGHTS

Southeast Alaska is far enough north to enjoy some of the Arctic "midnight sun" effect. In the course of the year, the number of daylight hours ranges from seven to eighteen and one-half hours. At summer's peak, however, most of the remaining five and one-half hours are in twilight, so the effective daylight is more like twenty-two hours. If you step outside at midnight on a clear night in midsummer, you can read a newspaper in the available light. On the longest day of the year, the sun rises at 4:05 A.M. (daylight time) in Ketchikan, 3:51 A.M. in Juneau, and 3:43 A.M. in Skagway; and sets at 9:32 P.M., 10:09 P.M., and 10:23 P.M., respectively.

In winter, the opposite conditions prevail. On the shortest day of the year, the sun rises at 8:12 A.M. in Ketchikan, 8:46 A.M. in Juneau, and 8:58 A.M. in Skagway; to set at 3:18 P.M., 3:07 P.M., and 3:01 P.M., respectively. It is dark going to work in the morning and dark again going home.

Although minimal compared with the Arctic, the seasonal fluc-
tuations in daylight make themselves felt in people's attitudes
and levels of activity. People seem to become increasingly ener-
gized as the days lengthen. By summer's peak, with near-perpet-
ual daylight, it is not unusual to put in a full day at the office and
then spend several more hours fishing or working on the house or
yard. The streets ring with the voices of children playing late into
the evening. With the onset of winter's darkness, the pace slows
and people seem to need more sleep.

Chapter 3
Southeast Past to Present

Fifteen thousand years ago, the watery trail now known as the Inside Passage was locked in an icy embrace. Glaciers flowed down the 10,000-foot peaks and scoured the valleys below. As the land warmed, the ocean waters gradually thawed. Rivers sprang from melting glaciers and coursed across the land, carrying a succession of unknown peoples who lingered along the coast as many as 9,000 years ago. Eventually — perhaps some 1,500 years ago, perhaps longer — groups of Tlingit Indians followed the waterways out of Interior Alaska and Canada and into the lush coastal forests of Southeast Alaska.

The Tlingit lived comfortably off the land. They formed in small villages along the coast where they could harvest the resources that the sea and land placed within their reach. They fished for salmon and halibut, collected seaweed from the beach, and picked the blueberries, salmonberries, and nagoonberries growing wild along the Southeast shore. They learned to use the forest cedar and spruce for shelter, tools, and complex works of art.

The Tlingit traveled the length of their 600-mile domain by wooden canoe. Occasionally they contacted the Haida Indians who lived to the south of them or the Athapaskans who ranged across Interior Alaska to the north. Secure in their rain-forest environment, the Tlingit peoples prospered and increased. By the middle of the eighteenth century, the Southeast Alaska coastline was one of the most heavily populated regions north of Mexico.

No white person had yet set foot upon the shore. On the day that the first sailing ship appeared off the Southeast coast, according to one Tlingit tradition, the villagers had sent several boys to the beach to see if the wild celery shoots had reached the height that meant the seaweed was ready to harvest. The boys came running back with the news that a huge white Thunderbird—in Tlingit mythology, a powerful spirit that created thunder by beating his enormous wings and lightning by blinking his eyes—was approaching from the sea. Most of the villagers fled. Those who stayed behind watched as the Thunderbird folded his wings and white men came ashore for the first time in Southeast Alaska.

In that instant, life along the Inside Passage changed irrevoca-
bly. The future of Southeast Alaska would be governed by the harvesting of resources as first furs, then gold, fish, timber, and even
the ice itself brought wave after wave of fortune hunters into the
coastal wilderness.

FIRST CONTACT

The men who rowed ashore from the white "thunderbird"
might have come from the *Saint Paul,* one of two Russian ships
that set out on an exploratory expedition under the command of
Vitus Bering in 1741. The North Pacific coast was an unknown
entity in the 1700s. European expeditions had unraveled the mysteries of much of the rest of North America (the English had been
settled in Hudson's Bay since 1670 and the Spanish were on the
California coast), but the northern region had remained obscure.
In 1725 the Russian czar Peter the Great had sent Bering on a
preliminary voyage to find out what lay to the east of Russia:
Were the continents of Asia and North America one and the same,
or were they separate? Sailing from the mouth of the Kamchatka
River in Siberia, Bering passed through what would come to be
called Bering Strait but turned back without sighting the Alaskan
coast. On his second voyage, in 1741, Bering left with two ships:
the *Saint Peter,* under his own command, and the *Saint Paul,* cap-
tained by Alexei Chirikof. Fifteen days out, they became sepa-
rated and never sighted each other again.

Chirikof, in the *Saint Paul,* was the first to glimpse the North
American continent. He sighted high wooded mountains near
Cape Addington off the west coast of Prince of Wales Island on 15
July 1741. Two days later he anchored in a bay (possibly where
Sitka is located today) and sent an armed party ashore. When the
men failed to return, a second landing party went to investigate.
They did not return either. On the day after that, two parties of
Tlingit paddled out to the ship in canoes, shouted something that
the Russians of course could not understand, and went back to
shore. Having no other landing boats at his disposal, Chirikof
turned back to Russia without learning the fate of his men.

Bering, meanwhile, proceeded in the same east-by-northeast
direction and sighted 18,000-foot Mount Saint Elias near Yakutat.
Anchoring near Kayak Island, to the southeast of Prince William
Sound, he sent two parties ashore to investigate the area and replenish the water supply. The shore parties found a few deserted

A 1741 Russian map shows Kayak Island and cloud-capped mountains. (Centennial Collection, Alaska Historical Library)

Native dwellings made of logs and rough planks, some underground storehouses, and signs of a recent cooking fire. They took away several household items, such as bundles of dried fish and a wooden box, and left some of their own possessions in exchange, among them reportedly some tobacco, a pipe, cloth, and an iron kettle.

One of the members of the shore expedition was the naturalist Georg Wilhelm Steller. In the short time that Bering allowed him to remain ashore, Steller collected specimens of plants and birds that were not native to Europe or Asia, among them a most important find: a dark blue jay with a high head crest known to be an inhabitant of North America. Steller realized that this bird—now called the Steller's jay—was proof that the new land was part of the North American continent and separate from Asia.

Bering, anxious about the deteriorating weather, turned the *Saint Peter* for Kamchatka as soon as the water casks were full, but encountered a massive storm in the Aleutians that drove the ship hundreds of miles off course. After battling the Aleutian weather throughout late summer and fall, he made a landing on one of the Commander Islands (west of the Aleutian chain) in November. The crew scraped pits in the bank of a ravine for shelter, collected driftwood for a roof, and settled in to try to survive the winter, keeping themselves warm with pelts from blue foxes and other animals that were plentiful around the island. The *Saint Peter* was blown ashore and they salvaged what they could from the wreck. Bering died in December, like so many of his crew a victim of exhaustion, exposure, and scurvy, the scourge of early seafarers.

When spring came, the survivors built a 40-foot craft from the wreckage of the *Saint Peter* and reached home port in little more than two weeks. Among their baggage were 900 sea otter pelts that had been collected during the stay in the Commander Islands. Richly colored, glossy, and luxurious, the pelts fetched astonishingly high prices from Chinese merchants, and before long the first wave of Russian fur traders set off to find the mysterious fur-rich lands to the east and their small marine inhabitant, the sea otter.

THE EUROPEAN EXPLORERS

In the years following the return of the Bering expedition, word trickled through the courts of Europe that the Russians had discovered a great land in the North Pacific that was rich in furs and possibly other treasures as well. A progression of exploratory voyages was soon under way to find this land, and to find the Northwest Passage between the Pacific and Atlantic oceans that rumors persistently claimed to exist. Between 1774 and 1800, sailing ships from Spain, Britain, France, Russia, and America glided among the misty waterways of Southeast Alaska. Some of them reached tentatively northward along the Gulf of Alaska to Prince William Sound and Cook Inlet, then passed through the Aleutian Chain to the Bering Sea and proceeded into the Arctic. Eventually, all came to the same conclusion: If the Northwest Passage lay in that direction, it would not be usable anyway. (It took until 1837 to prove that there was a passageway from the Arctic Ocean to the Atlantic, but so clogged with ice for much of the year that it was of little practical use.)

The early explorers bartered with the local inhabitants they encountered along their route, paving the way for the trading vessels that would soon follow. Besides the coveted furs, the sea captains brought out of Alaska the first examples of Southeast Alaska Native art and culture, and detailed sketches of Native villages. These items—woven blankets and baskets, carved wooden feast dishes, fishing equipment, and household tools, displayed today in museums of European capitals, give us a priceless portrait of the Tlingit and Haida peoples at the time of their initial contact with European culture. Among the legacies of the explorers were the place names they gave to many of the land forms in Southeast Alaska.

Juan Pérez was the first of the international boating community to follow the Russians into Alaska, sailing from Spain in the *Santiago* in 1774. With holdings in Mexico and California, the Spanish were in an excellent position to continue their explorations northward along the Pacific coast. Pérez proceeded far enough to sight Prince of Wales Island, which he named Santa Maria Magdalena. The following year he returned with two ships. He turned back because of a storm before reaching Alaska, but Lieutenant Juan Francisco de la Bodega y Quadra in the second vessel sighted Mount Edgecumbe at Sitka before scurvy forced him to retreat. On the way home he entered and named Bucareli Bay on the outside coast of Prince of Wales Island.

English sea captain James Cook reached Southeast in 1778 on the third of his remarkable explorations to the Pacific (the first two had taken him to New Zealand, Australia, and the Antarctic). In the ships *Resolution* and *Discovery,* he sighted and named Mount Edgecumbe off Sitka and Mount Fairweather off the Gulf

These Tlingit artifacts were sketched during a Russian voyage in 1805. (Centennial Collection, Alaska Historical Library)

of Alaska, and continued along the coast to the north until he was stopped by the Arctic ice. He then headed south to winter in the Hawaiian Islands, preparatory to continuing the search for the Northwest Passage the following summer, but was killed there in a dispute with the indigenous people.

The French explorations were carried out by Jean François Galaup de la Pérouse in the ships *Astrolabe* and *Boussole*. La Pérouse arrived in Southeast in June 1786. He sighted Mount Saint Elias and anchored for some days at Lituya Bay (south of Yakutat), surveying the inlet and trading with the local Tlingit. The trip ended in disaster when two of the survey boats were swept into the breakers at the entrance to the bay and all hands lost. La Pérouse left Alaska after the catastrophe and journeyed to the Kamchatka Peninsula where he arranged for his journals to be sent on to Paris, which was a good idea because when he turned south again the *Astrolabe* and *Boussole* vanished in the southern oceans.

The British returned to Alaska in 1793. Captain George Vancouver sailed from England with instructions to verify Cook's findings and make one more search for the Northwest Passage. Cook's voyages had pretty much convinced the British government that no practical waterway existed north of latitude 60° (to the north or west of the Gulf of Alaska), but rumors persisted that the elusive passage lay to the south of latitude 60° (i.e., in Southeast Alaska). Vancouver was also charged with charting the coast from the Columbia River to Cook Inlet. Having served with Cook on the last voyage, he was no stranger to the territory.

Vancouver's ships, the *Discovery* and *Chatham,* arrived in Southeast Alaska in July 1793. Throughout that summer, he and his four-man survey teams worked along the inlets and passageways of the Alexander Archipelago. They ran south in the fall to winter in the Hawaiian Islands, returned the following summer, and mapped their way south from Cook Inlet. When they left for England in August 1794 (arriving the following year), Vancouver took with him a set of charts so accurate that they were used for years after Alaska became a U.S. possession. Vancouver also provided many of the names for geographical features we use today (among them Chatham Strait, which he named for English statesman William Pitt Chatham, the Earl of Chatham, and Lynn Canal, which he named for his birthplace, King's Lynn, in Norfolk) and proved conclusively that there was no usable passage through North America between the Pacific and the Atlantic below or above latitude 60°. Besides successfully completing his mission, Vancouver accumulated a remarkable safety record. During the four and one-half years that the expedition was gone from England, the *Discovery* lost only six men out of a crew of one hundred: five through accidents and one from disease. The *Chatham* did not lose a single man.

THE RUSSIAN OCCUPATION

When the survivors of the *Saint Peter* staggered back to Saint Petersburg with their souvenir pelts of lustrous sea otter that fetched fabulous prices from Chinese traders, they touched off a fur stampede to the North Pacific. The onslaught consisted mainly of *promyshlenniki*—gangs of toughs who moved through the mountains of Russia, conquering villages and forcing villagers to pay a tribute in furs to the czar. The *promyshlenniki* had reached the coast of Kamchatka by the time of Bering's expedition, and when they saw the rich furs coming in from the unknown waters to the east, they recognized an unparalleled opportunity for profit.

The *promyshlenniki* built boats out of anything they could find and set out for the Commander Islands where Bering's party had been shipwrecked. The *promyshlenniki* were mountain men, not seamen, and many were swamped at sea in their unseaworthy crafts, but those who managed to complete the trip found their dreams come true—acres of sea otter available for the taking. The Russian opportunists gradually worked their way along the Commander Islands and onto the Aleutian chain, harvesting the sea

The unassuming sea otter caused a fur stampede to the North Pacific. (Centennial Collection, Alaska Historical Library)

otter as they went. They met little resistance from the indigenous Aleuts, who were gentle and unwarlike in nature. The Russians made it their practice to take the Aleut women and children hostage and force the Aleut men to hunt sea otter. In their lithe skin kayaks, which the Russians called *bidarka,* the Aleuts were much more efficient hunters than the Russians were anyway.

KODIAK COLONY

The Russian expeditions traveled farther and farther from Kamchatka as the hunting grounds were depleted, and the excursions became more costly. The fur traders gradually banded together in small companies to make the trips economical. In 1783, a merchant named Grigor Shelikof decided to establish a permanent hunting base on the Aleutian Islands that would make the fur-gathering business more efficient still. That summer Shelikof, his wife Natalie, and a small party of settlers founded the first Russian colony in Alaska on the southeast part of Kodiak Island. The Russians soon had a working settlement with houses, offices, and outbuildings. They organized the indigenous population into work parties to hunt sea otter, gather food, and perform other menial tasks. The idea worked tolerably well and the storehouses filled up with furs. Shelikof's company was the forerunner of the Russian-American Company, which would ultimately be granted a royal charter with exclusive rights to all trade and properties in Alaska.

By 1790, Shelikof had concluded he needed someone to manage the Alaska colony for him. Alexander Baranof was a natural organizer, gutsy and efficient, and experienced in trading with Siberian Natives. When at last he arrived at Kodiak, after a shipwreck in the Aleutians, he set about trying to improve conditions in the settlement. Sea otter were growing scarce and supplies, which had to be shipped out from Russia, were constantly running out. There was also the increasingly serious problem of trying to prevent traders from other countries, now familiar with the Alaska coast, from encroaching upon the Russian position. Baranof began to scout for a better location for the colony.

SAINT ARCHANGEL MICHAEL

The Russians established a small agricultural settlement at Yakutat in 1795, but Baranof's choice for a new headquarters was a natural harbor on the outside coast of Baranof Island. In April 1799, a convoy of Russians and Aleuts crossed the Gulf of Alaska to the new site in Southeast Alaska. Baranof negotiated with the chief of the local Tlingit Indians for land on which to build a fort. The site was on the harbor about 6 miles north of the present town of Sitka. The Russians and a detachment of Aleuts stayed to start the building, while the rest of the Aleut hunters went back to Kodiak with instructions to hunt along the way. Two days after their departure, they had rounded the northern shore of the island and were camped on the beach when they ate a meal of purple-black mussels that grew there in great profusion. Many of the Aleuts became violently ill and more than one hundred died—the first known case of paralytic shellfish poisoning in Southeast Alaska. From this event, the body of water became known as *Pogibshii,* the Russian word for deadly, and has come down to us as Peril Strait.

The Russians quickly completed a two-story barracks and various outbuildings, all enclosed within a wooden stockade. Baranof named the new settlement Saint Archangel Michael. The Russian outpost was simply a foothold in the midst of what had become an international trading center on traditional Tlingit ground. French, Spanish, British, and Yankee vessels had visited Sitka Sound for years. They traded cloth, beads, blankets, metal, and anything else they could get the Tlingit to take as payment for the profitable furs they had come to find. During the 1790s, twenty to thirty trading ships a year anchored at various harbors along the northern coast. Eventually, some of the sea captains found two other items that the local Indians would readily accept in exchange for furs: alcohol and arms.

The Sitka Indians tolerated the Russian settlement initially, but became increasingly angry about the way the Russians treated them, especially their women, and they got into disputes with the Aleuts as well. The situation became volatile. When Baranof left on a trip back to Kodiak three years after founding the Sitka settlement, he gave strict instructions to avoid giving offense to the Tlingit and to be continually on the alert.

On Sunday, 20 June 1802, when most of the Russians and Aleuts were away from the fort hunting, fishing, or picking berries in the woods, the Tlingit attacked. Wearing their fierce-looking wooden helmets and armed with guns and spears, the warriors emerged from the forest where they had been hiding and quickly overran the stockade. The Russians resisted the attack, but almost all were killed or captured. A few of those in the woods escaped to the water and were rescued by English and American boats anchored in the Sound. The Tlingit burned the buildings and the post was completely destroyed.

RETAKING SITKA

Baranof immediately made preparations to retake the Sitka outpost. In the summer of 1804, a second convoy left Kodiak for Sitka Sound. This time the party consisted of some 400 *bidarkas* carrying 800 Aleuts, plus two small sailing ships with 120 Russians. The expedition stopped at Yakutat to pick up two additional vessels that Baranof had commissioned for the attack. When they arrived at Baranof Island, they found the frigate *Neva* had arrived from Kodiak to assist.

The Tlingit retreated to a stronghold when the Russians began their cannon assault. The Russians landed 150 men on the beach, but were repulsed with ten killed and twenty-six wounded—including Baranof, who took a shot in the arm. After several days of alternating negotiations and bombardment, the Tlingit quietly

Chief Katlean's Raven helmet, worn in the 1804 battle with the Russians, is displayed in the Sheldon Jackson Museum in Sitka.

abandoned their fort during the night and slipped away to Chichagof Island to the north. Baranof ordered the Tlingit stronghold burned. He built a new stockade with houses, storehouses and other buildings within, calling the settlement New Archangel.

For the Tlingit, the hero of the occasion was the young chief Katlean, who led the battle against the Russians, fighting fiercely hand-to-hand and, according to tradition, swinging at his enemies with a mighty hammer. Remarkably, Katlean's raven-shaped helmet can be seen today in the Sheldon Jackson Museum in Sitka. (At Sitka National Historic Park, the actual battle site, you can view a film about the contest and the Russian settlement at Sitka.)

NEW ARCHANGEL

The year after retaking Sitka, the Russians had completed eight new buildings and cleared ground for gardens and livestock. Baranof had concluded a treaty with part of the Tlingit tribe, and while others remained hostile, relations had improved to the point that the Indians were invited to the settlement occasionally for feasting and presents. The main worry continued to be food. The climate was cool and damp, the Russian settlers were not farmers by trade or inclination, the soil was unproductive, and the crops were not a success. Baranof developed a penchant for buying ships with cargoes intact from Americans who happened into port.

Baranof invited the Tlingit to return to Sitka in 1821. In the intervening years they had caused periodic trouble for the colonists by interfering with the Aleut hunting parties, and Baranof thought the wisest course would be to let them return to their ancestral home. Besides, he needed their skills to provide game and fish for the Russian larders. The Indians settled around the Russian fort. They outnumbered the Russians, and the colonists were in constant fear of another uprising, but an uneasy truce prevailed.

In 1834, the Russians established a second outpost in Southeast Alaska. Redoubt Saint Dionysius was built to prevent the British Hudson's Bay Company, a fierce competitor for the Native fur trade, from using the Stikine River to gain access to the fur-rich Interior. The post was placed close to the mouth of the Stikine, at today's Wrangell.

The 1840s were the height of development for the colonists at New Archangel. The physical plant had grown to include a governor's residence atop Castle Hill, a clubhouse for lower officials, barracks and other housing, a library, an observatory, churches, a hospital, an arsenal, a wharf, and three schools, including an academy that trained students in surveying, navigation, engraving, and accounting; a finishing school for young ladies; and a theological seminary. There were shipyards that built steam vessels, a forge that fabricated plow blades and spades for Spanish farmers in California, and a foundry, sawmill, flour mill, and fish saltery. New Archangel was not only the center of commerce for the twenty-four Russian settlements that then existed in Alaska, the town was the largest port on the entire North Pacific coast. In the days when San Francisco was still a muddy hole in the Pacific, Sitka was a haven of culture for trading vessels from all over the world.

In the 1850s, a new industry was born: ice. Enterprising capitalists discovered that lake ice from Southeast Alaska could be packed in sawdust deep in a ship's hold and arrive in San Francisco intact. Over the next decade, tons of ice were sawed from freshwater lakes at both Sitka and Kodiak and shipped south. Fish and lumber were sent south, too, for sale in California, Mexico, and Hawaii. Other ships came north to be repaired in Sitka's well-equipped shipyards. On occasion there were fifteen vessels in the harbor at once, loading and unloading wares.

THE RUSSIANS OPT OUT

At length, Russia's expenses of maintaining the Alaska colonies began to outweigh the benefits. The fur trade diminished to almost nothing as the supply of pelts grew scarce. Provisioning remained a constant headache, as did the difficulties of maintaining a political presence so far from the mother country. Treaties had fixed the boundary between Russian-America and Canada in 1824 and 1825, but both British and American traders were pushing past the Russian boundaries into the Alaska Interior. Renewal of the Russian-American Company charter was in question, too. The Russian government had proposed to renew the charter for a twenty-year term beginning in 1862, but company officials were not pleased with new conditions that would exempt Aleuts and all other Alaska Natives from forced labor and allow them to participate in other industries.

The Russian government had never really intended to occupy Alaska. The settlements had come about through the activities of first the fur traders and then the Russian-American Company, which had represented the government's interests there while it gathered in the rich harvest of Alaska resources. If the company was no longer interested in governing the new settlements, neither was the government. The czar decided to give up the Alaska colonies. The question was, to whom? Both Britain and America were likely prospects. The czar opted to have the United States for a neighbor instead of England, Russia's enemy in the Crimean War.

The treaty of purchase was concluded by U.S. Secretary of State William Seward on 30 March 1867 and ratified that May. The purchase price was $7.2 million. The boundaries between the new possession and Canada would be the same as were agreed upon in the 1824–1825 treaties between Russia and Great Britain, with the lower extreme fixed at 54°40' north latitude and then following the natural boundaries of the Portland Canal and the Coast Mountains before turning due north at Mount Saint Elias.

At Sitka, the Russian flag was exchanged for the American on 18 October 1867. The Russians were promised citizenship rights in the new American territory, but most went home to Russia. The Aleuts went back to their native islands, and the Tlingit Indians were left to wonder what new indignities this new development would bring.

RACING FOR GOLD

Thousands of miles to the south of New Archangel—now called Sitka—gold had been struck near Sacramento, California, and the gold rush was under way. Prospectors fanned across California, exploring the creek beds and mountain canyons for gold. The search took them northward through Oregon and Washington and on into Canada and its bordering neighbor, Alaska.

In 1858, a discovery was made on Canada's Fraser River and thousands of prospectors surged into this area. The first strike to affect Alaska came three years later. A Hudson's Bay Company trader named Buck Choquette found gold on the upper Stikine River in Canada at a spot that came to be known as Buck's Bar. Prospectors flocked to Southeast Alaska to get to the new Stikine strike. Their destination was Wrangell, at the mouth of the Stikine in Russian territory. William Moore, an enterprising riverboat captain, was running a steamer upriver to the strike site with cargoes of optimistic prospectors.

THE CASSIAR

In 1873, word of a huge, new strike in Canada brought another wave of opportunists up the Stikine on their way to the Cassiar

Exhaustion was the only certainty about the Klondike rush for gold. (P.E. Larss Collection, Alaska Historical Library)

gold fields in the Interior. This time Wrangell ballooned from a quiet outpost to a booming tent city of 15,000. Captain Moore was on the scene again to move prospectors and their gear upriver where they could pack the 200-odd miles to the diggings. Other steamers, both British and American, carried passengers and goods as well. At the end of the season, the prospectors came downriver to Wrangell to patronize the stores, saloons, dance halls, and other boomtown delights. At the time, Wrangell was the busiest place in Alaska.

Prospectors picked around in both Canada and Alaska, searching for that next big strike. The first find in Alaska came in 1870 at Windham Bay on the mainland, 65 miles south of Juneau. Forty thousand dollars in gold is said to have been taken from the placers in that region. Gold mining was carried out near Sitka shortly thereafter and, in 1880, ore samples from Silver Bow Basin on Gastineau Channel led to the founding of Juneau, Douglas, and Treadwell and, ultimately, the largest gold mining operation in the world.

But the biggest gold boom was yet to come. The gold trail led onward to a region close to Canada's western border called the Klondike. At its center was the boomtown of Dawson on the Yukon River. The route to the gold fields lay through Southeast Alaska, and the migration of men and equipment was one of the greatest in history.

KLONDIKE MADNESS

The Klondike story began in August 1896 when George Washington Carmack and his two Indian companions, Skookum Jim and Tagish Charlie, found gold on a tributary of the Klondike River in the Yukon Territory of Canada. That winter, rumor spread that rich gold deposits had been found in the Yukon, and a few prospectors working nearby managed to get into the area by spring. On 17 July 1897, headlines in the *Seattle Post-Intelligencer* screamed that the steamer *Portland* was on her way with a "ton of gold" from the Klondike.

Those who reached Dawson had a lot of panning to do. (P.E. Larss Collection, Alaska Historical Library)

Prospectors trudge to the summit of Chilkoot Pass in 1898. (P.E.
Larss Collection, Alaska Historical Library)

All through that summer and the fall, prospectors stampeded
to the Klondike and the fields of gold. There were at least seven
ways to get into the Klondike, and not one of them was easy. The
safest route was also the longest: the all-water route that led from
Seattle to the port of Saint Michael on the far western coast of
Alaska where the Yukon River exited into the Bering Sea. There
prospectors boarded Yukon River steamers for the 2,000-mile
journey upriver to the gold fields. All the other possibilities involved a combination of water and land travel. There was the
White Pass Trail that left from Skagway at the head of Lynn
Canal, and the shorter, but steeper, Chilkoot Pass from nearby
Dyea. Both terminated in a system of treacherous waterways that
led to the Yukon River and Dawson. Or there was the Dalton
Trail from Haines, which also led to the Yukon headwaters; the
old Stikine River route; the Edmonton route through Canada; and
finally the gruesome climb over Valdez Glacier and into the Interior river systems from Prince William Sound.

The most popular routes were the White Pass and Chilkoot
trails. In the summer of 1897, Dyea, at the foot of the Chilkoot

Trail, consisted of a trading post and a couple of saloons. At Skagway, a log cabin had been put up by a homesteader by the name of
Captain William Moore. (Now there was a man with vision.) Dyea
and Skagway turned into boomtowns overnight as some 25,000
people prepared to pack up the gold trails with the required year's
worth of provisions. Over the Coast Mountains in Canada the
trails came together at Lake Bennett. Twenty thousand would-be
prospectors camped around the lake that spring of '98, constructing boats to carry them downstream to the Yukon. As soon as the
ice gave way on the lakes, 7,000 boats headed downriver on the
next leg of the journey. By midsummer, 18,000 people had arrived
at Dawson. By summer's end, many had started for home—broke.
Others went on down the Yukon to the next big strike in 1899.
The place was Nome where, rumor had it, there was gold on the
beach, just waiting to be picked up.

WHEN SALMON WAS KING

Simultaneous with the gold strikes, a new industry was
launched in Alaska: salmon. The first salmon canneries were built
in 1878 at the Tlingit village of Klawock, on Prince of Wales Island, and at Sitka. The canneries spread like wildfire up and
down the Southeast coast. Ketchikan grew from an Indian summer fishing camp to a salmon saltery in 1883 and a cannery in
1887. The next year the nearby Loring Cannery was finished.
Prince of Wales Island developed canneries at Craig, Kasaan, and
other sites. Three canneries were started near Haines in the
1880s. Wrangell got one in 1887 and another in 1889. In 1900 the
town of Petersburg was born with a salmon cannery and an
equally lucrative halibut industry that kept the fishing crews occupied over the winter.

Southeast waters were choked with salmon and Ketchikan
was at the center—the "Salmon Capital of the World." More than
a dozen canneries operated there in the 1930s. During the peak
years, the Ketchikan district alone packed more than two million
cases a year. The piper had to be paid, however, and by the 1940s
the years of overfishing had taken their toll. Today the empty,
sagging remnants of the great cannery buildings can be seen in
many quiet Southeast coves; picturesque, but forlorn reminders of
plentiful days gone by.

One result of the decline in the salmon runs has been the development of aquaculture. Fish hatcheries were introduced in

In the late 1800s, Southeast's supply of salmon seemed limitless.
(H.G. Barley Collection, Alaska Historical Library)

Alaska around 1900 but most projects were busts. Research and experimentation have since led to successful techniques for rearing salmon. The Alaska Department of Fish and Game built several hatcheries during the 1970s, and more than a dozen private, nonprofit hatcheries are operating or under construction in Southeast as well.

Hatcheries in Southeast Alaska rear and release all five species of salmon (plus steelhead trout) and contribute significantly to the commercial and sport harvest. The 1992 harvest included some three million private-hatchery-reared salmon, which returned more than $10 million to commercial fishing crews.

There are several opportunities for touring salmon hatcheries in Southeast. Three of the most accessible facilities are: the Sheldon Jackson College Hatchery in Sitka (see page 212), the Deer Mountain Hatchery in Ketchikan (page 166), and the Douglas Island Pink and Chum (DIPAC) hatchery in Juneau (page 233).

Mariculture, or ocean ranching, gained a foothold under a state program in the early 1990s and currently includes nearly thirty permitted farms on the Inside Passage. The majority of the operating farms produce Pacific oysters, grown from spat imported from the Lower 48. There is limited farming of blue mussels as well. Most mariculture takes place in the southern part of the Panhandle, particularly in the areas of Wrangell Narrows, Clarence and Sumner straits, and Prince of Wales Island.

CASHING IN THE FOREST

The wood products industry has played a role in the Southeast economy since Russian times. The Russian-American Company harvested the local timber for shipbuilding and for fuel. (Evidence of their clear-cutting practice can still be seen around Sitka today.) They also operated sawmills and exported lumber to South America and China.

Rafted logs await milling at the Tsimshian village of Metlakatla on Annette Island.

After the U.S. purchase of Alaska, additional sawmills were constructed to provide lumber for packing boxes needed by the salmon canneries. Development of the industry was hindered, however, by the absence of a civil government in Alaska to regulate ownership of the land being logged. The situation was clarified somewhat in 1884 when Congress passed the Organic Act, providing machinery for the regulation and administration of government in Alaska according to the laws of Oregon. In 1907, the federal government created the sixteen-million-acre Tongass National Forest—the largest national forest in the United States (since expanded to seventeen million acres)—incorporating most of the timber in the Alexander Archipelago. With management of the forest in the hands of the U.S. Forest Service, which could hold timber sales, private timber companies were able to get into business.

World War I brought demand for strong and lightweight Sitka spruce for building fighter planes. Mills at Craig and Ketchikan cut spruce for the war effort and supplied lumber for local fishing and mining operations. The demand for spruce reappeared during World War II for the same reason. The Alaska Spruce Log Program called for one hundred million board feet of timber to be cut annually from Prince of Wales Island. The logs were tied into enormous oceangoing rafts called "Davis Rafts," 280 feet long by 60 feet wide and 30 feet deep, that were towed to Puget Sound mills. In the 1950s, the forest industry began to surpass the declining salmon industry. The annual timber harvest in Southeast doubled and doubled again as pulp mills were constructed at Ketchikan and Sitka.

Today most of the timber cut from the Tongass continues to go to the pulp mills in Ketchikan and Sitka, which produce high-grade dissolving pulp used in manufacturing such products as rayon and plastic. High-quality logs go to sawmills for processing into cants or dimensional lumber, usually for export. The pulp companies operate the three primary sawmills, in Metlakatla, Ketchikan, and Wrangell. There are also independent sawmills at Haines and Klawock, and dozens of mom-and-pop operations that start up and close down according to the timber supply. In 1993 the wood products industry accounted for about 12.5 percent of the jobs in Southeast Alaska. This is an industry in transition, though, as evidenced by the anticipated closure of the Alaska Pulp Corporation mill at Sitka in late 1993.

In recent years logging the Tongass has engendered a storm of protest from environmental and commercial fishing organizations, with far-reaching results. Like all national forest lands, the Tongass is open to many different activities, from tourism and recreation to logging and mining—a policy known as Multiple Use Management. Under Multiple Use, the U.S. Forest Service is charged with managing the land in such a way that all of these activities can be carried out simultaneously without damage to timber, water, wildlife habitat, or recreational values. Critics charged the Forest Service with catering to the needs of the timber industry, especially the two pulp mills, at the expense of other values. At the heart of the controversy were prime watersheds— lush river valleys that contain the largest and most valuable stands of old-growth timber; prime wildlife and scenic habitat prized by hunters, tourists, and local recreationists; and important fish spawning grounds that the commercial fishing community depend upon for their livelihood.

The public controversy reached a climax in the late 1980s with a series of bills submitted to Congress to amend the policies governing timber sales and logging in the Tongass. Previous legislation, the Alaska National Interest Lands Conservation Act of 1980, had specified that 4.5 billion board feet of timber per decade would be made available for harvest in the Tongass, irrespective of market demand. Congress revoked that stipulation in the Tongass Timber Reform Act of 1990 and directed that the timber supply would be based on market considerations. They also addressed environmental and fishing concerns by declaring slightly more than one million additional acres in the Tongass, including a number of key watersheds, as wilderness areas or otherwise off-limits to logging. The act tightened requirements for no-logging buffer strips along salmon streams and repealed the Tongass Timber Supply Fund, an automatic $40 million annual appropriation that had been used for road building and other activities supporting the timber program.

Not all the logging in Southeast Alaska takes place on national forest land. The Alaska Native Land Claims Settlement Act of 1971 added a new dimension to the timber industry by granting Southeast Native corporations some 600,000 acres of land selected from the Tongass National Forest. Several Native corporations selected prime timber land and entered the logging and timber export business. Unlike timber cut from the national forest, which must undergo "primary processing" prior to export (usually into squared-off logs called cants), Native-owned logs can be exported in the round; most of the high-quality Native timber goes as raw logs to Japan.

SHORT-LIVED VENTURES

Through the decades numerous other ventures have stirred the economy in various locales, but they have been short-lived. Whaling was one of the industries that touched Southeast Alaska briefly. In 1880, Northwest Trading Company of Portland, Oregon, built a shore-based whaling station on Killisnoo Island opposite the Tlingit village of Angoon. The company harvested whales from local waters and reduced the carcasses to oil, bone meal, and fertilizer. A second company started a whaling station on the southeast tip of Admiralty in 1907, and a third set up shop at Port Armstrong on the southern end of Baranof Island. All had shut down by 1923.

The Killisnoo plant, however, turned to another resource that proved profitable for several more years: herring. In 1882, the whaling station was converted to a herring reduction plant to process the plentiful, small, oily fish into fish meal. Quite a market developed for the meal, first as fertilizer and then as a food additive for livestock and poultry. A second product, herring oil, was valued as a superior industrial oil for manufacturing such varied products as leather, cosmetics, and ink. Eventually seventeen herring reduction plants operated in Southeast Alaska and processed millions of pounds of herring a year. The industry gradually declined as the herring were fished out, and the last plant closed in 1966. Herring also figured in food industries. Herring salteries had operated on a small scale at least since 1894. The 1920s saw a great demand for salted and pickled herring, but this industry declined as competition appeared from East Coast and foreign producers. Commercial production ended in 1953. Today's limited herring industry consists of two products: bait, which is processed whole and frozen, and roe, exported to Japan as a delicacy.

Copper provided a fleeting boom in the Ketchikan area. Copper claims had been located on Prince of Wales Island as early as 1867, and mining was under way on both sides of the island by 1900. The boomtowns of Coppermount and Hadley grew up around the copper industry. High costs and depleted ores closed the smelters by 1908, and the copper-mining industry faded away—taking Coppermount and Hadley with it. Marble provided a flurry of activity in the same region in 1912, when the Vermont Marble Company began quarrying at Tokeen on Marble Island, off the west coast of Prince of Wales. The white Tokeen marble was used in many buildings in the Pacific Northwest, including the Alaska Capitol at Juneau. The industry folded when the Depression cut into the building market.

Fox farming swept Southeast in the 1920s. With furs fetching high prices, some bright entrepreneur realized that the little, tree-studded islands in Southeast Alaska would make ideal fox pens. Food would be easy to come by in the form of scraps from the many nearby salmon canneries and the water perimeter would prevent the foxes from escaping. The U.S. Forest Service leased the islands for as little as $25 per year. One or two pair of blue fox—which provided pretty, sooty brown pelts with bluish hairs beneath—could stock the entire farm in just a few years. Many fox farms operated in the Tongass in the 1920s, but by the mid-1930s the price of furs had dropped again and the foxes were left to run wild.

SOUTHEAST TODAY

Today mining, timber, and fish—the traditional resource-extractive industries operating in Southeast Alaska—continue to form a cornerstone of the economy. But they operate in a much more heavily regulated environment than in the past. Increasingly, they compete with one another and with other industries, such as tourism and mariculture, for the most valuable resources of the forest and sea. Wilderness—valued historically for the extractable elements it contained—has itself become a resource, with a vocal, national constituency.

Together, the wood products industry and the commercial fishing/seafood processing industry account for roughly one quarter of the jobs in Southeast Alaska. At present, mining produces only 1 to 2 percent. A rising metals market and technological advances sparked renewed interest in mining, but the future remains uncertain. The Greens Creek Mine on Admiralty Island—which started production in 1989 and generated more than eight million ounces of silver per year, making it the largest lode-silver mine in the United States—suspended operation in the spring of 1993 pending higher metal prices. Several former gold mining properties are being actively explored and evaluated for possible redevelopment; development companies have initiated the permitting process for reopening the Kensington Mine in Berners Bay and the Alaska Juneau property in Juneau.

The City of Topeka *rides at anchor while tourists step ashore at Glacier Bay in 1895. (Alaska Historical Library)*

The tourism industry, which now accounts for about 7 percent of jobs, was born in Southeast Alaska soon after the great naturalist John Muir visited the country for the first time in 1879. Muir landed in Wrangell and canoed into Glacier Bay with his Presbyterian missionary friend Hall Young. Muir's accounts of the ice-locked wilderness were so inspiring that steamship companies began to offer summer tours up the Inside Passage. The first was the steamer *Idaho,* which came north in 1883. On board was a twenty-seven-year-old journalist named Eliza Ruhamah Scidmore, whose descriptions of the voyage appeared in national newspapers and magazines and later in a guidebook to Alaska. The tourism industry was launched.

The early steamships were oases of comfort with carpeted lounges, crystal chandeliers, starched linen, and elegant food. The ships called at mining towns and cannery sites along their route to deliver supplies, which passengers found interesting and entertaining. By 1889, 5,000 tourists a year were making the trip up the Inside Passage. The practice continues today, but the number of visitors who pass along the same route has swelled to more than a quarter of a million a year.

The number-one employer in Southeast Alaska today is government. Roughly one-third of the Southeast work force earn their annual wages from federal, state, or local government. In Juneau, the capital of Alaska since 1906, one out of every two working people is an employee of either state, federal, or local government.

SOUTHEAST HISTORY IN BRIEF

1741   Alexei Chirikof, sailing for Russia with the Bering expedition, makes the first recorded sighting of Alaska 15 July 1741. Two landing parties go ashore, possibly near Sitka, but fail to return. Vitus Bering anchors at Kayak Island. Shore parties inspect deserted Native dwellings and collect several household items.

1774   Spanish explorer Juan Pérez sights Prince of Wales Island.

1775   Spanish explorer Bodega y Quadra sights Mount Edgecumbe.

1778   Captain James Cook visits Southeast Alaska on his third voyage of exploration in the Pacific for England.

1783   Russian merchant Grigor Shelikof establishes a Russian settlement on Kodiak Island.

1786   La Pérouse sights Mount Saint Elias and surveys Lituya Bay for France.

1793-   Captain George Vancouver charts the Alexander Archipel-
1794   ago for England.

1795   Russians establish a small agricultural settlement at Yakutat.

1799   Russians settle at Old Sitka.

1802   Sitka Tlingit attack and destroy the Russian post.

1804   Russians retake Sitka and build a new fort at the present site.

1824-   Treaties fix boundaries between Russian-America and
1825   Canada.

1834   Russians establish Redoubt Saint Dionysius at Wrangell.

1839   British lease mainland coast from Russia; Redoubt Saint Dionysius passes into British hands as Fort Stikine.

1861   Buck Choquette discovers gold on the upper Stikine River in Canada; prospectors flock to Wrangell.

1867   United States purchases Alaska from Russia.

1873   Wrangell balloons to 15,000 people with a new gold strike in the Canadian Cassiar.

1877   First mission school in Alaska opens at Wrangell.

1878   First salmon canneries in Alaska built at Klawock and Sitka.

1879   S. Hall Young founds a Presbyterian mission at Haines.

1880   Joe Juneau and Richard Harris find gold on the Gastineau Channel and stake the townsite of Juneau. First Southeast whaling station begins operation on Killisnoo Island.

1882   U.S. Navy vessels shell and burn village of Angoon.

1883   Steamer *Idaho* brings tourists up the Inside Passage.

1884   Congress passes Organic Act providing minimum framework for administering government in Alaska.

1887   Father William Duncan and Tsimshian followers found Metlakatla on Annette Island.

1896   George Washington Carmack, Skookum Jim, and Tagish Charlie strike gold in Yukon Territory, precipitating a rush to the Klondike.

1897   Skagway takes shape as a tent city of 10,000 people. Peter Buschmann homesteads along Wrangell Narrows to found Petersburg.

1898   Porcupine becomes the center of a rich gold-mining district.

1900   White Pass and Yukon Route is completed from Skagway to Whitehorse. Copper mining booms on Prince of Wales Island.

1903   U.S. Army constructs Fort William H. Seward at Port Chilkoot, Haines.

1906   Capital of Alaska transferred from Sitka to Juneau.

1907   New sixteen-million-acre Tongass National Forest is largest in the United States.

1912   Alaska is granted territorial status. Marble quarries begin production on Marble Island.

1913   First territorial legislature's first law gives women the right to vote.

1917   Cave-in floods all Treadwell mines except one.

1925   Glacier Bay is proclaimed a national monument.

1941   Sitka hosts 30,000 military personnel with an army base and naval air station.

1943   Haines Highway links Haines with the Alaska Highway.

1944   Closure of the Alaska-Juneau Mill ends hard-rock mining in Juneau.

1948   Steve Homer initiates ferry service between Haines, Skagway, and Juneau.

1959   Alaska achieves statehood.

1963   First vessels of the Alaska Marine Highway fleet come on line.

1971   Alaska Native Land Claims Settlement Act awards Southeast Native corporations 550,000 to 600,000 acres of land.

1978   Klondike Highway connects Skagway with the Carcross and the Alaska Highway. Presidential proclamation designates Misty Fiords and Admiralty Island national monuments to be managed by the Forest Service.

1980   Alaska Lands bill reaffirms national monument status for Misty Fiords and Admiralty Island and designates these areas and twelve others as wilderness. Wilderness lands within the Tongass National Forest now equal 5.5 million acres.

1982   Alaskans rescind vote to move state capital from Juneau to Willow. White Pass and Yukon Route railway suspends operations.

1989   White Pass and Yukon Route reopens as summer excursion train to Fraser. Greens Creek Mine, the largest lode-silver mine in the United States, begins production.

1990   Congress passes Tongass Timber Reform Act, which designates an additional 296,080 acres of Wilderness in the Tongass National Forest and makes major changes to Tongass timber program.

1993   Greens Creek Mine suspends operation.

other Native groups. The Haida were the unquestioned masters of canoe building. Red cedar, the preferred wood for dugout canoes, was more plentiful in the southern region where they lived, and they were known up and down the Northwest coast for their large, well-built, beautifully decorated craft. A Haida seagoing canoe could easily measure 70 feet in length and carry fifty to sixty men. (The early European explorers frequently found their vessels overshadowed by the Indian canoes.) The Tlingit and Haida regularly canoed down the coast of British Columbia to Puget Sound, some 700 miles away.

HOUSING

The traditional Native houses were shared by several families. They were constructed of rough cedar planking set horizontally and notched at the corners. The structures contained a low doorway, but no windows, and a bare earth floor. An opening at the top let out smoke from the central fire pit that served for both cooking and heating. A raised wood platform around the perimeter of the house provided space for seating during the day and sleeping at night. Some houses contained two of these platforms, one above the other. The platforms were also used to store wooden boxes, sleeping mats, blankets, clothing, weapons, hunting and fishing gear, and other belongings. Dried fish, meat, and other foodstuffs hung from the ceiling.

With no ventilation except the smoke hole, these traditional dwellings were fairly aromatic. The early traders who observed some of these structures before the houses were adulterated with European goods and ideas reported themselves much bothered by the darkness and acrid smoke that permeated the interior. The visitors felt invariably either too hot or too cold, depending upon their distance from the fire.

Replicated Native community houses can be seen today at Haines (Port Chilkoot), Wrangell (Chief Shakes Island), and Ketchikan (Saxman and Totem Bight). Another, at Kasaan on Prince of Wales Island, will be outside your itinerary unless you are traveling in your own boat. A replicated house interior is part of the permanent display at the Alaska State Museum in Juneau.

FOOD GATHERING

Food was plentiful and varied along the Northwest coast. The primary staple was fish: salmon, halibut, herring, trout, and a small, oily member of the smelt family called eulachon (*hoo*-ligan). The forests were generous with bears and deer, and mountain goats were available for the price of a climb. There were birds of all types, and bird eggs. In addition to fish, the sea provided several types of seaweed, seals, the occasional whale, and all manner of shellfish. The land produced wild rhubarb, wild peas, wild rice, and nearly every imaginable form of berry. If necessary, even the hemlock forest could be eaten. With the bark peeled away, the soft cambium layer beneath could be scraped off, cooked, and consumed.

The Tlingit and Haida Indians were superb fishermen. The European explorers quickly discovered, to their astonishment, that the Natives could outfish them handily, even with their "primitive" gear of wood and bone. In fact, the Indian fishing equipment, while fabricated from natural materials, was highly efficient. Nets were fashioned out of twined cedar bark or spun nettle fibers, and lines were made from spruce roots, cedar bark, or kelp stems. Fishing methods depended upon the quarry. Salmon were speared, netted, or trapped. Herring and eulachon were netted or brailed out of the water with long-handled rakes.

Carved wooden halibut hooks in the Wrangell Museum show the beauty that accompanied an efficient design.

The breadth of their ingenuity can be seen in their method of catching halibut. The traditional halibut set consisted of a wooden hook with a stone or bone barb (later metal, fashioned from nails), a stone weight to hold it down because halibut are bottom dwellers, and a line leading to the surface with an inflated seal bladder or wooden float at the end to mark the location of the set. Two men in a canoe could watch over several halibut sets at once. The hooks were baited with squid or octopus, lowered into position, and left to do their work. When a halibut took the bait, the surface float would bob and jerk, signaling the fishermen to paddle over and haul the fish aboard. The wooden hooks discriminated between halibut, a flat fish, and other bottom feeders, and even controlled the size of halibut that could be caught.

Tlingit and Haida halibut hooks were objects of beauty as well as efficiency. The unbarbed arm of the V-shaped hook was carved in the figure of an animal or human. Perhaps the carvings represented spirits that were called upon to assist the fishing effort, or perhaps they simply attracted the halibut's eye. The wooden floats that marked the lines also were carved into shapes, usually of animals or birds. Most of the museums in Southeast Alaska have displays of carved halibut hooks and other Native fishing gear.

The Tlingit and Haida smoked or dried most of their fish for preservation. The eulachon, however, was valued most for its oil. The flesh of this small fish is so oily that a dried eulachon can be lighted like a candle, hence the nickname "candlefish." Southeast Alaska Natives used eulachon oil as a dipping sauce and mixed it with berries and other foods to preserve them over the winter. To obtain the oil, the fish was allowed to decompose for several days and was then boiled in water. Most of the oil collected on the surface of the water where it could easily be skimmed off. The remainder was obtained by pressing the cooked fish in a basket. In the old days, eulachon oil was frequently stored in the long, hollow kelp stems that are plentiful in Southeast waters.

The Tlingit and Haida were not the only Alaska Natives to enjoy the oil: so much eulachon oil was traded to the Athapaskans that the trade routes to the Interior became known as the "grease trails." Dieticians now know that eulachon oil is rich in iodine and vitamins and was important to the Native diet. It is still a precious commodity among Southeast Natives.

Until the Europeans came, Southeast Natives had no iron except the few bits that drifted ashore from distant shipwrecks, and no pottery. Their cooking vessels consisted of wooden boxes and tightly woven baskets. They placed water and the food to be cooked in a basket or box and dropped in stones that had been heated in the fire. They also practiced pit cooking, wrapping or layering their fish with seaweed or leaves.

SOCIAL STRUCTURE

The Southeast coastal Natives observed a rigid social structure that emphasized kinship lines. The concept of lineage permeated every aspect of their lives and was manifested in their works of art. It is thanks to this strong adhesion to kinship that we can admire today the great totem poles, the beaded blankets, the carved serving dishes, and all of the other items, both ceremonial and quotidian, that have been marked with the animal crests denoting family line.

EAGLE AND RAVEN

As you travel throughout Southeast Alaska and observe the artifacts of Tlingit and Haida culture, you will quickly notice that Eagle and Raven are the dominant motifs. Every individual in Tlingit or Haida society was (and still is) born into one of two great social divisions, known as Eagles and Ravens (northern Tlingit use Wolf interchangeably with Eagle). These two groups are called moieties or phratries—anthropological terms meaning tribal subdivisions. Tlingit and Haida societies are matrilineal, so each child automatically assumes the moiety of the mother, but must marry into the opposite moiety. Thus, every set of parents consists of one Eagle and one Raven with all of the children belonging to the mother's group.

KINSHIP CLANS

Both Eagle and Raven moieties are subdivided into several kinship clans that identify themselves by totems: animal names and crests that were adopted long ago because they had special significance for the groups they represent. For example, Frog and Beaver are common clans of the Raven moiety; while Grizzly Bear, Killer Whale, and Wolf are Eagle clans. Clans represent specific lineages, like branches of a family tree, that theoretically could be traced back to the time of their migration to and throughout Southeast Alaska. Thus, each individual is born into one moiety and one clan, for example Eagle and Killer Whale, both according to the mother's group.

Traditionally, clans controlled such property rights as were acknowledged by the coastal Indians. They owned the right to use specific salmon streams, berry patches, hunting grounds, and house sites; as well as the right to employ the clan crest and other designs, songs, dances, and names. The head of each clan was an important and powerful chief whose responsibility was to look after the clan and its property and act as spokesman.

House Groups

Clans were further subdivided into as many house groups as were necessary to accommodate all the clan members and their families in a particular village. The community house was the minimum political and social unit in all Southeast Native societies, and all houses were ranked according to prestige and importance. The head of the most important house in a village was automatically the village chief. Within each house lived various families and individuals of like clan and moiety. Each house had a name, usually relating to one of the clan's totemic crests or to a physical feature of the structure. Dog Salmon House, House of Many Levels, and House with Sand All Around would be examples. Because of intermarriages between clans, the same clan might own houses in several different villages, and each village was made up of at least two and usually several different clans, all of which vied to be most important.

Kwans

Historically, the Tlingit, the largest of the Native groups, were arranged into several different geographical groups called kwans. The precise number of kwans in Southeast Alaska that existed at the time of the first contact with Europeans is uncertain but seems to have been at least thirteen. The kwans took their names from a prominent river or bay in their region. Each contained a number of permanent villages.

Tlingit kwans were fairly cohesive units. The Chilkat Tlingit, for example—the Chilkat-kwan—from the Klukwan area were reputed to be fierce and warlike, the most powerful of all the kwans. Their principal village of Klukwan, on the Chilkat River north of Haines, is still an important Tlingit village. The Chilkat controlled the mountain passes that lead to the Interior, traded with the Interior Athapaskans, and were known up and down the coast for their skill at weaving the famed Chilkat blankets from the hair of mountain goats. Other well-known kwans included the

Stikines, near Wrangell, who controlled the river trade that passed up the Stikine River to Interior Canada, and the Sitka Tlingit.

CLASS

Underlying the fabric of moiety, clan, house group, and kwan was the fundamental question of social class. Southeast Native society ranked all individuals into roughly three classes: nobility, including clan chiefs and their heirs and families; commoners, who comprised the majority of the population; and slaves, who were born into servitude, purchased from neighboring groups, or captured in raids on other villages. Social status was of the utmost importance to Southeast Natives. Rank could always be improved
• through the acquisition of wealth and prestige, the pursuit of which was a continuous and passionate undertaking.

THE POTLATCH

The various Tlingit and Haida groups did not live in isolation, but traveled around Southeast and beyond on trading missions or social visits. Sometimes they went to war against other groups to capture slaves or property, or to avenge a past slight. Occasionally they journeyed to another village to attend a potlatch, which was a party thrown by a clan chief on some meritorious occasion (perhaps to erect a totem pole, celebrate a marriage, dedicate a new house, or perform memorial rites) for the purpose of bringing honor to himself, his house, and his clan.

In the old days, a potlatch could go on for weeks with feasting, singing, dancing, and storytelling. Gift-giving was an important aspect of the potlatch, and the esteem of the potlatch chief was measured by the amount of wealth that he distributed to his guests. Clans saved for years to accumulate the wealth necessary to throw a potlatch, and often the rise in status was about the only thing they had left when it was over. It was more than enough, however, because an astute potlatch host could expect to get everything back—with interest—by the time the necessary reciprocal potlatches had been held.

Potlatches are still given on occasion in Southeast Alaska, and they are an apt reflection of a culture balancing the traditional with the contemporary. Feast dishes of roast turkey and sheet cakes might be presented alongside smoked salmon, pickled kelp, and berries served with eulachon oil. Gifts could be blankets, cases of soda, or cash.

Summer was the trading season. The coastal Tlingit followed the Stikine, Taku, and Chilkat river systems into the mountains to trade with the Interior Athapaskans. They exchanged eulachon oil for such items as durable moose and caribou hides, then went south to barter these things plus thick Chilkat blankets for the superior cedar canoes of the Haida. When the Hudson's Bay Company established a trading post in British Columbia in 1831, the Tlingit and Haida ventured even farther for the chance to trade furs for manufactured goods such as iron tools and cooking utensils, cloth blankets, beads and buttons, rifles, tobacco, sugar, molasses, and flour.

THE RAVEN CYCLE AND OTHER MYTHS

The Southeast Coast Indians enjoyed a rich tradition of stories and myths, passed down orally from one generation to the next, that helped to explain the natural phenomena that surrounded their forested home. Prior to contact with the Russian colonists, they did not practice any organized religion, but tried to stay on the right side of the various spirits that inhabited the earth in the form of animals, fish, trees, water, winds, and other natural elements. They did have a shaman among them whose job was to interpret spirit signs and, in his role as healer, to intercede with the supernatural beings on behalf of the sick.

The most important myths involve Raven, who winged his way into the mythology of many Indian cultures, both inside Alaska and out. In Tlingit mythology, there are actually two Ravens: Yehl, the Great Raven, also called Nass Raven, is the creator figure. From his home above the Nass River (at the southern border of Southeast Alaska), which the Tlingit believe to be their original homeland, he controlled the sun, the moon, and the stars.

Scamp Raven, his grandson, is known as the trickster, and most of the Raven stories pertain to him and his usually comical adventures. It was Scamp Raven who manufactured the earth out of mud and rocks, and then stole the sun, moon, and stars away from Nass Raven so that the world would have light. He also acquired fire, got the tides under control, painted birds their various colors, and accomplished many other feats. Scamp Raven is a much-beloved character. He has a rather coarse sense of humor and something of a mean streak; he loves to play tricks on people.

He is basically lazy and a glutton, in an endearing, human sort of way.

Many totem poles in Southeast depict characters and episodes from the Raven myths. So that you can better appreciate these poles on your travels through Southeast, here are very abbreviated versions of some of the best-known tales.

"HOW RAVEN STOLE THE STARS, THE MOON, AND THE SUN"

All of the light in the world was kept by a man (Nass Raven) who lived at the head of the Nass River. He kept the light hidden in various boxes and bundles inside his house and guarded them closely. Scamp Raven wanted some light for the world and he thought and thought how to go about getting the light away from the man on Nass River. The man had a beautiful daughter, but she always had her slaves with her so Raven was not able to approach. Finally he thought of turning himself into a hemlock needle and slipping into her glass of water. She swallowed the needle and then grew large with child, which is how Scamp Raven happened to be born into the household.

The girl's father loved the baby dearly and gave him everything he asked for. One day the baby cried and cried and simply would not be comforted until his grandfather reluctantly let him play with the bag of stars. Raven rolled the bundle around and around on the floor and when he was positioned beneath the smoke hole in the roof, quickly untied it. All of the stars flew out the smoke hole and escaped into the heavens.

Raven's grandfather was extremely cross about losing his precious stars, but when again the baby cried and cried, he relented a second time and gave him the moon to play with. The same thing happened and the moon took its place in the sky. When Raven finally got hold of the box of daylight, he flew with it up the smoke hole and enjoyed his new world full of light.

"HOW RAVEN STOLE WATER"

In the beginning there were no lakes, no streams, and no rivers; no water anywhere except at Petrel's house where there was a natural spring. Raven wanted water for the world and he thought and thought of a way to get some of that water from Petrel.

Raven went to visit Petrel, who was courteous but very suspicious. He would not let Raven anywhere near the spring. In desperation, Raven invited himself to spend the night at Petrel's house, but still he was not able to approach the spring. The next morning he got up very early and found a pile of dog excrement that he smeared over the poor sleeping Petrel and his blankets. Then he woke Petrel up and, with a great show of commiseration, pointed out that the unfortunate bird had dirtied himself in the night. Petrel, humiliated, went off to bathe. Raven took the opportunity to drink as much water as he could and then escaped out the smoke hole.

As he flew, Raven spat out the water in his beak and the Nass, the Stikine, the Chilkat, the Taku, and the Alsek—all the great rivers of Southeast Alaska—took shape beneath him. Little drops fell here and there as well, forming the smaller salmon streams.

"RAVEN AND TIDEWOMAN"

Tidewoman, or Tidewatcher, lived high on a cliff where she controlled the tide. Raven decided that she kept the tide too high and people could not gather enough food on the beach. He vowed to do something about that. He went down to the water and gathered some sea urchins, then approached Tidewoman and asked her to lower the tide. When she refused, he pricked her bottom with a sea urchin spine. "Ouch!" she cried, and she let the tide down just a little bit. Raven stuck her with another sea urchin spine. "Oh! Ouch!" she cried. "Please don't stick me anymore!" The tide receded a little farther. Raven stuck more spines in her bottom until Tidewoman promised to make the tides rise and fall every day so that the people could collect the food they needed.

"RAVEN AND THE DAUGHTERS OF THE FOG"

Raven created the salmon streams when he stole the water from Petrel, but unfortunately, the salmon refused to go up them and the people could not catch the fish to eat. One day when Raven was wondering what to do about this he noticed a fine-looking woman sitting beside one of the streams. He decided to place her at the head of the stream so that all the salmon would rush upstream to look at her. This worked just fine, and now all of the salmon travel up the streams every fall to see the beautiful women, the Daughters of the Fog, who live there.

OTHER TALES

Both Tlingit and Haida mythology includes the giant Thunderbird responsible for lightning and thunder. The Thunderbird had enormous wings and a large curved beak. He lived on a mountain-top and when he was hungry flew down to the sea and returned with a whale in his talons. The thunder was caused by his great wings beating the air, and lightning flashed from his eyes when he blinked.

One Raven story explains why something does not exist, in this case "Why There Is No Large River Near Sitka." According to this tale, Raven alighted one day near Sitka in a place that he thought would make a fine river. The tide was out and there were clams all over the beach. As Raven walked about to get the lay of the land, the clams kept squirting, making so much noise that Raven could not hear himself think. "Stop squirting, you clams!" he yelled, becoming increasingly irate, but the clams paid no attention. Next Raven picked some blueberries and stuffed them down the necks of the clams, but that did no good either. Finally he flew away in a huff, vowing not to make a river there after all.

This last Raven story, "How Raven Lost His Beak," concerns Scamp Raven, who was hungry one day and looking for an easy meal. He noticed some men fishing for halibut and decided to make his dinner from the bait on their hooks. For a long while he succeeded at this and was feeling very pleased with his cleverness when his beak caught on one of the hooks and came completely off.

The fishermen took home the curious object they had brought up on their halibut hook. That night, Raven turned himself into human form, wrapped himself with a blanket to cover the hole in his face, and went to their house. He asked to examine the object they had found, pretending he might be able to identify it. When they showed him the beak, Raven clapped it back on his face and flew away.

ART AND ARTIFACTS

Food was so easily gathered in the coastal forest that the Tlingit and Haida had time for other pursuits. One of them was art, which they managed to integrate into virtually every aspect of their daily lives. There is a fine line between producing a utilitarian object such as a basket or a wooden bowl that is beautiful for its workmanship and design, and making a functional object beautiful by enhancing it with decorative design. The Southeast Indians did both, and some of the most delightful art objects in museums today were created for everyday use. The Tlingit and Haida also used their sophisticated design sense to create objects that were strictly ceremonial, such as totem poles; or strictly decorative, such as carved metal bracelets. These art forms have undergone a revival in recent years and continue to be practiced today.

Men were the artists and artisans in traditional Tlingit and Haida culture, with one exception: basketry was women's work. Women also wove the fabulous Chilkat blankets, but men created the pattern boards that the women followed to make the design.

BASKETRY

Southeast Alaska Natives produced two types of baskets: cedar bark baskets woven from the stringy inner bark of the cedar tree, and spruce root baskets. The latter were the most difficult, requiring years of practice and immense skill, not just in the weaving, but in preparing the materials. First the roots had to be collected; the smaller roots were preferred. These were roasted in the fire so that their outer covering could be removed by pulling the roots through a forked stick. Then each root was split into still smaller strands with the aid of a long thumbnail. The smooth and shiny outer portion was set aside for the part of the design that would show, and the inner layer used for the rest of the weaving.

Years of practice were required to weave a spruce root or cedar bark basket. (Alaska State Museum, Alfred A. Blaker)

The rings on top of ceremonial potlatch hats indicated the status of the wearer. (Alaska State Museum, Alfred A. Blaker)

Spruce root baskets could be woven watertight. Before contact with other civilizations brought pottery and iron vessels, the Natives used baskets to carry water and for cooking. Special needs called for special shapes. Very small baskets were carried around the neck when berrying, leaving both hands free to pick the fruit. When full, the small basket was upended into a larger basket borne on the back, which was in turn emptied into an even larger model for transporting the berries back to camp. The Indian women of the northern Panhandle were known for weaving large, flat, floppy baskets that they placed beneath the bushes to catch the berries as they fell. Their baskets were so finely woven and flexible that they could be folded and stored for the winter.

To decorate their baskets, the women bleached or dyed tall grasses and overlaid the woven spruce roots with stripes, zigzags, or other geometric designs. For a black pattern, they buried the grass in black mud or steeped it in a solution of hemlock bark. Yellow dye could be made from moss, blue from a solution of urine and copper ore, red from urine that had stood in an alder dish.

Spruce root was also used for weaving hats. Ordinary hats were roughly lampshade-shaped, made of coarser roots, and left undecorated. Wealthy and important people wore larger hats that were more finely woven and decorated with a painted crest design. The weaver's talent was put to the test with the potlatch hats worn by clan chiefs on ceremonial occasions. The potlatch hat was one of the most important symbols of Southeast Indian society. They also were decorated with painted crests, but their distinguishing feature was a series of flat cylinders stacked one on top of the other to form a topknot over the crown. These potlatch rings signified the number of potlatches that the wearer had given during his lifetime and thus symbolized his status in Tlingit or Haida society.

The museum collections of Southeast Alaska, especially the Alaska State Museum in Juneau, Sheldon Jackson Museum in Sitka, and the Tongass Historical Society Museum in Ketchikan contain fine examples of cedar bark and spruce root basketry.

BENTWOOD BOXES

Southeast Alaska and other Northwest Coastal Indians crafted a style of wooden container known as the bentwood box. The boxes, used for storage, packing, carrying, and cooking, were formed out of a single cedar plank that was folded or bent in three places and joined at the fourth corner. The artist added a bottom and sometimes a removable lid, and decorated the finished box with carved or painted crest designs.

To construct a bentwood box, the artist first chiseled or adzed the plank to the correct thickness and then routed out the inside surface opposite the points where the bends would be made. The board was steamed until it could be bent to shape and the ends joined with wooden pegs or spruce root stitching (also used to mend wooden canoes). Iron nails were used in later years. This method of construction produced a sturdy but beautiful box with the soft lines of rounded corners. Look for the seamed corner and nearly invisible spruce root stitches when you see bentwood boxes in museums.

CHILKAT BLANKETS

Art historians look upon Chilkat blankets as the crowning glory of Tlingit artistic design. The shawl-shaped ceremonial and dance robes featured a complicated geometrical pattern that demanded extraordinary skill to achieve. Only a handful of contemporary weavers have mastered this nearly lost art.

Chilkat blankets were woven from mountain goat hair. The weaver spun the wool by hand by rolling the strands of hair be-

The shawl-shaped Chilkat blankets are the highest expression of Tlingit art. (Jorgen Svendsen)

tween the palm of her hand and her thigh. For added strength, the yarn of the warp (the fixed, vertical part of the weave) was wound around a strand of cedar bark. (You can see the reddish brown bark in the long fringe that hangs from the bottom of the blanket.) The yarn was worked with the fingers—not shuttles—on a simple, upright frame, following a pattern board created by one of the male artists of the village.

The colors of the intricate design were black, yellow, and blue-green, set against the cream background of the natural goat hair. To obtain the colors, the wool was dyed in various concoctions similar to those used to dye grass for decorating baskets. Black usually came from hemlock bark, yellow from a type of moss, and blue-green from urine and copper.

The art of weaving the Chilkat blanket was not limited to the Chilkat Tlingit, but they were considered the masters of the craft. The goat wool was more readily available to them in their northern villages than to some of the other Tlingit groups. The original art form is thought to have originated with the Tsimshian peoples, who used a similar technique to create a different type of robe. It is not known when the present style of blanket was first developed, but Captain Cook acquired geometrically styled goat hair robes that may represent the early stages of the art form when he visited the Northwest Coast in 1778.

Chilkat blankets have always been coveted by Southeast Natives as objects of beauty and status. They signified wealth and were very valuable trade items. Collectors covet the prized blankets today. You will find several on display in museums and cultural centers.

Button blankets came into use after traders introduced plain woolen blankets into Southeast Alaska late in the eighteenth century. The Indians adapted the blankets for ceremonial use by decorating them with red trade cloth and bits of abalone shell. Commercially manufactured buttons, glass beads, and sequins were added to the crest designs when they became available.

TOTEM POLES

Totem poles are at once the most familiar and most misunderstood form of Southeast Native art. Part of the false impression can be attributed to the grotesque and gaudily painted poles in curio shop windows, seeming as they do to symbolize some mysterious religion or primitive Native rite. In fact, traditional Haida and Tlingit poles were never worshipped as religious objects, and they were not gaudy. For the most part, they were bare cedar with painted accents of the typical Southeast Alaska palette: black, red, and blue-green. As the poles aged, they were allowed to return gracefully to their natural state, never being touched up or restored, so that in time they sprouted bits of grass and woolly moss blankets. In later years, when the art form was in danger of being lost, efforts were made to retrieve and rehabilitate the best of these poles.

Many visitors, upon seeing a particular totem pole, will ask what it "says." What is the story carved in the pole? For many poles, there is no story at all. For others, the answer can be given only by the carver or the person who commissioned the pole.

The Lincoln Totem, carved about 1883, bears likeness to the U.S. president. (R.N. De Armond)

Totem poles were carved and erected for several different purposes or occasions. None of them involved worship in any sense; they were not religious objects. Some were memorial poles erected to honor important individuals upon their deaths. Many memorial poles were comparatively simple: a plain shaft topped by a crest figure representing the individual's clan. The crest figure might be Eagle, Raven, or one of the other totems such as Bear, Beaver, or Frog. Some early poles were mortuary poles, which were similar to memorial poles except for a niche carved in the back of the pole to contain the ashes of the deceased.

Totem poles also were carved to commemorate a particular event, such as the building of a new house, the giving of a potlatch, or an occasion of even more widespread significance. One of the most famous poles in Southeast was commissioned by a Tongass Island chief about 1883 to commemorate his clan's first sighting of a white man many years before. The carver evidently used a likeness of Abraham Lincoln as a model for the figure of the white man at the top of the pole, which is why the pole has come to be called the Lincoln Totem pole. The pole is more properly known as the Proud Raven pole from the Raven crest carved at the base. The original carving, weathered but still Lincolnesque, stands in the State Museum in Juneau. (There is a replica at Saxman Totem Park in Ketchikan.) A last type, the ridicule pole was erected to shame publicly a family or individual who had failed to pay a debt or otherwise broken a trust. When the debt was paid, the pole was taken down.

Whatever the type of pole, the dramatic carvings on the column served to remind the Native viewers of events, people, and legends from their collective history. With no written language, this was a significant contribution to the continuation of the culture. Totem poles are "story poles" only in the sense that the figures carved on them acted as symbols or memory aids to remind the storyteller of the principal characters and events he was relating.

Totem poles were carved by artists commissioned by the clan chief. The chief decided what figures he wanted on the pole and the artist executed the design. Red cedar was the preferred wood, although yellow cedar (Alaska cedar) was acceptable in the north where red cedar was not available. The Haida, especially, who had very large trees at their disposal, frequently hollowed out the back of the log to reduce weight and guard against splitting. The artist was left with a half-round shell approximately 10 inches thick on which to carve his designs. (Be sure to look at the backs of totem poles, too.) The artist shaped the figures on the pole by chipping off small, uniform bites of wood with an adze. The Southeast Natives look upon fine-textured, even adzing as an indication of the carver's skill.

The next step was paint, applied sparingly. In earlier days, the paint was a version of egg tempura using pulverized salmon eggs for a binding medium. Soot, graphite, or charcoal ground and mixed with the salmon eggs produced black paint. Red was made from red ochre, and the blue-green came from copper sulfide.

Originally, wood-carving tools were polished stone, bone, or shell, but trade with the Europeans brought sharp iron blades that cut through the cedar like butter. The metal blades enabled carvers to create larger and more complex designs, culminating in totem poles up to 65 feet tall. Most of the poles now seen in Southeast Alaska were carved in the latter half of the nineteenth century when trade with Europeans and Americans had brought considerable wealth to local Native groups and touched off a renaissance of Native carving.

Once erected, totem poles were generally not taken down (except for ridicule poles), even if the villagers moved to a new site. The poles were simply abandoned. Most of the totem parks around Southeast today stem from the 1930s when the Civilian Conservation Corps, working in conjunction with the U.S. Forest Service, undertook to collect old poles from abandoned sites and restore them to public view. Over the course of the project, more than one hundred totem poles were restored, duplicated, or carved from memory and placed in parks around Southeast.

Southeast's largest and most accessible totem pole collections are at Sitka National Historic Park and at Saxman Totem Park and Totem Bight State Historic Park in Ketchikan. At Sitka the poles are spaced along a beautiful trail within the Tongass National Forest. There is an exhibit center where you can watch carvers and other craftspeople work and see a film about the history of Sitka and the Tlingit culture. The Totem Bight site in Ketchikan has a spectacular beach setting, but Saxman is closer to downtown. Ketchikan also houses the state's largest collection of original, unrestored totem poles at the Totem Heritage Center. Totem parks also can be found at the villages of Hydaburg, Kasaan, and Klawock on Prince of Wales Island.

There are also many individual poles to be seen as you walk around Southeast towns, and several new poles have been erected in recent years. Alaska's tallest totem pole—132 feet, 6 inches—stands in the village of Kake on Kupreanof Island. The pole was carved in the 1970s at the Indian Arts Center in Haines.

OTHER CARVING

The Tlingit and Haida carvers—always men in those days, but no more—were kept busy. Besides bentwood boxes and totem poles, many other utilitarian and ceremonial objects were decoratively carved with clan crests or other significant totemic designs. The posts supporting the house roof beams frequently were patterned in designs that celebrated the history of the clan. There were elaborate wooden serving dishes for special feasts, "grease dishes" to hold eulachon or seal oil, enormous sheep horn spoons with handles carved of black goat horn, dance rattles shaped like birds, and ceremonial wooden hats with crest animals carved on top. Intricate dance masks, some with moving parts that the wearer controlled by strings, represented birds, animals, or spirits. All these objects—and more—are displayed in museums throughout Southeast Alaska.

In the early 1800s, the Haida developed a new art form: argillite carving. Argillite is a black shalestone that was discovered around 1820 on the Queen Charlotte Islands of British Columbia. The Haida artists found that the new substance could be carved and polished to a high luster that the traders frequenting the Northwest coast found attractive. The Natives began carving boxes and ceremonial dishes from argillite, sometimes adding decoration of ivory, abalone shell, or operculum to the traditional crest designs. Later they found that miniature totem poles of argillite proved profitable in the tourist trade. Haida argillite carving is considered one of the highest art forms of the Northwest Coast.

BASIC COMPONENTS
OF TOTEMIC DESIGN

Almost every object in Southeast Native life, whether ceremonial or strictly utilitarian, lent itself to adornment. Sometimes the design was carved into the wood of the object, and sometimes it was painted on top. The designs were generally totemic, meaning that they represented the clan totems, or crests. The crests served to signify ownership of the object and they engendered a sense of pride, in much the same way that a coat of arms created pride and allegiance in medieval Europe. Perhaps more than anything else, they turned plain household implements into objects of beauty

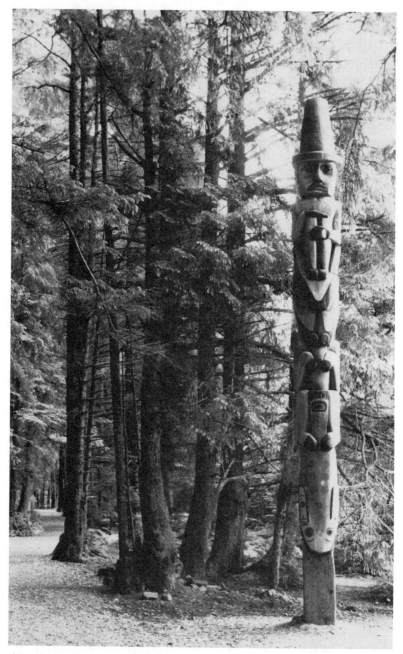

A totem pole merges with the woodland setting at Sitka National Historic Park.

and delight. Looking at an exquisitely carved halibut hook or a perfectly proportioned dish, in the shape of a seal, for example, it is easy to believe that these early artists worked primarily out of love for the materials, their tools, and the designs they were creating. Surely they felt great joy in filling their workaday world with beautiful objects.

Tlingit and Haida designs may all look the same to you at first—you will not be able to distinguish one totem from the next. In time, though, you will become practiced at picking out the identifying characteristics of each totem, which will add enormously to your pleasure in viewing Native art.

If you want to learn more about totemic design, I strongly recommend Hilary Stewart's *Looking at Indian Art of the Northwest Coast* (University of Washington Press). The author uses wonderfully explicit illustrations to break down the elements of totemic design into understandable bits.

THE TOTEMS

Whether painted on canoes or spruce root hats, or carved into the soft cedar of totem poles or storage chests, Native designs consist of the same basic totemic motifs. Only the format differs according to the shape of the object. The basic crest figures are most easily recognized in three dimensional form as they appear on totem poles. Whether the carving is Tlingit, Haida, or Tsimshian,

This sea lion feasting bowl, from the Sheldon Jackson Museum, is a fine example of the carver's art.

there are certain distinguishing features that you can look for in each crest animal. Usually the identifying characteristic is a particular body part, but a characteristic pose or an object frequently associated with that animal may be part of the design convention as well.

Raven can probably be considered the most important design figure because he appears so frequently, either as one of the two major totems or in his mythological guise. Either way, Raven is usually portrayed as birdlike with wings. His distinguishing feature is a long, straight beak.

Eagle's beak is shorter than Raven's and curved downward. Frequently he is shown with large claws. Occasionally you will see a double-headed eagle, such as the one on the totem pole in front of the Pioneers' Home in Sitka. This does not represent the Eagle crest, but the Russians in Alaska.

Bear is an important family crest. He is usually sitting upright on his haunches, in the attitude of a begging dog. He has upright ears, prominent teeth, large nostrils, and no tail. Sometimes a bear represents not a clan crest but a story, such as "Kats and His Bear Wife." This popular Tlingit legend tells of Kats, whose life was saved by a female grizzly bear that appeared to him in human form. Kats and the bear woman lived together as husband and wife, but he was killed by their cub children.

Beaver is similar to Bear in overall shape and begging-dog attitude, but he has very large front teeth for gnawing. He also has a distinctive paddle-shaped tail that frequently is turned up in front of him and decorated with cross-hatching. Beaver sometimes holds a stick between his front paws.

Wolf often assumes the begging-dog pose, with these differences from Bear or Beaver: a pointed snout, pointed ears, and a long tail. Sometimes his tongue lolls out of his mouth.

Frog generally looks exactly like a frog, with a large, toothless mouth; short legs; and a squat body, sometimes with spots.

Killer Whale is the easiest totem to identify. Look for a blunt head sometimes with prominent teeth, a forked tail, and a circular blowhole. The telling dorsal fin protrudes from his back. Usually Killer Whale is placed vertically on the totem pole, head down, but sometimes he rides crosswise on top.

Halibut does not appear as frequently as some of the other totems, but is eminently recognizable with close-set eyes that are off-center, mouth to one side, and flatfish body.

Humans are occasionally portrayed on totem poles as figures from legends or notable events. They can be distinguished from animals by their ears, which are located on the sides of the head

Grizzly Bear

Double-headed Eagle

Raven

Beaver

Frog

Wolf

Killer Whale

Halibut   *White Man*

instead of the top. White men are typically given beards, clothes, and curly hair. Native women wear lip ornaments called labrets, which were popular in early days. Haida poles are frequently topped by one or two human figures wearing tall potlatch hats. They are the "watchmen" on the lookout for enemies.

APPLIED DESIGNS

The same techniques for carving animal designs onto a log could be applied to other surfaces and shapes, such as wooden serving vessels. A bowl could be shaped like a halibut, for example, with a broad tail at one end, a head with two offset eyes and crooked mouth at the other end, and the body hollowed out to form the cavity. Or a grease dish made to hold seal oil could be formed in the shape of a seal, with head protruding from one end and flippers on the sides.

When the totemic patterns were applied to flat surfaces, such as painted house screens, the designs had to be adjusted to fit. Once the principle was established of letting each totem be represented by stylized body parts, however, the problem was solved. The body parts were simply rearranged as necessary to fill up the given space in a pleasing manner. Sometimes the animal was simply "split" down the backbone and spread open to create a symmetrical design in one plane. The head appeared at the center of the design, with one side of the body shown to the left and the other side to the right. Many silver bracelets are carved this way.

Sometimes the totem was just shown in a single profile, or as a double profile. Sometimes all of the necessary features were there, but out of order. This rearrangement of body parts can approach pure abstraction, as in the case of Chilkat blanket designs, which only experts can interpret. Always, though, the key design elements are there if you know where to look.

DESIGN COMPONENTS

Regardless of their media or subject matter, Southeast totemic artists adhered to certain conventional motifs. The components of this art form have undergone scholarly analysis in recent years, and certain names and definitions have come to be accepted as standard. The fundamental shape in Southeast Alaska totemic art is called the ovoid—the slightly rounded rectangle that is re-

Killer Whale is portrayed with a double profile on a painted housefront in Angoon.

peated over and over within a single design. Eyes are usually contained within an ovoid; sometimes the whole face or head is an ovoid shape as well. The ovoid illustrates the design principles of Native art: corners are rounded, lines are curved, and everything is gently smoothed to make a flowing, pleasing shape.

The U-form frequently appears as an upside-down U, usually with a flattened top. This shape forms the ears of many crest animals and is used in details of tails and wings. The U-form can be divided in half to form a split U, a favorite device for feathers. U-forms can vary greatly in size and proportion. Some are tall and narrow, as for feathers, and others short and wide at the base.

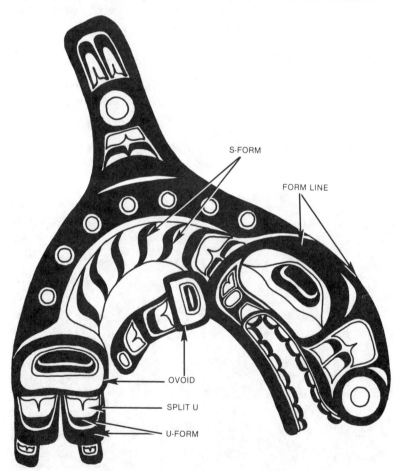

Jumping Killer Whale patterned after the design on a Tlingit hide shirt in the Berne Historical Museum.

The S-form is primarily used to fill up space or act as a bridge from one line to another. It, too, can vary in shape. A series of S-forms often represents ribs or a backbone.

All of these various components that make up a totemic design are contained within a continuous form line that defines the structure by outlining the major body parts. In a painted design the form line is usually black, while the secondary features are red or blue. In carved designs, the outermost surface of the wood becomes the form line while secondary motifs are recessed. Like all parts of the design, the form line is always curving, to create a continuous, controlled, flowing form.

In both carved and painted designs, the artist places a small face where two body parts join. This device is often seen in the figure of Beaver, where his tail joins with his body. The face also appears as the blowhole in Killer Whale. A face appearing within wings, however, indicates the power of flight. Within an eye, a face represents the life-force.

INTO THE CORPORATE ERA

After the first contact with the Russians when Chirikof's party went ashore, presumably near Sitka, in 1741, the Indians of Southeast Alaska saw ships from many nations. They traded furs for articles they did not have, such as cloth, iron tools, kettles, and pots. These manufactured goods, and the practice of trading with the outsiders, changed the pattern of their lives. They began to fit canvas sails onto their seagoing canoes; they adopted white men's garments in place of their own sewed skins and cedar bark shirts. But even when the Russian-American Company settled into Sitka, forcing the local Tlingit to abandon their homeland and camp in the shadow of the Russian community, the life-style of the majority of the Tlingit and Haida Indians living on the coast was not severely disrupted.

Clear, cataclysmic devastation came in the form of smallpox, the scourge of aboriginal peoples. The English sea captain Nathaniel Portlock believed he saw many pockmarked faces when he visited near Sitka in 1787. He concluded the Spanish had brought the disease with them a dozen years before during the Pérez explorations. In 1836, smallpox broke out among the Tlingit in the southern range of the territory, perhaps spread northward from the British territories in Canada. This time the disease ran rampant through the Southeast coast and island chain. An esti-

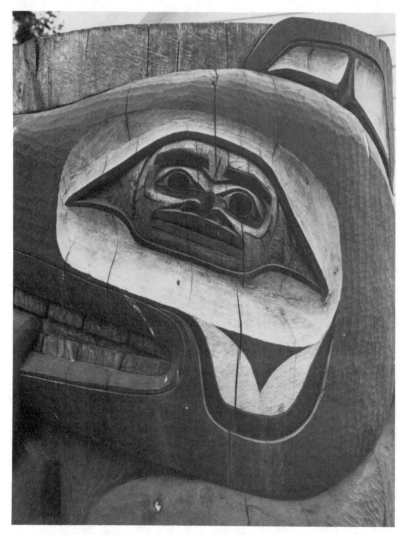

A small face within an eye usually represents the life-force. This is one of the Tired Wolf houseposts at Saxman.

mated 50 to 60 percent of the Indian population—thousands of people—died. The smallpox spread from settlement to settlement along the coast to the north, eventually reaching the peoples of Bristol Bay, the Kuskokwim River, the Yukon River, and Norton Sound.

The U.S. purchase of Alaska from Russia had little immediate effect upon the Tlingit and Haida. The trading posts were more of an interruption to their life-style, as was the coming of missionaries. The discovery of gold and the birth of the commercial fishing industry in the late 1800s brought a substantial increase in the white population of Southeast Alaska and the development of new permanent communities. The Indians moved from their traditional villages to camp near the bustling mining towns or canneries where they could barter for goods or earn wages.

In the first years of U.S. possession, there were few laws to protect the white population and even fewer for Natives. In 1902, the Tlingit petitioned to attend white schools in Juneau and Ketchikan but were refused entrance. In 1912, they organized the Alaska Native Brotherhood with the aim of winning citizenship. This right was finally recognized in 1924. The same year, Tlingit attorney William Paul, Sr. won a seat in the territorial legislature.

Native peoples from all over Alaska gradually gained political sophistication and power. In 1971 their long efforts were rewarded by passage of the Alaska Native Claims Settlement Act, which awarded a cash and land settlement to reimburse the various Native groups for aboriginal lands that had been usurped by the U.S. government. Village, urban, and regional corporations were formed to manage the new resources. In Southeast Alaska, the final land selections for Native corporations will total 550,000 to 600,000 acres. Much of the acreage has been selected from prime timberland and many Native corporations have entered the logging industry on a large-scale basis.

Chapter 5
Common Plants of the Inside Passage

The topography of the Inside Passage region consists of deep salt-water passages adjacent to mature coastal forests and high mountains, all occurring within a few thousand feet. This wide range of habitats existing in close proximity is one of the principal characteristics of Southeast Alaska.

HABITATS

From shipboard, the flora of the Inside Passage appears to consist solely of evergreen forest, but there are actually five distinct communities of vegetation. Marshlands or tidal flats made up of grasses, sedges, and other herby vegetation lie close to the saltwater shore and along estuaries and riverbanks. Small willows and alder also grow at this low elevation and, in some locales, tall black cottonwoods.

The evergreen forest extends from sea level to timberline at 2,000 or 3,000 feet. The coastal forest of Southeast Alaska is the natural extension of the forest that stretches all along the Pacific coast from northern California to Cook Inlet in Southcentral Alaska. The southern forests are composed primarily of Douglas fir, but the dominant species in Alaska are western hemlock and Sitka spruce. There is also a scattering of red cedar, Alaska cedar, and mountain hemlock.

Except where they have been disturbed by humans, Southeast forests are generally more than 150 years old. Some of the mature trees are more than 200 feet tall. Shrubs, ferns, and young trees grow beneath the tall cover, and the forest floor is littered with a thick layer of fallen logs and moss. These mature old-growth forests are called climax forests. They are in a natural cycle of growth and decay, which means that every stretch of woods con-

Forest openings reveal wet muskegs with low-growing shrubs and stunted trees. (U.S. Forest Service)

tains many large, healthy trees; some small, young trees; and the remains of dead and dying trees that eventually will decompose to nourish the next generation.

In the forest openings are wet muskegs with pools of freestanding water. This community is characterized by natural bonsai—stunted, deformed trees that may be 200 years old—as well as mosses, sedges, and low shrubs such as Labrador tea, high bush cranberry, blueberry, and crowberry. The primary trees are lodgepole pine (also called shore pine) and mountain hemlock.

Above the spruce and hemlock forest lies a subalpine transition zone of scrubby trees such as mountain hemlock and a mat of low-spreading vegetation. Past the tree line, above 2,500 feet, begins the true alpine tundra community of tiny, low-spreading plants, such as heather, crowberry, nagoonberry, and alpine azalea, that grow amongst the rocky outcrops.

Vegetation grows rapidly with the increasing daylight of spring. Within the space of a few weeks, muddy hillsides are transformed into impenetrable salmonberry thickets that tower overhead. In the autumn, the process is reversed. The leaves linger on the berry bushes, turning yellow and mottled brown, until a late fall wind blows up, baring trees and bushes to winter.

The five most important conifers and some of the other common plants of the Inside Passage follow.

TREES

WESTERN HEMLOCK

Western hemlock is the most prevalent tree in Southeast, forming more than 70 percent of the coastal spruce/hemlock forest. These tall evergreens can grow to 190 feet with a 5-foot diameter trunk. The needles are dark green and shiny on top, dull on the underside. Unlike spruce needles, they are short, soft, flexible, and rounded

Western hemlock

at the tip. They grow along two sides of the twig only, so the western hemlock twig is flat. The branches have a feathery appearance compared with the stiffer spruce; the tips are slender and curve down, especially when the ⅜- to 1-inch cones have formed on the ends.

Better-quality hemlock logs are used for general construction lumber. Poor-quality hemlock goes into pulp. Although hemlock makes one of the best paper pulps, the mills in Southeast produce dissolving pulp, which is further processed into rayon, cellophane, and plastics.

Sitka spruce

SITKA SPRUCE

The Sitka spruce is Alaska's official state tree and makes up 20 percent of the Southeast coastal forest. The tree can attain 225 feet in height and 8 feet in diameter, although 160 feet high and 3 to 5 feet in diameter is more typical. The needles are dark green on top, but silvery blue below. They are short, stiff, and sharp, and grow all around the twig, like a bottlebrush. If you squeeze your hand around a spruce tip, you will say "Ouch!" Not so with the hemlock. The 2- to 4-inch cones—considerably larger than the hemlock's—hang from the branch tips.

The fast-growing Sitka spruce is one of the most valuable trees in Alaska. Like hemlock, better-quality spruce is cut into lumber. Spruce is an important wood for aircraft and glider construction, boats, ladders, and other items that require strength combined with light weight, and its excellent acoustical properties make it suitable for guitar faces and piano sounding boards. Lesser-quality wood goes into dissolving pulp.

MOUNTAIN HEMLOCK

Mountain hemlock is the alpine counterpart to western hemlock. Although found at sea level, the mountain hemlock extends to 3,500 feet—higher than the western hemlock or Sitka spruce cares to grow. The tree is smaller than the western hemlock, normally 50 to 100 feet high, but capable of stretching to 125 feet. In muskeg bogs and subalpine communities where soils are infertile, the tree takes on a severely stressed shape with very short branches, bonsai bends, and weathered, gray bark. At times mountain hemlock hugs the ground, spreading horizontally as a low-lying shrub. The needles of mountain hemlock are similar to those of western hemlock: shiny green, short, and soft. The difference is that they grow around the entire circumference of the twig. The cones resemble those of western hemlock but are longer. They are dark purple before they mature, deepening eventually to brown.

WESTERN RED CEDAR

Western red cedar grows in the southern part of the Panhandle, approximately from Petersburg south, mixed in with the rest of the spruce/hemlock forest. The foliage of this aromatic tree is much different from that of either spruce or hemlock, the needles forming flat, fanlike sprays with ½-inch elliptical cones appearing near the ends of the twigs. The wood from the red cedar resists rot and insects and is widely used for fence posts, shakes, shingles, and boats. The Tlingit and Haida Indians used this wood for their canoes, houses, and totem poles, and wove mats and baskets out of the stringy bark. The red cedar commonly grows to 100 feet and sometimes to 130.

ALASKA CEDAR

Alaska cedar, known also as Alaska cypress or yellow cedar, exists throughout the coastal forest but is not nearly as common as spruce or hemlock. Smaller than the western red cedar, the Alaska variety grows to a maximum height of 100 feet. The leaf structure consists of the same flat, fanlike spray, but the tiny cones (less than ½-half

Alaska cedar

inch in diameter) are nearly round and more gray-colored than brown. The durable wood is soft and easy to work—the Coastal Indians habitually used Alaska cedar for their carved canoe paddles. Today Japan imports quantities of Alaska cedar, and U.S. manufacturers use the lumber for windows, doors, and boats.

LODGEPOLE PINE

Lodgepole pine, or shore pine, is the only pine native to Alaska. In Southeast Alaska, it usually appears as a twisted, scrubby specimen growing in the muskeg swamps of forest openings. In this mode the pine attains only a few feet of height, often spreading horizontally rather than vertically. In better growing conditions, though, lodgepole pine can shoot straight up to 40 feet. An inland variety found around Haines and Skagway grows to 75 feet. The tree is dark green with typical pine needles growing in pairs with a sheath at the base. The cones are up to 2 inches long. Many local residents prefer this resinous pine at Christmas time, but they are too few to be harvested commercially.

ALDER

Red alder

Alder is the most common deciduous tree in Southeast Alaska. It appears from the size of a shrub to a small tree in places where the ground has been disturbed: along roads and ditches, on avalanche scars, by rivers and streams, on logging sites, and where glaciers have retreated. The smooth, gray-barked wood has long been used for smoking fish and game and is easily gathered for firewood. Alder is also preferred for some types of Native carving.

Three species of alder are present in Southeast. All have smooth, gray bark; shiny, dark green leaves with serrated edges; and small, dark, nutmeg-shaped nuts. The largest and most abundant species is red alder, which grows to 40 feet. Sitka alder is slightly smaller, growing to 30 feet. This species grows along with red alder at lower elevations, but exists by itself at elevations above 1,000 feet. The third variety, thinleaf alder, is found only in the northern part of the Panhandle, from Juneau to Skagway, where it grows mixed in with willows along streams.

Alder is known as a pioneer species, meaning that it follows disturbances to the ground such as avalanches or roadbuilding, quickly takes root, and improves soil conditions. When the evergreens appear and overtake them in size, the shade-intolerant alders disappear.

WILLOW

Willows grow along with alders beside stream beds, beaches,

and roads. Like alders, they quickly take over sites that have been logged, burned, or otherwise cleared. Their light, gray-green leaves are smooth and oblong. In spring, they develop fuzzy caterpillar-shaped catkins that spread tufts of white fluff everywhere. There are many varieties of willow in Southeast. The Scouler willow is most common, followed by the Sitka willow and Barclay willow. In size the willows range from shrubs to small trees.

BLACK COTTONWOOD

The stately black cottonwood, the largest deciduous tree in the area, reigns over the river valleys on the mainland of Southeast Alaska, including the Stikine, the Taku, and the Chilkat. The black cottonwood grows alongside the alder and willow trees but towers above both at 80 to 100 feet. In 1965 a champion specimen was found near Haines (about 5 miles west of Klukwan on the Klehini River). The tree measured 101 feet in height with a circumference of 32 feet 6 inches.

At first glance the cottonwood might be taken for an alder, since the two usually grow side by side. The cottonwood is much larger, though, and the leaves are smooth around the edges, in contrast with the toothed leaves of the alder. The handsome cottonwood provides welcome color in the fall when the leaves turn golden. In late autumn and winter bald eagles gather by the thousands in the cottonwoods along the Chilkat River near Haines to feed on spawned-out salmon.

MOUNTAIN ASH

The colorful European mountain ash, introduced as an ornamental in many Southeast towns, grows to 40 feet. Its clusters of tiny white flowers are among the first blooms to appear in spring; in fall its scarlet berries attract flocks of Bohemian waxwings and other migrating birds. The delicate foliage contains numerous small, yellow-green leaves on a slim stem. The leaves turn bronze in fall. The bark is light gray and smooth. A rare na-

Mountain ash

tive species of mountain ash grows as a tall shrub to about 15 feet in forest openings. It is smaller and less showy than the introduced tree.

A handful of other trees exist in Southeast Alaska but are less commonly seen or exist only in isolated spots. They include the dwarf Douglas maple (the only maple in Alaska), Pacific silver and subalpine firs, Pacific yew, quaking aspen, western paper birch, and Pacific serviceberry.

BERRIES AND OTHER FOREST PLANTS

Berrying is an important recreational activity in Southeast Alaska, an excuse to be with friends and enjoy the wild forest trails. Around late June, the berry fanatics begin cruising the roads and trails to sniff out the best patches for the summer's gathering. The two-pound coffee can makes an excellent berrying pail. You punch holes in the sides, thread them with a long scarf, and knot the ends. The scarf goes over your neck and the pail hangs in front of you, freeing both hands for picking. The bounty in Southeast Alaska includes blueberries, salmonberries, thimbleberries, and nagoonberries. Southeasterners bake them in pies, shortcake, and crisps and freeze a supply for muffins and sourdough pancakes throughout the winter. The remainder goes into jam and jelly—Christmas presents for favored friends and relatives in the Lower 48.

Berry picking is more than recreation for some older Alaska Natives, whose culture was once heavily influenced by the cycle of food gathering. For them, collecting a quantity of berries in summer and preserving them for winter use is virtually a ritualistic necessity. I once was acquainted with an elderly Tlingit woman who had the use of only one eye and such severe arthritis that she could barely hobble with the use of a cane. At berrying time she asked to be carried to the berry patch where she would spend hour upon hour gathering in her winter's fruit.

SALMONBERRY

The pink, star-shaped blossoms of the salmonberry peek through the bright green leaves in early May, a welcome sign of spring. These berries grow profusely along trails, on open hillsides, and in forest clearings. When the prickly canes reach their full summer height—easily 10 feet—they form a nearly impenetrable barrier. The fruit, which appears about July, appeals to both humans and bears. The large, pendulous berries, shaped like boysenberries or black-berries, vary in color from salmon-orange to dark red. The mild fla-vor is slightly tangy.

PACIFIC RED ELDER

When the salmon-berries are already blos-soming, the red elder, or elderberry, springs to life with clumps of lacy, white blossoms. This berry reaches the size

Salmonberry

of a small tree in Southeast, with brittle, woody branches and long, narrow leaves. In late summer, grapelike clusters of shiny red berries form in place of the flowers—much to the delight of the crows. But the bitter fruit affects some people adversely. (The European elderberry that forms the basis for the excellent elder-berry wines is not present in Southeast.)

Red elders add color and grace to many Southeast gardens. They are common in open areas of the forest or on the fringes of communities: a scarlet splash against the dark green spruce and hemlock.

BLUEBERRY

Several varieties of blueberry and huckleberry thrive in South-east. All the varieties form compact shrubs that can reach 6 feet in height. The stems are woody; there are no thorns or prickles. The oval leaves are small and light green, and the spring blos-soms, yellow-pink to bronze-pink, depending upon the variety, hang down in the shape of a bell. The berries vary in color from blue to nearly black.

The fruit of the early blueberry is covered with a light-colored powder or bloom while that of the Alaska blueberry, often called a huckleberry, is shiny blue-black. Both varieties grow together. The red huckleberry, much appreciated for its bright color and good jam-making qualities, is rarer. Most people simply mix the various varieties together since they grow side by side in the woods. Two dwarf varieties grow on the muskeg at higher elevations: the dwarf blueberry and the bog blueberry. Both are low, spreading shrubs that never attain more than a couple of feet in height.

Some years the blueberries have a tendency toward worminess. Nothing to be squeamish about—just dump your berries in a pail of water when you get back from the woods and soak them for a few hours. The worms (which are minuscule) become starved for oxygen and crawl out.

OTHER BERRIES

Blueberries and salmonberries may be the most plentiful berries in the Panhandle, but they are by no means the only ones. Wild cranberries are a tangy bounty in fall. There are two creeping varieties that grow in bogs and alpine areas, and a high bush variety that appears in the forest and grows to 12 feet. The sparse, three-lobed leaves turn color with the seasons. The large (⅜ to ½ inch), elliptical, translucent fruit is a beautiful yellow-orange in summer and turns brighter with time. Locals prize the high bush cranberries for jelly or syrup. Unfortunately, they are not plentiful except along streams on the mainland. The western thimbleberry has large, maple-shaped leaves. The flat, white blossom forms an edible pinky red berry shaped like a thimble. The shrub grows to 5 feet.

Southeast has several edible currants and gooseberries and several ground berries. The latter include the crowberry (sometimes called mossberry), a low, heatherlike plant with shiny, round, black berries that grows in bogs and upper tundra regions, including the rocky cliffs of the Juneau Ice Field at 5,600 feet. The rare nagoonberry appears in low-lying meadows and bogs. This is a delicate little plant, growing 2 to 10 inches off the ground, with three-lobed leaves and a red fruit shaped like a rounded, shiny raspberry—coveted for jam, jelly, or wine (Southeasterners have been known to share *anything* except the location of their secret nagoonberry patch). Small wild strawberries can be found in beach areas.

Avoid the poisonous baneberry, which has large, coarsely toothed, lobed leaves and round red or white fruit, several to a stem. The bush grows in woods and thickets to 3½ feet. As few as six berries have been known to cause dizziness, increased pulse, and stomach pain.

DEVIL'S CLUB

Devil's club might be
called the ogre of the
woods: a primitive-look-
ing plant with enormous
leaves and treacherous
spines. This common in-
habitant of the spruce/
hemlock forest under-
growth grows to 10 feet.
The elephantine leaves,
which measure up to a
foot in diameter, are
prickly on the underside.
Even worse, the tall,
snaking stalks are
equipped with sharp,
poisonous spines that
can make a painful sore

Devil's club

if they become embedded in your skin. Although it can block your
path through the forest very unpleasantly, the plant is quite
handsome at a distance. In spring pale greenish-white flowers develop on tall stalks and turn into bright red berries (not edible) in
the fall. Devil's club is one of the few hazardous plants in the
Southeast woods. There is no poison ivy or poison oak in Southeast forests.

COW PARSNIP

The cow parsnip also has gigantic leaves. This plant appears
along roadsides and in meadows, forest clearings, and many a do-
mestic garden where it is not wanted. The hollow green stem is
striated like celery or rhubarb, hence the plant's two other names:
wild celery and Indian rhubarb. Cow parsnip bears tight clusters
of tiny white flowers in the spring—so large and compact that
they resemble a flat head of cauliflower.

Cow parsnip smells strongly "weedy," and the scent lingers on
skin and clothing for hours. Many people are allergic to this plant;
for particularly susceptible people even superficial contact can
cause painful blisters on the skin. For those not allergic, the stems
are edible and formed part of the Native diet in earlier times. But
beware of confusing cow parsnip with deadly poison water hemlock, which has a similar-appearing flower.

Skunk Cabbage

Skunk cabbage

Bright yellow skunk cabbage is the unsung champion of the boggy forests of Southeast Alaska, the first plant to appear through the waning snow in spring. The flower appears first, shaped like a yellow calla lily with a green stalk in the center. The leaves come up later. They are bright green and they grow, and grow, and grow throughout the spring and summer until they are nearly 5 feet tall.

Skunk cabbage thrives in wet conditions. You will see the familiar shape in drainage ditches, swamps, and bogs. The plant sometimes gives off a strong odor, hence the name. Although the Tlingit used skunk cabbage for pit baking, the leaves contain large amounts of oxalic acid and should not be eaten.

Wildflowers

Despite a rainy disposition, Southeast Alaska grows a full complement of wildflowers. A list of the commonly appearing varieties appears on pages 100–101. Below are a few of the better-known specimens that you may encounter during your rambles through the coastal forest.

The lovely blue-violet lupine grows to 4 feet tall along the coastal shore, along highways and roads, and in alpine areas. One of the most extravagant displays appears opposite the highway just north of the Juneau airport, in the vicinity of Brotherhood Bridge. The showy fireweed, with magenta blossoms, grows to 9 feet along roadsides, riverbanks, and in meadows. Along forest trails, the bunchberry, a dwarf form of dogwood, forms a single greenish-white flower with four petals in spring and a red fruit in fall. This common ground cover in the spruce and hemlock forest stands no taller than 8 inches.

Both the yellow stream violet and the blue Alaska violet grow in Southeast. They prefer damp locations. Southeast has many varieties of buttercup, a red-orange columbine, a purple-blue wild flag or iris, a wild rose, the delicate blue forget-me-not—Alaska's state flower—and a wild beach pea with red-violet flowers. Among the other species one has special interest: a rare (outside of coastal Alaska) chocolate lily that grows in open grassy flatlands. This purple-brown lily grows

Chocolate lily

to 24 inches. The bulb is covered with ricelike pellets that are edible when cooked. The local Native peoples included the pellets in their diet, accounting for the lily's other name: Indian rice.

If you visit Southeast in early fall you might enjoy searching for clumps of Alaska cotton grass. Local residents like to use this tufted grass in dried floral arrangements.

COMMON WILDFLOWERS OF SOUTHEAST ALASKA

Cotton grass/Alaska cotton, *Eriophorum* species *
Skunk cabbage, *Lysichitum americanum* *
False hellebore, *Veratrum eschscholtzii*
Indian rice/Chocolate lily, *Fritillaria camschatcensis* *
Alp lily, *Lloydia serotina*
False lily-of-the-valley, *Maianthemum dilitatum*
Wild iris/Wild flag, *Iris setosa* *
White bog orchid, *Habenaria dilitata*
Ladies' tresses, *Spiranthes romanzoffiana*
Heart-leaf twayblade, *Listera* species
Fairy slipper/Calypso, *Calypso bulbosa*
Coral root, *Corallorrhiza mertensiana*
Moss campion/Cushion pink, *Silene acaulis*
Dwarf water lily, *Nymphaea tetragona*
Yellow pond lily, *Nuphar polysepalum*
Mountain marigold, *Caltha leptosepala*
Marsh marigold, *Caltha palustris*
Western columbine, *Aquilegia formosa* *
Monkshood, *Aconitum delphinifolium*
Yellow anemone, *Anemone richardsonii*
Narcissus-flowered anemone, *Anemone narcissiflora*
Cut leaf anemone, *Anemone multifida*
Cooley buttercup, *Ranunculus cooleyae*
Eschscholtz buttercup, *Ranunculus eschscholtzii*
Creeping buttercup, *Ranunculus repens* *
Western buttercup, *Ranunculus occidentalis* *
Sundew, *Drosera* species
Roseroot/King's crown, *Sedum rosea*
Grass of Parnassus, *Parnassia palustris*
Fringe cup, *Tellima grandiflora*
Alaska boykinia/Bear flower, *Boykinia richardsonii*
Laceflower, *Tiarella trifoliata*
Purple mountain saxifrage, *Saxifraga oppositifolia*
Luetkea/Alaska spirea, *Luetkea pectinata*
Goatsbeard, *Aruncus sylvester**
Marsh fivefinger/Cinquefoil, *Potentilla palustris*
Silverweed, *Potentilla egedii* var. *grandis*
Yellow dryas, *Dryas drummondii*
Eight-petaled dryas/Mountain avens, *Dryas octopetala*
Nootka lupine, *Lupinus nootkatensis* *
Prickly wild rose/Nootka rose, *Rosa nutkana* *

Beach pea, *Lathyrus maritimus*
Cranesbill/Northern geranium, *Geranium erianthum*
Touch-me-not, *Impatiens noli-tangere*
Stream violet/Yellow violet, *Viola glabella* *
Alaska violet, *Viola langsdorffii* *
Fireweed, *Epilobium angustifolium* *
Dwarf fireweed, *Epilobium latifolium* *
Western/Poison water hemlock, *Cicuta douglasii*
Cow parsnip, *Heracleum lanatum* *
Ground dogwood/Bunchberry, *Cornus canadensis* *
Pink pyrola/Wintergreen, *Pyrola asarifolia*
Single delight/Shy maiden/Wax flower, *Moneses uniflora*
Labrador tea, *Ledum groenlandicum*
Alpine azalea, *Loiseleuria procumbens*
Aleutian heather/Mountain heather, *Phyllodoce glanduliflora*
Alaska moss heather, *Cassiope* species
Bog rosemary, *Andromeda polifolia*
Pixie eyes/Wedge-leaved primrose, *Primula cuneifolia*
Rock jasmine, *Androsace septentrionalis*
Star flower, *Trientalis europaea*
Shooting star, *Dodecatheon* species
Broad-petaled gentian, *Gentiana platypetala*
Jacob's ladder, *Polemonium pulcherrimum*
Forget-me-not, *Myosotis sylvatica* *
Monkey flower/Wild snapdragon, *Mimulus guttatus*
Coastal paintbrush/Yellow paintbrush, *Castilleja unalaschcensis*
Mountain paintbrush, *Castilleja parviflora*
Lousewort, *Pedicularis* species
Poque/Broomrape, *Boschniakia rossica*
Butterwort/Bog violet, *Pinguicula vulgaris* var. *macroceras*
Twinflower, *Linnaea borealis*
Valerian/Mountain heliotrope, *Valeriana* species
Mountain harebell/Bluebell, *Campanula lasiocarpa*
Bluebells of Scotland, *Campanula rotundifolia*
Dandelion, *Taraxacum* species *
Goldenrod, *Solidago multiradiata*
Fleabane, *Erigeron* species
Arctic daisy, *Chrysanthemum arcticum*
Arnica, *Arnica* species
Seabeach senecio/Seabeach groundsel, *Senecio pseudo-arnica*
Yarrow, *Achillea borealis*

* Very common

Chapter 6
Wildlife of the Inside Passage

The coastal forests and waterways of Southeast Alaska nurture a huge variety of creatures. A few of them, such as the bald eagle, grizzly bear, and humpback whale, are so seldom seen in most of the continental United States that their numbers in Alaska seem an embarrassment of riches and, for lovers of wildlife, probably worth a trip in themselves.

The continued richness of wildlife resources—15,000 bald eagles, 25,000 brown bears—can be attributed to the relatively vast expanse of habitat that still exists in an undisturbed state in Southeast Alaska. Where natural habitat gives way, be it from logging, mining, roadbuilding, tourist activities, or simply the gradual encroachment of towns and marinas, wildlife decreases. Animals lose nesting areas and cease to bear young; they become poisoned by unnatural substances in their environment and die; they lose sources of nourishment or resting spots and fail to reproduce. In the case of brown and black bears, they become a threat to the safety of humans and are destroyed.

So far, wildlife populations for major species in Southeast Alaska remain strong. Even the sea otter, long missing from these coasts, appears to be returning. Living in close proximity to these wild creatures—seeing them in their natural habitat, observing their seasonal comings and goings—remains one of the greatest of pleasures of living along the Inside Passage.

These are a few of the wildlife forms that are common to Southeast Alaska.

LAND ANIMALS

BLACK BEAR

The black bear, the smallest and most common species of bear in America, exists in the forests of much of Alaska. In Southeast, the black bear is at home on all of the mainland and most of the islands. Exceptions are the northernmost islands, including Admiralty, Baranof, Chichagof, and Kruzof. One of the highest concentrations occurs on Prince of Wales Island, across Clarence Strait from Ketchikan, where you might well glimpse one of these animals ambling across one of the logging roads that bisect the island.

An adult black bear measures approximately 26 inches at the shoulder and can weigh up to 200 pounds in summer when feed is plentiful. Although called *black* bears, the animals range in color from deep black to brown and even cinnamon, a fact that frequently causes them to be confused with their larger brown grizzly cousins. A very rare glacier variety with smoky blue fur appears sometimes in the northernmost part of the Panhandle around Yakutat.

Black bears spend most of their time in summer browsing through open forested areas where they can find the salmonberries, blueberries, and other shrubs they like to eat. You are not likely to see one unless you happen to be in the forest, too. In late summer and fall, they turn to fishing for spawning salmon along shallow rivers and streams. In winter, when food is scarce, they enter a state of semihibernation characterized by a drop in metabolic rate. They are easily awakened, however, and may even leave their dens for short periods.

Spring may be the best time to spot black bears as they feed on tender new growth along beaches and in open meadows and hillsides. Look for clearings on the mountainsides (such as slide or avalanche scars) where the new vegetation has grown. The dark-colored animals are visible against the bright green cover or as they cross lingering patches of snow. The Anan Creek Bear Observatory near Wrangell provides an excellent opportunity to view both black and brown bear (see page 190).

BROWN BEAR

The large brown bear, known also as the coastal brown bear and grizzly, lives throughout the Southeast mainland and on the northern islands, especially Admi-

Grizzly bear

ralty, Baranof, and Chichagof. Small populations occur on Wrangell and Etolin islands in the southern Panhandle. The concentration of brown bears on Admiralty Island is estimated at approximately one bear per square mile, one of the highest in the world. In summer, some of these Admiralty Island bears can be viewed from an observatory at the Stan Price Bear Sanctuary at Pack Creek (see page 241).

Brown bears and grizzlies used to be considered separate species, but biologists now believe them to be the same. Nevertheless, bears living inland with primarily a vegetable diet (usually called grizzlies) tend to be smaller than coastal bears that feed on protein-rich salmon during the summer and fall.

Color is not a good test for distinguishing a brown bear from a black bear, since both species vary in color. Brown bears range from dark black-brown to blond. Size is a better indicator. Mature males weigh from 500 to 900 pounds, and large coastal bears can reach 1,400 pounds. The brown bear also has a prominent hump over the shoulders (actually an extension of the powerful front leg muscles) and a round, massive head.

SITKA BLACK-TAILED DEER

This abundant game animal provides winter meat for many Southeast families. The Sitka black-tailed deer is a member of the coastal mule deer family, which is native to the entire Pacific Coast from northern California through Southeast Alaska. The Sitka species is small, the average adult weighing from 100 to 150 pounds. The reddish-brown summer coat turns dark gray in winter. The name comes from the small flag of a tail which is black on top and white beneath.

Home for these animals varies with the season. After the fawns are born in May and June, the deer move out of the forest and up to the alpine meadows where they feed during the summer months (the opposite of the bears, which come down from the mountains in the summer to feed off berries and salmon). When fall frosts limit the available food, the deer return to the forest and remain there throughout the winter and early spring, foraging among leaves and shrubs. In deep snow conditions they may be forced down onto the beach to search for dried grass or, in extreme conditions, seaweed. In spring and early summer, they move to the beach to nibble new grass and other succulent plants. You may see them there with their new spotted fawns, especially in the early morning, as you glide by in your ship.

Moose

Moose are found in only the mainland river valleys of Southeast Alaska. The largest herd is located at the northern end of the Panhandle around Yakutat. Smaller herds roam near Haines, Berners Bay (on the mainland between Haines and Juneau), and in the drainages of the Taku, Stikine, and Unuk rivers. You stand a good chance of encountering the large animals if you explore these rivers by small boat. Otherwise, you can only hope to spot them from the air or see them grazing on the flats at the river mouths as you pass by on your ship. Ferry passengers occasionally sight them on the large sandy flats at the entrance to the Katzehin River in Chilkoot Inlet, on the way to Haines and Skagway.

Moose weigh up to 1,600 pounds. They spend much of their time knee-deep in swamps or shallow ponds, where they munch on willow twigs, weeds, and grass. Although slightly ludicrous in appearance with a mule-shaped body, small ears, and an improbably long nose, the animals are greatly respected for their strength and ferocity, especially in defense of their young, and for their excellent meat. Many local hunters set off resolutely every fall to "get their moose" to fill the freezer.

Mountain Goat

If you have sharp eyes or binoculars, you may be able to pick out a group of mountain goats in the high rocky outcrops that border the Inside Passage. The goats are mighty small to the naked eye—you have to look for small white dots that appear about half an inch high against the gray rock. You may be lucky and see them closer up, especially in Glacier Bay or Tracy Arm Fjord near Juneau.

Mountain goats make their home in the most rugged and inaccessible parts of the Coast Mountains. Their hooves are fitted with cushioned pads that allow them to clamber up and down

Mountain goat

the sheer rock walls. They have all-white shaggy coats, long chin whiskers, and short black horns—in contrast to the light-colored and curved horns of Dall sheep, with which they are frequently confused (Dall sheep are not native to Southeast anyway). Mountain goats spend the summer in high meadows where they feed off grasses and alpine shrubs. In winter they forage along the wind-blown ridges that are free from snow. Some may climb down to tree line and nibble at the hemlock trees.

RED SQUIRREL

You are likely to catch sight of red squirrels whisking along the spruce branches above your picnic table or hear them scolding you for some imagined transgression. This forest native measures only 11 to 13 inches long to the tip of its bottlebrush tail. The belly is white and the back and tail brown to rust. A white ring around each eye enhances an already bright countenance.

True to their reputation, red squirrels spend the summer months putting food by, collecting spruce cones and piling them in heaps for winter use. They make their nests in the trunks of trees and sometimes in dense foliage, but once the young are raised the squirrels live a solitary existence, each within a prescribed territory.

The red squirrel is Alaska's most common squirrel. The only other species in the state are the Arctic ground squirrel of the tundra and the northern flying squirrel that inhabits the spruce/hemlock forests throughout Alaska. The latter species is nocturnal, however, and you are unlikely to see one.

GRAY WOLF

The gray wolf population is thriving in Alaska. The densest accumulations occur in Southeast, where they inhabit the mainland and major islands except for Admiralty, Baranof, and Chichagof. The animals range in color from black to near white, with those in Southeast usually somewhat darker than those in the north. The wolf is a good deal larger than the average dog or coyote, the adult male weighing 85 to 118 pounds (the coyote weighs 25 to 40 pounds). In the north, wolves feed primarily on moose and caribou. In Southeast Alaska, their diet consists of deer and goats as well as small animals, such as squirrels and the occasional bird or fish.

Historically the wolf has been trapped and hunted in Alaska for different reasons. The thick pelt, used for parka ruffs, can bring good money to the hunter. In northern and interior parts of Alaska, wolves have been considered a threat to game animals (especially moose and caribou) sought by sport hunters and depended upon by resident subsistence hunters, including Alaska Natives, for food. Until the early 1970s, in fact, the wolf earned a $50 bounty from the state of Alaska, and the state has sanctioned aerial wolf hunts and other predator-destruction programs for the purpose of protecting declining game species. The controversy over game management policy has heightened in recent years and spilled into the national arena as wildlife organizations and other groups have come to the defense of the wolf.

Unless you venture into the remote areas of Southeast, you are not likely to see a wolf. But it is not uncommon for kayakers and other independent boaters to spot the occasional animal prowling the shoreline in search of a meal, or to hear its captivating howl in the night.

Coyote

The coyote is a relative newcomer to Alaska, having migrated out of Canada's interior. First noted at the beginning of the twentieth century, their numbers now range as far north as the Brooks Range. In Southeast Alaska they appear to exist on the mainland only and are not especially prevalent. The coyote is about one-third the size of a wolf, averaging 30 pounds, with a coat that varies from tan to gray.

The coyote's appetite for sheep and chickens has given it a bad reputation in the Lower 48. In Alaska, where there are few sheep or chickens to prey upon, the coyote is forced to eat birds, squirrels, and the like. There was a $25 bounty in the state until 1969 that resulted in some hunting. Today coyotes are only occasionally trapped for their pelts and otherwise not much bothered.

Other Animals

A raft of other animals inhabit the coastal forest. The porcupine is much in evidence in Southeast, as dog owners will testify. Although nocturnal, the porky often can be glimpsed plodding along forest trails and even on the highway. The forest provides both shelter and sustenance, spruce bark (the inner layer) being a principal food. In the woods you will see vertical bare patches on the trunks of trees where a porcupine has dined off the bark. In summer porcupines augment their diet with leaves, tender branches, and buds.

Beaver pelts have been prized since the days of the Russian occupation and were used as a trade medium for many years. So many beaver were taken after the U.S. purchase of Alaska that they were protected in 1910. Beaver are still trapped, but under state regulation. In Southeast, beaver are most abundant near Yakutat and Juneau, but they live on other river drainages on the mainland, too, where they dam streams to satisfy their requirements for 2 to 3 feet of water year-round.

Of the other fur-bearing animals, the versatile land or river otter is at home on land as well as in both salt and fresh water. You can distinguish the river otter from the sea otter by the muscular tail, which makes up one-third of the animal's total body length of 40 to 60 inches. The dark brown fur includes some gray on the chin and throat. River ot-

River otter

ters are wonderful swimmers and can dive to at least 60 feet. In winter, they seem equally suited for snow and ice, where they run and slide and slip and tunnel just like human children. They eat fish, supplementing their diet with shellfish and occasional birds. They might show up anywhere. I once watched a pair frolicking among the boats in the Wrangell harbor.

Southeast's other fur-bearing animals include the wolverine, marten, mink, and ermine, which dresses in brown for summer but switches to white in winter. The sea otter, whose luxurious fur brought Russian traders to Alaska in the first place, has begun to reappear in Alaska waters after years of protection. These creatures once occupied the entire Pacific coast from northern Japan through the Aleutian Islands and along North America to Baja California. Reintroduced in Southeast Alaska during the late 1970s, they may be a familiar sight again one day. Your best chance of seeing them is probably around the northwest Chichagof and Yakobi islands area, near Elfin Cove.

Mammals not found in Southeast Alaska include the caribou and the Arctic fox, which frequent the Arctic tundra in the northern part of the state; the polar bear, which lives near the edge of the Arctic ice; and the big-horned Dall sheep, whose territory is the high mountains of Alaska's Interior and northern British Columbia.

MARINE MAMMALS

Many species of whale inhabit the waters off the Alaska coast. Some are year-round residents, while others arrive for the summer months after wintering in the more temperate waters off Hawaii or Baja California. Some whales are toothed, meaning they have large teeth that they use to catch—but not to chew—sizable prey that they then swallow whole. The others are baleen whales, which feed primarily on tiny shrimplike organisms called krill. The krill is strained from the water by strips of bonelike material hanging from the whale's upper jaw. It was this baleen, or whalebone, that was so essential for ladies' undergarments and, along with whale oil, caused the creatures to be pursued by whalers in the nineteenth century. Ironically baleen whales, the giants of the deep, feed on krill and microorganisms, while the smaller whales, porpoises, and dolphins feed on meaty sea mammals and fish.

Since they are mammals, all whales must surface frequently to breathe air. They exhale through blowholes on their backs. Accompanied by a great deal of water vapor, the exhalations look like small geysers and are commonly known as spouting or blowing, hence the traditional lookout's cry, "Thar she blows." Often you will see the spout first, which will be your clue to look for the whale.

HUMPBACK WHALE

The humpback, a baleen whale, returns to Inside Passage waters every spring after wintering off Mexico or Hawaii. Unlike most other whales, humpbacks come in close to shore to feed in the bays and fjords that outline the coast. They are a familiar and beloved sight in Southeast, and you are almost certain to see some of these elegant creatures as you cruise along the Inside Pas-

Humpback whale

sage. One group of approximately forty whales feeds around Frederick Sound, the large east-west channel at the south end of Admiralty Island, which is rich in krill from late July through early August. Other concentrations occur near the north end of Chichagof Island and in Glacier Bay. The humpbacks also follow the herring runs in Auke Bay and Lynn Canal north of Juneau, and in Seymour Canal on the east side of Admiralty Island. When fall comes, the humpbacks turn south for warmer waters to breed and bear their young.

The humpback reaches 45 to 50 feet in length and is dark-colored except for the grooved belly. Three characteristics distinguish this acrobatic whale: long pectoral fins, or flippers, which measure up to 14 feet; the huge lobed tail that lifts completely out of the water on a dive; and the hump that lies in front of the small dorsal fin.

In recent years, biologists have focused considerable attention on characteristic humpback behavior such as breaching, when the whale leaps clear out of the water. Some scientists think breaching may be a warning behavior or territorial display, but its significance is not yet fully understood. Humpbacks also practice a sophisticated feeding technique known as bubblenet feeding, which, experts believe, helps the whales herd together small prey, such as herring. A whale (sometimes a pair of whales or more) dives beneath the prey and swims around them in an upward spiral while exhaling through its blowhole. This creates a "net" of bubbles in the water that contains the confused fish. The whale dives again and surfaces through the center of the bubble ring with open jaws, scooping in the feed. Scientists have documented other cooperative feeding techniques and recorded a specific humpback song believed to aid in this process. Researchers identify specific whales by the distinguishing patterns on their tail flukes.

GRAY WHALE

Whale watchers tend to associate the gray whale, a baleen, with the California coast. Great numbers of gray whales are observed every winter as they migrate southward along the coast to their winter breeding grounds in the lagoons of Baja California. But in spring they reverse the journey and spend June through October off northern Alaska, where they feed on small shrimplike crustaceans that live near the ocean floor. That makes a round trip journey of 12,000 miles. Gray whales do not stay around Southeast Alaska like the humpbacks do, but they are frequently spotted as they pass through inside waters in early summer and late fall.

You probably can distinguish the gray whale by the pointed head that is usually covered with barnacles. There is no dorsal fin, and the flippers are much smaller than the humpback's. This whale is equal to the humpback in size, reaching a maximum length of 50 feet, but colored mottled gray instead of black.

MINKE WHALE

The only other baleen whale common to Southeast is the minke or piked whale. The minke is the smallest baleen whale in the Northern Hemisphere, occasionally reaching 33 feet in length. These whales are grayish black on the top side, with a white stomach. Look for a large sickle-shaped dorsal fin placed far back on the body.

Minkes are migrating whales and are found in many oceans from southern California to the Bering and Chukchi seas, where they spend their summers. When they are in southern waters, they feed on krill, but their northern diet shifts to mackerel, cod, and herring.

KILLER WHALE

The killer whale, or orca, is unmistakable. In the first place, this whale has striking black and white markings, including a sparkling white chin, white flanks, and a white patch on either side of the head. Then, the male has an enormous triangular-shaped dorsal fin that stands out of the water like a shark's. In adults, the dorsal measures up to 6 feet. Whereas other

Killer whale

whales may be traveling solo, killer whales are almost always seen in groups, or pods, containing as many as twenty-five or thirty whales. Herds of 150 have been observed.

A toothed species, orca feed on almost anything that moves in the ocean. Little is safe from this swiftest of whales that can swim at twenty-five knots and more. These "wolves of the sea" habitually go after seals, porpoises, squid, and many varieties of fish. They have even been observed attacking a swimming moose. Like land-based wolves, they are also capable of organizing their numbers to hunt down whales larger than themselves. Orcas themselves have no natural predators.

Killer whales average 23 feet in length and weigh eight to nine tons. They range all over the world and are frequently seen in the inside waters of Southeast Alaska. Chatham Strait and Stephens Passage are likely places to spot them.

DALL PORPOISE

Dall porpoise, another black-and-white sea creature commonly seen in Southeast, seems to delight in cavorting in the bow waves of fishing boats and pleasure craft. The Dall porpoise has a black body with white underside markings that extend halfway up the sides and sometimes tip the end of the tail and dorsal fin. How can you tell them from killer whales? First, the killer whale averages three times as large as the Dall porpoise, which reaches a maximum length of 7 feet. Second, the porpoise's dorsal fin is insignificant compared to the large upright triangle of the orca. Finally, the porpoise delights in swimming close to the bow of your boat, but you are more apt to spot the killer whale off in the distance, chasing after something to eat.

HARBOR PORPOISE

Harbor porpoise frequent coastal bays and river mouths from the Arctic coast of Alaska to southern California. The smallest of the whale, dolphin, and porpoise family, they reach no more than 5 or 6 feet in length. They are colored dark brown to gray and sport a triangular dorsal fin toward the center of the back.

Usually this porpoise is seen alone, in pairs, or in small groups, but it sometimes travels in larger company. You may see harbor porpoise swimming near the surface of the water, but probably not near your ship.

HARBOR SEAL

The resident species of seal in Southeast is the harbor, or spotted, seal, which is at home in both the North Atlantic and Pacific oceans. It is a hair seal, as opposed to either a fur seal or sea lion, and the only such seal in Southeast. Like all hair seals, harbor seals are true seals: they have no ears and cannot rotate their hind flippers forward, making them clumsy on land. They are thus primarily water creatures, touching down on land to rest and bear their young. The harbor seal averages 5 to 6 feet in length and varies in color from yellowish gray to blue gray with dark spots. The coat of stiff hair is used for parkas, moccasins, purses, and the like, which are available in the curio shops of every town.

Harbor seals feed on fish and shellfish—everything from herring to crab. They curry great disfavor within the commercial fishing industry by damaging or stealing salmon caught in nets or on trolling gear. A $2.00 bounty was in effect from 1927 and raised to $3.00 in 1939, but was removed south of Bristol Bay in 1967. The Federal Marine Mammal Protection Act of 1972 limited seal hunting (and that of all marine mammals) to Alaskan Indians and Eskimos.

You might spot harbor seals anywhere—in the open water, in a protected harbor, on rocky offshore outcrops, or on sandy beaches. They rest with their pups on icebergs in such places as Tracy Arm and Le Conte Glacier.

STELLER'S SEA LION

The brownish black sea lion is the largest of the eared seals—bulls reach 13 feet in length and weigh up to 2,400 pounds. They have tiny, visible ears and, unlike the true seals, they can rotate their back flippers forward, making them more mobile on land.

The sea lions' province is the coastal waters from the southern end of the Panhandle to the Bering Sea. They favor remote areas with shallow, rocky bottoms where they can find the herring, rockfish, octopus, and shellfish that make up their diet. Like the smaller harbor seals, Steller's sea lions are fond of salmon and are a nuisance to the commercial fishing industry. Like seals, sea lions have been protected from indiscriminate hunting since 1972 and can be harvested only by Indians and Eskimos.

Although the Steller's sea lion population has declined drastically in other parts of Alaska and worldwide since the 1960s, their numbers appear stable in Southeast. They congregate at rookeries and haul-out spots at various periods of the year. (The Alaska ferries pass right by one haul-out spot, Benjamin Island, at the entrance to Lynn Canal north of Juneau, en route to Skagway and Haines.) I have seen them gamboling in the Juneau harbor in winter.

FISH AND SHELLFISH

SALMON

All five species of salmon exist in Southeast waters: the king salmon, known also as the Chinook; the coho, or silver; the sockeye, or red; the chum, or dog; and the pink, humpback, or "humpie." The species differ from one another in several respects, including size, color, shape, anatomical details, and spawning season. They share one of the most dramatic life cycles in nature.

All species of salmon are anadromous, meaning that they spend part of their lives in fresh water and part in the sea. After hatching in the gravel stream beds, the salmon pass the next segment of their lives feeding and growing in the freshwater stream. The amount of time varies according to the species, from almost none in the case of pink and chum salmon to up to three years in the case of cohos. They then migrate downstream to salt water where they spend, again according to the species, from two to three years or more roaming the North Pacific. When they reach maturity, they migrate back to the stream in which they were hatched to spawn. Before reaching fresh water they eat voraciously because they will eat little once they start their upstream dash. It is at this point, while they are moving toward the stream mouth, that they become the targets for commercial and sport fishing.

The salmon spend as much as a few weeks at the entrance to the stream while their bodies readjust to fresh water. Then they begin the exhausting uphill battle to the spawning grounds. When their instincts tell them that they have reached the place, the once beautiful salmon—now battered, torn, and mortally weary—carry out the spawning ritual. The females scrape a series of shallow nests, called redds, in the gravel with their broad tails and deposit several thousand eggs. The males spill their milt over the eggs, and the females brush gravel over the top. That is the end. Both males and females will die, usually within two weeks.

The fertilized eggs remain in their gravel incubators developing into embryos called alevins and then baby salmon called fry. When the fry are mature enough to swim downstream, they are known as smolt. The smolt head out for the few good years in the great Pacific; then the cycle begins again.

The king salmon, Alaska's official state fish, is considerably larger than the other four species, commonly exceeding 30 pounds and frequently exceeding 50 pounds. The largest king salmon on record, taken in a fish trap off Prince of Wales Island in 1939, weighed approximately 126.5 pounds. (The salmon was not weighed until after it had been cleaned, so the weight is only an estimate.) This giant salmon is on display at the Clausen Museum in Petersburg. A record sport-caught king (93 pounds) was caught at Kelp Bay on the northeast coast of Baranof Island in 1977.

In Southeast, the king salmon runs extend from May through July. The major spawning runs are up the Stikine River near Wrangell, the Taku south of Juneau, and the Alsek south of Yakutat. Kings are capable of extremely long freshwater migrations. The northern kings that spawn in the headwaters of the Yukon River travel more than 2,000 miles to their spawning grounds.

King salmon are commercial favorites because of their large size and good flavor, and they retail for several dollars per pound. Their flesh may be either red or white—why, no one knows. Although there is little difference in flavor, the white kings have always been undervalued because the flesh is not "salmonlike" in appearance. Local residents fish for kings year-round. A winter-caught king is considered a delicacy because of the flavorful fat that builds up over the winter months.

Next in size to the king is the coho, which reaches 35 pounds. Appreciated by anglers for its aggressive response to the hook, the coho is also valuable on the commercial market. The cohos enter the spawning systems from August through November, and sport fishing is good from July through September.

Sockeye salmon are the "money fish" of the Bristol Bay fisheries, where enormous quantities are netted, canned, and frozen. The nickname "red salmon" comes from the spectacular coloration that the sockeye acquires while spawning: a brilliant red body and an olive green head. The sockeye is small compared with the king or coho, weighing only 4 to 8 pounds in maturity. The fish also differs in eating habits, preferring a diet of marine plankton, chiefly small crustaceans. This makes the sockeye an elusive target for anglers, who rarely hook the fish in salt water and never on bait. The fly fisherman sometimes succeeds and comes away with a good prize because the sockeye is extremely desirable for eating fresh, home canning, and smoking.

The chum, or dog, salmon is the widest-ranging of any Pacific salmon. This species is found from the Sacramento River in California to the Mackenzie River in Canada, and in Japan. The fish takes its other name from the large doglike teeth that develop during the spawning season. Chums weigh up to 18 pounds in maturity (some grow to 30), but are not sport-fishing favorites because they seldom strike a lure. Most commercially caught chum are netted. Unlike kings, cohos, or sockeyes, the young chum salmon do not spend a long time in fresh water, but feed in the estuary for a few months and then go out to sea.

Pink salmon are the smallest of the Pacific salmon, averaging only 3½ to 4 pounds. They are also the shortest-lived, maturing at two years. They set off for the spawning grounds from late June to mid-October. Most pinks spawn within a few miles of the coast; some even spawn within the intertidal zone of the stream mouth. Like chums, the pinks spend no time in fresh water after they emerge from their gravel incubators. The fry swim up out of the gravel and head immediately downstream to salt water.

Despite such spunk, the pinks were not well regarded by either sport or commercial fisheries until recent years, when the lack of availability of other species tempted some commercial fishermen to concentrate on the increasingly plentiful pinks (reared very successfully in hatcheries). Pink salmon now constitute 80 to 90 percent of the commercial salmon harvest in Southeast Alaska. They are netted, for the most part. Their flesh is softer and less flavorful than coho or king, making them most suitable for canning. The nickname "humpy" comes from the spawning males, which develop a pronounced hump on their backs after they enter fresh water.

PACIFIC HALIBUT

Like the salmon, the halibut has traditionally been an important fish in Southeast Alaska. The Tlingit and Haida Indians elevated halibut

Halibut

fishing into an art. Their beautiful, carved wooden halibut hooks were proportioned to catch only halibut of the desired size, and their fishing skills were the envy of the early European explorers. Like so many things in Alaska, halibut come in exaggerated proportions. Sport-caught halibut weighing more than 300 pounds are brought in by sport fishers every year. The largest on record is a 495-pounder caught near Petersburg.

Halibut are flounder, or bottomfish, which accounts for their flat and generally goofy appearance. The fish starts out looking perfectly normal, but after about six months the left eye migrates across to join the right, and the halibut spends the rest of its days with both eyes on one side of its head. Then the fish turns over so the two eyes are uppermost, and what seems to be the top (the dark side) is actually the right side . . . very fishy indeed. Left to their own devices, halibut live many years—one specimen was estimated to be forty-two years old.

Halibut is an excellent eating fish. The flesh is firm, beautifully white, and mild tasting, and it freezes well. If you are lucky enough to catch a halibut for your table, here are two typically Alaskan things to do with it. Get some Krusteaz buttermilk pancake mix, add enough beer to make a batter that will not slide off your chunks of halibut, and deep fry. Or, cut your fresh, filleted halibut into small serving pieces and cover with white wine for up to two hours. Drain and roll in dry bread crumbs (preferably from homemade bread). Place in one layer in a buttered baking dish. Mix together two parts sour cream to one part mayonnaise and one part finely chopped onion and spread over the top, reaching clear out to the edges. Sprinkle with paprika and bake at five hundred degrees for fifteen to twenty minutes or until light brown on top and bubbling. This dish, called "Halibut Caddy Ganty," was made famous by the kitchen of the Gustavus Inn (near Glacier Bay). I pass it on with the kind permission of the chefs.

TROUT

There are two important kinds of trout in the Southeast region. The cutthroat, which takes its name from two red stripes below the mouth, is found from Southeast Alaska north to Prince William Sound in sizes up to 17 pounds. In fresh water the trout, like others of the family, frequently follow the salmon runs and feed on the new eggs. The cutthroats also are found in salt water.

Rainbow trout live in the river drainages as well as in freshwater lakes where they have been introduced. Some rainbows are seagoing, in which case they are known as steelheads. There is no difference between the two except that one lives in salt water and the other in fresh. The rainbow or steelhead is closely related to the Atlantic salmon and weighs up to 20 pounds. The world-record steelhead, however, was caught near Ketchikan in 1970 and weighed 42 pounds, 2 ounces.

DOLLY VARDEN

Silver-green Dolly Varden are members of the char family. Many anglers contend that they are in fact Arctic char, but the scientific community says not: Although closely related, they differ anatomically in certain respects. (The true Arctic char does not exist in Southeast. Its realm is to the north in the coastal regions of the Alaska Peninsula, Bering Strait, and the Arctic.)

Dollies have an unusual life cycle. Like salmon, they spawn in fresh water and migrate downstream to salt water in their third or fourth year. Once at sea, however, they return every winter to a freshwater lake. Those that were spawned in a lake system return there. Those that were not have to find themselves a suitable lake. When mature, at five to six years, the dollies return to their original streams to spawn. Many survive the spawn, however—perhaps as many as 50 percent—and return to sea.

Fully grown Dolly Varden reach up to 22 inches and weigh 3 pounds. When fresh out of the water, they have a pattern of small red spots on their sides, which fade with time. They are easy to catch on spinning gear and well worth taking home for the frying pan or smoker. Their flesh is a delicate pink in color, like salmon, but troutlike in texture; the flavor falls nicely in between.

ARCTIC GRAYLING

The Arctic grayling is a true Alaskan, dependent upon clear, cold streams and lakes that exist only in the north. The greatest concentrations are found in rivers on the north side of the Brooks Range. Other populations exist in the Cook Inlet region and parts of the Interior. In Southeast Alaska, grayling have been introduced successfully in some lakes, among them Antler Lake in the Juneau area; Big Goat, Tyee, and Manzoni lakes in the Ketchikan vicinity; and several on Prince of Wales Island.

Grayling grow slowly, reaching only 12 inches in six or seven years. Fully mature grayling might reach 20 inches, and some larger ones have been reported. Their diet consists of insects and the like, which makes them a fly-caster's delight. If all of these things did not make the grayling special, appearance would. The troutlike body has a dark purple back and silvery green sides. On top is an enormous fanlike dorsal fin with reddish purple spots on a green background.

PACIFIC HERRING

This productive little fish has been an important contributor to the Southeast economy. The original Indian inhabitants of Southeast harvested both herring and herring roe for food. Herring roe are sticky, and the female herring deposits them—usually in late

March to early April—on grass, kelp, or other surfaces in the intertidal area. The Tlingit learned to place spruce boughs in the water at the spawning grounds, and the herring obligingly covered the branches with their sticky eggs. The laden boughs were then removed from the water and hung out to dry. Natives still gather herring roe in this manner.

The commercial herring fishery was launched in 1882 when the first herring reduction plant was built at Killisnoo on Admiralty Island. The products were fish meal, used as a fertilizer and food additive for livestock, and oil, which was used as an industrial lubricant and detergent. The herring industry peaked in 1937 when seventeen plants processed more than 251 million pounds of herring in Alaska. Salted and pickled herring was also produced in Southeast, especially during World War I. Both industries gradually declined, the last reduction plant closing in 1966. Today herring are harvested for bait and for roe, which is frozen and exported to Japan.

The Japanese specialty market made the herring sack roe fishery very lucrative—fetching $1,000 to $1,500 per ton in some years. A glut of herring on the market, coupled with the depressed Japanese economy, caused prices to drop to $100 per ton by 1992. During the peak years the Sitka sack roe fishery, the most important in Southeast and third largest in Alaska, received national media attention for the intense, derbylike atmosphere that prevailed. The Alaska Department of Fish and Game regulates the fishery a little differently now; the 1993 season lasted eight days and took the quota of 9,700 tons. The roe fishery does not waste the rest of the fish. Since 1983, it has been illegal to discard the herring carcasses; they are sold for fertilizer and the like.

Blue-green Pacific herring average 9 to 10 inches in length. They run in schools of up to a million fish, which are in turn pursued by salmon and other predators. One stretch of coastline north of Juneau has been dubbed the "milk run" by local fishermen who drag the area for the salmon that habitually chase after the herring that frequent that stretch of water every spring.

There are many other species of fish in the fresh- and saltwater systems of Southeast Alaska, from the tiny eulachon that was an important source of oil for Southeast Natives, to rockfish, sculpin, cod, and other bottomfish. The U.S. Forest Service publishes a small pamphlet, *Common Fresh and Saltwater Fishes of Southeastern Alaska,* that is a handy reference guide to the many local species.

CRAB

If you own a boat and a crab pot in Southeast Alaska, all that remains is to find just the right place to set it down. Toss in a few fish heads, set the pot on the way to your favorite fishing grounds, and pick it up at the end of the day. Dinner that night might include any of the three

King crab

varieties of crab that inhabit the Southeast coast: king, Dungeness, and tanner.

The famous Alaska king crab is not a true crab at all, as evidenced by the fact that the spiny, spiderlike legs fold backward behind the body instead of forward and in front, like the Dungeness. True crab or no, the king crab is a fine prize for the table. By far the largest of the crabs, kings can grow to 24 pounds, although 7 or 8 pounds is the average commercial size. At that, they measure 3 feet from leg tip to leg tip. The meat is sweet and firm, not unlike lobster. Besides having excellent flavor, king crab is easy to eat. No messy cracking, picking, and sucking—you just snip open the shell of the leg with kitchen shears and slide out the meat. The small body is usually ignored.

Dungeness crab is the familiar Cancer shape, a true crab, with eight forward-folding legs and two short claws. Compared with the king, the Dungeness has a large body, but full of good meat. Locals disagree about which of the crabs is better eating, but I vote for the rich and succulent Dungeness.

Tanner crab, usually marketed as "snow crab," looks something like a cross between the king and the Dungeness. This true crab has long, spindly legs. You frequently see the bulbous claws sold separately in the frozen food section of the supermarket. The leg meat is delicious but tends to flake into small bits as you remove it from the shell.

ABALONE

It takes a hardy diver to brave the frigid waters to harvest abalone. Abalone are abundant, though, the length of the Alexander Archipelago, and occasionally they can be plucked from the bottom at very low tides. The species of abalone that inhabits Southeast rarely grows larger than 5½ inches. The meat is sweet and tender.

BIVALVES AND PARALYTIC SHELLFISH POISONING

In addition to crab and abalone, the Inside Passage yields several varieties of shrimp (including the tiny Petersburg species), cockles, scallops, octopus, sea cucumbers, sea urchins, mussels, and at least four varieties of clam. A word of warning here, however: *No bivalves (clams, mussels, cockles, scallops) in Southeast Alaska can be considered safe from the deadly paralytic shellfish poisoning, at any time of year* (unless they are sold commercially, in which case they will have been tested and certified safe). Paralytic shellfish poisoning (PSP) is caused by a toxin produced by a tiny organism known as a dinoflagellate (a similar dinoflagellate causes the sea condition known as the red tide). This organism is ingested by the shellfish, which absorb and store the PSP toxin in their bodies. The toxin does not harm the shellfish but is poisonous to humans. Some shellfish retain the toxin longer than others; clams and mussels are the worst.

Symptoms of PSP show up only *after* the shellfish has entered the digestive tract, so do not try to "see if the clams are poisonous" by holding one to your mouth and waiting for your lip to go numb. The symptoms usually occur within thirty minutes of eating the infected shellfish. They can include: a tingling or burning sensation on lips, gums, tongue, or face that gradually spreads to other parts of the body; dryness of mouth, nausea, vomiting; in later stages, shortness of breath, choking sensation, slurred speech, lack of coordination. If death occurs, which is seldom the case but does happen, the direct cause will be respiratory paralysis. There is *no antidote* to paralytic shellfish poisoning. If you experience any of the symptoms after eating shellfish, induce vomiting immediately and call a doctor.

Many longtime residents of Southeast Alaska eat clams every year from beaches that they consider safe. I do not. I used to, occasionally, but I found that worrying about PSP took all the pleasure out of eating the clams anyway. Now I save clam and mussel eating for places where I know they are safe, and, in Southeast Alaska, I console myself with crab, shrimp, halibut, trout, and five kinds of salmon.

tors of today's Tlingit and Haida Indians awarded the bird a central role in their mythology and celebrated its character in songs, dances, and artistic designs.

Until you see one up close, you could confuse the raven with the Northwestern crow, which also lives in Southeast year-round. Both are black all over. The raven is much larger—measuring more than 2 feet in length, against the crow's 17 inches. The raven also has a much larger bill than the crow's and a pronounced brow. And the raven produces a throaty, melodious *klok* or *kla-wock* that is entirely different from the raucous *caw-caw* of the crow.

STELLER'S JAY

The saucy Steller's jay, dressed in an electric blue and black plaid coat and black head crest, stays in Southeast year-round. I have often watched the case of two or three

Steller's jay

Steller's jays taunting a bald eagle. While the eagle rests stoically on a spruce limb, the jays flap about from branch to branch, chattering imperiously. Eventually the eagle gives up in disgust and flies away. Despite their bickering and bullying ways, I like these handsome birds.

The Steller's jay takes its name from the Bering expedition of 1741. When Vitus Bering set out to explore the uncharted sea to the east of Russia, he took with him the naturalist Georg Wilhelm Steller. With the ship anchored off Kayak Island near Yakutat in order to replenish the water supply, Steller went ashore to collect specimens of plants and birds not found in Asia or Europe. Among his finds was a brilliant blue, high-crested jay that he recognized as native to North America. The Steller's jay was proof that Bering had found a land that was separate from Russia.

BLUE GROUSE

The blue grouse, another year-round resident, dwells in mature forest stands and among the dwarf trees dotting the muskeg in alpine areas. Also called the spruce hen, this grouse has a brown-to-gray and white speckled body shaped like a small chicken, a black tail with a band of pale gray at the top, and the feathered legs common to the grouse and ptarmigan family. The females build their nests on the ground, and it is not unusual to come upon a hen with her clutch of chicks as you are walking through the woods or grassy openings in early summer. In winter the grouse are up in the trees. During the mating season the woods echo with the muffled *huh-huh-huh* of the courtship call. The sound is produced by air sacs on each side of the male's neck and is responsible for the grouse's other nickname, "the hooter."

The blue grouse is the most common species in Southeast (others include the spruce grouse and ruffed grouse). It is the largest of the grouse and a popular game bird, with the males often reaching 3½ pounds.

ROCK PTARMIGAN

Ptarmigan are closely related to grouse and similar in appearance, but smaller (⅔ to 1½ pounds) and have feathered feet. Of the three species of ptarmigan in Alaska, only the rock ptarmigan lives in Southeast. (The willow ptarmigan, the state bird, inhabits most of the rest of the state.) In summer, the ptarmigan is a mottled brown with white wings, but winter brings out an all-white coat except for a bit of black on the tail and (in the male) a band of black through the eye. Ptarmigan are nomadic in winter, wandering from slope to slope in search of a meal of birch buds or willow.

CANADA GOOSE

The Vancouver Canada goose is the largest of the several subspecies that frequent Alaska, weighing as much as 16 pounds in the fall. Many are year-round residents of the Southeast tide flats. One of the largest congregations frequents the Mendenhall Wetlands State Game Refuge in Juneau, where you can often observe them feeding, long necks curved down to the ground. The Canada goose is

Canada goose

unmistakable: a large bird with brownish gray back and wings, a long, black neck and a black head with white cheeks.

Canada geese mate for life. The Vancouver variety nests in shore grass, under conifers, or in muskegs. They are rare among geese in that they have even been known to nest in trees to protect their young from predators.

DUCK

Several varieties of duck brave the Southeast winters. Among the year-round residents are the ubiquitous mallard, the fancy-dress harlequin, the common merganser, and the red-breasted merganser. The white-winged scoter and surf scoter are familiar sights in Southeast. They raft upon the salt water in large groups.

RUFOUS HUMMINGBIRD

In spring the rufous hummingbirds arrive from their warm winter home in Mexico. Decked out in his orange coat and irridescent red throat, the male is a cheery sight after the drab, dull days of winter's end. The female wears green and lacks the brilliant red throat. They haunt Southeast gardens, impatiently awaiting the bright blossoms of summer. In late fall the hummingbirds, which measure no more than 3½ inches long, depart on their long journey south.

PESTS

Unfortunately, the winged creatures of Southeast Alaska are not limited to the bird family. Most of the stories you have heard about insects in Alaska are not true—at least about Southeast Alaska. The gigantic mosquitoes that swarm around your head and drive even four-footed animals loco are creatures of the northern tundra with its inviting pools of freestanding water. Southeastern insects are more apt to be too small to swat.

Usually there is enough breeze along the Inside Passage to keep insects at bay. If not, and the bugs are pesty, your best bet is to roll down your sleeves, button your collar, put on a hat, smear yourself with whatever brand of repellent is popular this year, and try to relax. Nothing seems to draw biting or stinging insects more readily than an overheated, sweaty, enraged human being.

Basically, the pests fall into three categories. Mosquitoes really are not that troublesome in most parts of Southeast Alaska and especially urban areas. Those that are around seem to be slow-moving and somewhat dim. In your hotel room at night, for instance, they are easy to hunt down and kill. Campers get the worst of them, and bug netting on your tent is certainly in order.

White-sox, on the other hand, are vicious, tiny, black, biting flies that swarm about your body and try to crawl under your clothes. Failing that they are happy to bite *through* your clothes. White-sox (the name comes from their silvery legs) can produce a nasty bite; on some people, the raised red spots can itch for days. You do not necessarily feel the bite at the time, though.

The bite you *do* feel at the time—a prolonged prick—comes from the no-see-um. Your skin swells up immediately and the itch comes and goes for days. These gnatlike insects like the damp—a nice sweaty forehead sends them into ecstasy. They will light on any exposed piece of skin—ears are an especially favorite meal. More than other pests, no-see-ums seem tuned to your state of mind. If you can stay calm and go about your business, they may not be a bother; but start getting anxious about them, perspiring and breathing heavily, and they will fulfill your worst fantasies.

Scientists now think these biting beasts may be attracted to the carbon dioxide that humans expel. Hold your breath!

COMMON BIRDS OF SOUTHEAST ALASKA
(PRESENT DURING AT LEAST TWO SEASONS)

Common loon, *Gavia immer* *
Arctic loon, *Gavia arctica*
Red-throated loon, *Gavia stellata*
Red-necked grebe, *Podiceps grisegena*
Homed grebe, *Podiceps auritus*
Black-footed albatross, *Diomedea nigripes* †
Sooty shearwater, *Puffinus griseus* †
Fork-tailed storm-petrel, *Oceanodroma furcata* †
Leach's storm-petrel, *Oceanodroma leucorhoa* †
Pelagic cormorant, *Phalacrocorax pelagicus*
Great blue heron, *Ardea herodias*
Whistling swan, *Olor columbianus*
Canada goose, Vancouver, *Branta canadensis fulva* *
White-fronted goose, *Anser albifrons*
Snow goose, *Chen caerulescens caerulescens*
Mallard, *Anas platyrhynchos* *
Pintail, *Anas acuta*
American green-winged teal, *Anas crecca carolinensis*
American widgeon, *Anas americana*
Greater scaup, *Aythya marila*
Lesser scaup, *Aythya affinis*
Common goldeneye, *Bucephala clangula*
Barrow's goldeneye, *Bucephala islandica*
Bufflehead, *Bucephala albeola*
Oldsquaw, *Clangula hyemalis*
Harlequin duck, *Histrionicus histrionicus* *
Common eider, *Somateria mollissima*
White-winged scoter, *Melanitta fusca deglandi* *
Surf scoter, *Melanitta perspicillata* *
Black scoter, *Melanitta nigra*
Common merganser, *Mergus merganser* *
Red-breasted merganser, *Mergus serrator* *
Sharp-shinned hawk, *Accipiter striatus*
Bald eagle, *Haliaeetus leucocephalus* *
Marsh hawk, *Circus cyaneus*
American kestrel, *Falco sparverius*
Blue grouse, *Dendragapus obscurus* *
Rock ptarmigan, *Lagopus mutus* *
Sandhill crane, *Grus canadensis*
Black oystercatcher, *Haematopus bachmani*

Semipalmated plover, *Charadrius semipalmatus*
Black-bellied plover, *Pluvialis squatarola*
Greater yellowlegs, *Tringa melanoleuca*
Lesser yellowlegs, *Tringa flavipes*
Spotted sandpiper, *Actitis macularia*
Black turnstone, *Arenaria melanocephala*
Northern phalarope, *Phalaropus lobatus*
Common snipe, *Capella gallinago*
Short-billed dowitcher, *Limnodromus griseus*
Western sandpiper, *Calidris mauri*
Least sandpiper, *Calidris minutilla*
Pectoral sandpiper, *Calidris melanotos*
Rock sandpiper, *Calidris ptilocnemis*
Dunlin, *Calidris alpina*
Glaucous-winged gull, *Larus glaucescens* *
Herring gull, *Larus argentatus* *
Thayer's gull, *Larus thayeri*
Mew gull, *Larus canus* *
Bonaparte's gull, *Larus philadelphia*
Arctic tern, *Sterna paradisaea*
Common murre, *Uria aalge* *
Pigeon guillemot, *Cepphus columba* *
Marbled murrelet, *Brachyramphus marmoratus* *
Rock dove, *Columba livia* *
Great horned owl, *Bubo virginianus* *
Short-eared owl, *Asio flammeus*
Rufous hummingbird, *Selasphorus rufus*
Belted kingfisher, *Megaceryle alcyon* *
Western flycatcher, *Empidonax difficilis*
Violet-green swallow, *Tachycineta thalassina*
Tree swallow, *Iridoprocne bicolor*
Barn swallow, *Hirundo rustica*
Steller's jay, *Cyanocitta stelleri* *
Black-billed magpie, *Pica pica*
Common raven, *Corvus corax* *
Northwestern crow, *Corvus caurinus* *
Chestnut-backed chickadee, *Parus rufescens* *
Brown creeper, *Certhia familiaris* *
Dipper, *Cinclus mexicanus* *
Winter wren, *Troglodytes troglodytes* *
American robin, *Turdus migratorius*
Varied thrush, *Ixoreus naevius*
Hermit thrush, *Catharus guttatus*

Swainson's thrush, *Catharus ustulatus*
Golden-crowned kinglet, *Regulus satrapa*
Ruby-crowned kinglet, *Regulus calendula*
Water pipit, *Anthus spinoletta*
Bohemian waxwing, *Bombycilla garrulus*
Starling, *Sturnus vulgaris* *
Orange-crowned warbler, *Vermivora celata*
Yellow warbler, *Dendroica petechia*
Yellow-rumped warbler, *Dendroica coronata*
Wilson's warbler, *Wilsonia pusilla*
Pine grosbeak, *Pinicola enucleator*
Common redpoll, *Carduelis flammea*
Pine siskin, *Carduelis pinus* *
Red crossbill, *Loxia curvirostra* *
White-winged crossbill, *Loxia leucoptera* *
Savannah sparrow, *Passerculus sandwichensis*
Dark-eyed junco, *Junco hyemalis* *
Tree sparrow, *Spizella arborea*
Golden-crowned sparrow, *Zonotrichia atricapilla*
Fox sparrow, *Passerella iliaca*
Lincoln's sparrow, *Melospiza lincolnii*
Song sparrow, *Melospiza melodia* *
Lapland longspur, *Calcarius lapponicus*

* Year-round resident
† Outside waters

Chapter 7
Sights along the Waterway

As you travel along the Inside Passage, you will observe a variety of wildlife, from seabirds to breaching whales; tall granite mountains; velvety green islands; and blue glaciers tumbling to the sea. But there is much more to Southeast Alaska than breathtakingly beautiful scenery, and your shipboard vantage point will allow you to observe the workings of life in this northern rain-forested land.

For people who inhabit the communities along these waterways, the Inside Passage is a transportation corridor, a lifeline to the outside world. There are few connecting roads along the shore. All day long, the narrow passageways hum with activity as vessels work their way north and south. Fishing boats are frequent sights in the summer and fall. You will see them with nets spread in the water and unloading the catch at the dock. Passenger cruise ships are another summertime phenomenon. More than twenty vessels make scheduled visits to Southeast Alaska from May through September of every year. Alaska Marine Highway ferries and commercial tugs and barges are year-round denizens of the waterway.

You may notice that the water itself is not as empty as it first appears. Southeast Alaska is still relatively free of man-made debris, but nature has strewn the water with old logs and clumps of seaweed. The occasional iceberg passes by on a one-way journey to oblivion. There are interesting navigational aids along the route, especially in the narrow channels, and floats to mark the location of private and commercial crab pots. On the shore clear-cuts indicate where the timber industry has been at work. You may pass staging areas where logs are rafted together for the trip to the mill or see tugs with a raft in tow. Always there are unexpected little scenes that are visible only from your special shipboard view: a homesteader's cabin tucked in the trees at water's edge; a sailboat riding at anchor in a quiet cove; an ancient cemetery with marble monuments poking above the grass; a cluster of abandoned cannery buildings; a glimpse of weathered totem poles guarding their secrets of the past; a derelict boat marooned on the tide; a secret beach, perfect moon of sand—can you ever find it again?

If you travel the Alaska Marine Highway System during the summer months, a U.S. Forest Service shipboard interpreter will be on board your state ferry to point out and explain sights along the route. The interpreter program is a cooperative arrangement between the state of Alaska and the U.S. Forest Service. The Forest Service provides the interpreters as well as maps, books, brochures, and films for their shipboard presentations. The Alaska Marine Highway System provides passage, accommodation, and meals. The Forest Service personnel present films and short, informal talks on such topics as bald eagles, humpback whales, glaciers, and the Tongass National Forest; they also give historical introductions to each Inside Passage community. Through such exercises as "eagle counts" while traveling through some of the especially narrow passages, they involve you in the passing scene.

The interpreters are equipped to answer questions about virtually every facet of life in Southeast Alaska, from where to find a campground to what date the Russians settled in Sitka. They maintain extensive information files on board and a library of books and pamphlets about Southeast Alaska that they will lend to you during the voyage.

TROLLERS, GILL-NETTERS, AND SEINERS

In late spring, when the snow leaves the mountains, the collective thoughts of Southeasterners turn to salmon. Sport fishermen dig favorite rods out from behind the piles of skis, while commercial fishermen begin sharpening hooks and mending nets. Along about May, the docks erupt in a frenzy of hull scraping and painting.

Commercial fishing is heavily regulated by the state of Alaska, both as a means of protecting escapements to ensure adequate future runs and as a way to comply with national and international fishing treaties that allocate certain types of harvest. Under the Limited Entry Program, the state licenses commercial salmon fishermen according to the type of gear they use, then limits the

A troller cruises slowly along, outriggers extended over the water. (Alaska Department of Fish and Game)

number of those licenses. This controls the total amount of gear actually in the water. Then, during the fishing season, the Alaska Department of Fish and Game determines how long the commercial harvest will last in each location, based on the strength of the runs. Depending on the type of gear, the allowable fishing periods, called "openings," can be as brief as a few hours. The days are long gone when commercial fishing crews could go out in spring and fish until they couldn't stand it any longer.

Three types of boat are used for salmon fishing in Southeast. Two of them use nets to trap the salmon, while the third employs hooks. You are likely to see all three as you travel around Southeast in the summer.

TROLLERS

Trollers fish with baited hooks or lures that are trailed through the water from long poles extended from the side of the boat (sometimes from the front as well). Each pole has a heavy stainless steel line attached to it with several hooks, so that an average-sized vessel might drag up to sixty hooks through the water at one time. You can recognize the troller by the long poles, or outriggers, extended horizontally over the water. When the boat is not actively fishing, the poles are pulled up to a vertical position alongside the center mast. Power-trollers are equipped with hydraulically powered winches that haul in the heavy gear. On hand-trollers, operators crank in the lines by hand.

Troll-caught salmon, usually kings or cohos, are the highest-quality fish on the market. They are removed from the line as soon as they strike and immediately killed, gutted, and iced in the hold where they stay until they are unloaded at a cold storage facility for further tidying up and freezing. These salmon end up in the fresh or fresh-frozen case in your supermarket or on the menu of the best seafood restaurants across the country. Only a small percentage of salmon leaves Southeast Alaska in an unfrozen or uncanned state. Those that do come from the troll fishery. (A trawler, incidentally, is something else entirely: a large fishing vessel that pulls a net bag through the water. There are no salmon trawlers in Alaska.)

GILL-NETTERS

Gill-netters are the smaller of the two net-fishing salmon boats employed in Southeast Alaska. The net is wound around a large spool-shaped reel on the stern or bow. With the boat in position, the operator lets the net out in a line stretching across the current from the boat. The end of the net is marked with a buoy. The top of the net is supported by floats and the bottom, fixed with weights, hangs straight down in the water like a curtain. The salmon, heading for their spawning stream, swim into the net headfirst. The size of the mesh prevents them from swimming forward, and when they try to back out they are caught by the gills, hence the name gill net. After a time the fisherman hauls in the net over the reel and plucks out the salmon (called "picking salmon").

Gill nets are designed to selectively catch fish. Smaller fish escape by swimming through the mesh openings, and larger specimens knock up against the net and swim away undamaged. The nets come in different sizes of mesh in order to target specific species. Gill-netted salmon can sustain some damage and are primarily destined for canning. The salmon are iced on board and usually sold in the round.

On some gill-netters, known as bow-pickers, the reel is mounted on the bow of the boat instead of the stern. Whether

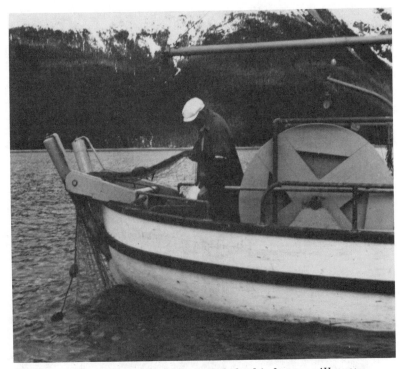

*The spool-shaped reel on the stern labels this boat a gill-netter.
(Alaska Department of Fish and Game)*

bow-mounted or stern-mounted, the reel is what to look for to identify a gill-netter. Newer boats are made of aluminum or fiberglass and have a long, low profile something like a large riverboat with a cabin. Some boats are outfitted for both trolling and gill-netting, so they have both poles and drum.

The gill-net fishery is very concentrated and intense. Openings may be for only a few days a week, and crews work around the clock. During one of these openings, so many gill-netters may be crowded into one inlet that your ship will be forced to weave through an obstacle course of boats and nets.

Purse Seiners

Purse seiners are the volume vessels of the fleet. They fish by deploying a large circular net called a seine and harvest primarily pink and chum salmon (some sockeye) destined for canneries. These 58-foot vessels are the largest of any salmon fishery: Whereas a troller or gill-netter can be operated by a one- or two-person crew, a seiner needs a crew of six.

Using a 19-foot power skiff, the seine crew deploys the net out in a circle from the mother boat. After a suitable period of time (minutes or hours, depending on the circumstances), they tighten the bottom of the net with a drawstring—called "closing the purse"—and haul the net and contents aboard. Some of everything will be inside: seaweed, sea urchins, jellyfish, halibut, sharks, cod, and—they hope—a substantial quantity of salmon. They keep the salmon and return the rest to sea.

Purse seining is at once the most efficient and least discriminating method of harvesting salmon. The fish are iced and off-loaded directly to cannery tenders (large vessels that transport ice and supplies to the fishing grounds and fish to the cannery) or cannery docks for cleaning and processing. The seiners are the major source for canned Alaska salmon.

Seiners are the largest boats in the fleet. Look for the circular power winch. (Alaska Department of Fish and Game)

Seiners are easily identified—look for the boom with circular power winch at the top that hoists the net onto the large afterdeck. When the vessels are underway, the huge net with its floats will be coiled on the afterdeck, and the power skiff rides upside down on the stern. Should you be sightseeing by plane during a seine opening, you might look down on the delightful sight of seine nets scribing perfect circles on the water.

LONGLINERS

Southeast enjoys good halibut fishing, too. Petersburg is the halibut capital of the region, but you will see the big halibut boats (up to 60 feet) in many Southeast harbors. Commercial halibut fishing involves the use of longlines. A longline is made up of a series of 1,800-foot (approximate) line lengths, called skates, to which leaders with baited hooks are attached. The skates are tied together to form one line several miles long. A large halibut boat might have 15 miles of gear in the water.

The line is laid down on the bottom of the ocean (halibut are bottom feeders) and the ends marked with floats. When the halibut have had a chance to get on the hooks, the line is reeled in over a drum at the gunwale (side) or stern, and the halibut are lifted off. The fish are iced in the hold and taken to a cold storage plant where they are processed and frozen for shipment to the Lower 48.

The halibut harvest in Southeast Alaska is regulated by the North Pacific Fishery Management Council. The allowable harvest has been very small in recent years, and as a result the few halibut openings have been short and intense. During these dangerous derby-style openings, exhausted crews work around the clock under brutal conditions, and accidents result. The local consumer suffers as well, as fresh halibut is available only during a few short periods a year. A new policy, still under consideration but expected to be approved and implemented by 1995, would assign an Individual Fishing Quota, or IFQ, to each qualifying fisherman. The fisherman could harvest the quota anytime throughout the year, which would eliminate the derby openings and provide fresh halibut to the consumer year-round. The downside: Some fishermen would not qualify for IFQs and would be eliminated from the industry. Also, the IFQs, like Limited Entry Permits, would become marketable commodities. Critics fear the industry would become controlled by larger fishing interests at the expense of the small, independent operator.

PROMISE OF PROFITS

Commercial fishing has become big business in Alaska, requiring enormous capital investment with only the promise of substantial profits. In 1993, a power-troll permit for Southeast Alaska cost around $35,000. Seine and drift gill-net permits cost $80,000 to $90,000 (by contrast a Chignik seiner, in Southwest Alaska, could pay up to $500,000). A new fishing vessel, equipped with modern electronic navigation devices and fish-finding equipment, costs $100,000 to $1,000,000, depending on the type. To those payments must be added the cost of fuel, insurance, and supplies.

Thanks to improved management, successful hatcheries, and a series of mild winters, the total annual catch in all of Alaska has exceeded 100 million salmon for the past several years. The 1991 catch in Southeast Alaska of 69.2 million salmon was the largest on record, exceeding the average statewide catch for some years; the average catch in Southeast for 1983 to 1992 was 45.8 million salmon. But 1993 illustrated the cyclical and somewhat mysterious nature of fisheries when the pink salmon simply failed to show up in some areas of Southeast. Prices, too, have been poor in recent years. The average price paid to fishermen in 1992 ranged from $2.25 per pound for troll-caught king salmon to $0.16 per pound for seine-caught pinks. Now add into this equation the heavy regulations: During the 1992 season, for example, trollers were allowed a total of four and one-half days of fishing for king salmon, the prime money fish. In this economic and regulatory climate, a top seiner (a "highliner") might gross $200,000 a season; a top power troller or gill-netter might gross around $50,000–$60,000. The average operator of a commercial fishing vessel may not even meet expenses.

Despite the soul-searching and upheaval in the industry, commercial fishing still enjoys an aura of romanticism. Being offshore and independent, living in concert with the natural elements—these aspects of the life-style haven't changed. And, despite the specter of six-figure boats and batteries of equipment, there is still room in the industry for the small-scale operator who goes out in a small boat with a couple of handlines and brings in a few salmon. For less than $10,000, you can purchase a hand-troll permit and participate in the life-style of the commercial fishery. The average hand-troller grosses less than $5,000 all summer—not a living, but enough to make expenses and justify the pleasure of working in Alaska's beautiful outdoors.

CLEAR-CUTTING

As you cruise among the larger islands such as Chichagof and Prince of Wales, you will see bright green, squared-off patches on the hillsides amid the surrounding darker green forest. These are areas that have been clear-cut: evidence of the timber industry at work. The bright green color indicates the new growth taking form where the old trees were cut. The clear-cutting is carried out on both private lands (most owned by Southeast Native village and regional corporations) and national forest lands.

Clear-cutting is the method most commonly used for harvesting spruce and hemlock stands in the Tongass National Forest. Clear-cutting means cutting down every tree within a specified area, as opposed to removing only selected specimens and leaving the rest. Logging companies favor clear-cutting in the difficult terrain of Southeast Alaska for obvious reasons: They can concentrate all the road building, cutting, and hauling in one area. Selective cutting requires such techniques as helicopter logging, which is dangerous, expensive, and inefficient.

Clear-cutting, according to the timber industry, increases the productivity of the forest by replacing uneven old-growth stands of mixed value with easy-to-harvest trees of uniform size and spacing. And, the new stands have a higher percentage of spruce than old-growth forest because clear-cutting makes way for the full sunlight that the more desirable spruce requires. By the time a clear-cut patch has regenerated and matured, the tree mix will be 50 percent hemlock and 50 percent spruce, versus 70 percent hemlock and 30 percent spruce in the old stands. In 90 to 125 years, the patch will be ready to harvest again.

Clear-cutting remains controversial. Critics consider the practice unsightly, wasteful, and damaging to the environment, and they charge logging companies with leaving too much timber and debris on the ground. Clear-cuts, plus the extensive road networks required to support them, risk damaging salmon-spawning streams from erosion and debris, destroy wildlife habitat, and compromise virgin wilderness—forever. Over the years, management changes have lessened these effects in the national forest by reducing the maximum allowable size of a clear-cut from more than two thousand acres to just one hundred; the average size of a clear-cut in the Tongass today is fewer than eighty acres. The Tongass Timber Reform Act passed by Congress in 1990 stipulated additional changes in industry practices to safeguard

A-frame hoists lower bundles of logs into the water for the trip to the mill.

salmon streams. Logging companies must now leave 100-foot no-logging buffer strips along both sides of salmon streams and tributaries. Private landowners such as Native corporations are not bound by federal regulations, however; they fall under state jurisdiction. The Alaska Forest Practices Act requires buffer strips but does not regulate the size of clear-cuts, and some Native corporation logging practices have been greatly criticized.

You may see other signs of the logging industry during your trip through Southeast. A-frame hoists at the water's edge are used to lower bundles of logs into the water, where they are formed into log rafts for the trip to the mill. The logs are corralled by a perimeter of boom logs chained together in the shape of a rectangle. The log rafts are towed to the mill by powerful tugboats, called "bullboats" because they "bull" the logs around.

Most hemlock logs cut from the Tongass, and some spruce, wind up at pulp mills at Sitka and Ketchikan, where they are turned into high-grade dissolving pulp used in industrial processes such as the manufacture of rayon or plastic. High-quality spruce logs are taken to sawmills and processed, usually for export to Japan.

NAVIGATIONAL MARKERS

You will notice several types of navigational marker along the Inside Passage route. Some are red, some green, some blinking, others not. All these markers are navigational aids that the Coast Guard has positioned to mark safe passageways through difficult channels or harbor entrances. Most of them are buoys that are anchored to the ocean floor. Their color, markings, shape, and number are all clues to how the passage should be navigated.

Coast Guard crew members hoist a lighted buoy aboard a tender for routine maintenance. (U.S. Coast Guard)

The color of the buoy indicates to which side the boat should pass. Red buoys are kept on the right, or starboard, side of the vessel when returning from sea (in other words, inbound, heading upstream, or entering the harbor), as in the mariner's expression, "red right returning." Green buoys are kept to the left, or port, side. When outbound, or heading out to sea, the situation is reversed. Buoys painted with red and white vertical stripes mark the center of the channel and can be passed on either side. Port and starboard buoys are also numbered consecutively from the beginning of the passage to the end. Red buoys are always even-numbered; green buoys always odd-numbered. Midchannel markers are not numbered but may be lettered. In very shallow or narrow channels, such as Wrangell Narrows between Wrangell and Petersburg, mariners must thread their way from buoy to buoy very carefully to avoid running aground.

Shape provides a further indication of buoy type. Regular red buoys, called nuns, are pointed or cone-shaped on top. Green buoys, called cans, are can-shaped or cylindrical. Lighted buoys are topped with battery-powered red, green, or white lights that flash intermittently at night to give mariners their position. They are also identified with reflective markers called daymarks—square-shaped, green, and odd-numbered for port; triangular, red, and even-numbered for starboard.

Groups of small, round floats that you see bobbing on the surface of the water, usually red, are not navigational aids, but buoys marking the location of commercial crab pots.

LIGHTHOUSES

With their tall white towers and red roofs, lighthouses are among the most picturesque sights along the Inside Passage. There are several on the route from Prince Rupert to Skagway. Congress provided for the building and maintenance of lighthouses in U.S. waters as early as 1789, but none was constructed in Alaska until 1900. Before then the only navigational warning light on the entire Alaska coast was the seal oil lantern burning in the cupola atop the governor's residence on Castle Hill in Sitka (replaced by a simple post light after the mansion burned in 1894). Eventually, twelve lighthouses stood watch over the Inside Passage. Originally all the lighthouses were manned by a lighthouse keeper (sometimes a family) who lived in splendid isolation

The Cape Decision lighthouse is one of twelve that stood sentry over the Inside Passage. (U.S. Coast Guard)

from the usual cares of the world. Today the lights are automated. The last manned light station in Alaska was Five Fingers, which was fully automated in the summer of 1984.

From south to north, the lighthouses you will pass along the Inside Passage include: Tree Point, Dixon Entrance (lighted 30 April 1904); Mary Island, Revillagigedo Channel (lighted 15 July 1903); Cape Decision, Sumner Strait (lighted 15 March 1932); Five Fingers, Stephens Passage (lighted 1 March 1902); Point Retreat, Lynn Canal (lighted 15 September 1904); Sentinel Island, Lynn Canal (lighted 1 March 1902); Eldred Rock, Lynn Canal (lighted 1 June 1906); Cape Spencer, Cross Sound (lighted 11 December 1925). You will also pass the Canadian Green Island and Lucy Island lighthouses just out of Prince Rupert.

The original lenses from some of these lighthouses are displayed in museums around Southeast. Check the Tongass Historical Society Museum in Ketchikan, the Juneau Douglas City Museum in Juneau, and the Sheldon Museum in Haines.

THE NARROWS

The Inside Passage contains two very narrow stretches of water. Wrangell Narrows and the connecting passages of Peril Strait challenge navigators and prove greatly interesting to passengers. You have ample opportunity to study the navigational aids marking your passage as your ship negotiates the twists and turns between looming shores. Few cruise ships travel these constricted waterways, but Alaska ferries pass through them on their scheduled runs between Wrangell and Petersburg, and to Sitka. If possible, schedule your trip so that you make the passage in daylight. If you must make the trip at night, it is worth getting out of bed to watch as your ship glides between the red, green, and white blinking lights that mark the route.

WRANGELL NARROWS

Winding like a narrow ribbon for 21 miles between Mitkof and Kupreanof islands, Wrangell Narrows terminates at Petersburg and empties into Frederick Sound. At one point this chute of rushing water closes to 100 yards. More than seventy navigational markers guide the helmsman through the passage. Passing through Wrangell Narrows brings you so close to shore that you can almost reach out and grasp an evergreen. Darkness transforms the waterway into a maze of winking colored lights that Alaskans have dubbed "Christmas Tree Lane." Your ship glides silently between them as dark cliffs loom overhead.

The passage is so squeezed—an average ½-mile wide at high tide—that the current rips through the narrows at up to 8 miles an hour with every tidal change. The tide enters and exits from both ends. The channel was dredged to an average low-tide depth of 26 feet in the 1940s, but has since silted in another 4 feet. The shallowest point is currently 19 feet. Large ships, such as the Alaska Ferries, do not attempt Wrangell Narrows unless the water measures at least 2 feet above average low tide.

Wrangell Narrows is the preferred route between Wrangell and Petersburg for all types of vessel—fishing boats, tugboats with log rafts, state ferries, and private cruisers. There is ample room for small craft to pass, but large ships remain in radio contact with each other and pass at prearranged wide spots in the road. Fog is the helmsman's worst enemy in Wrangell Narrows. Even with radar, ship captains delay passage until the next tide, if possible, rather than grope their way through the maze of markers. If thick fog descends en route, the best choice is to anchor well off to the side and wait for it to lift.

PERIL STRAIT

Peril Strait is a diagonal cut between Baranof and Chichagof islands formed by an ancient fault. The waterway, which serves as an inside route to Sitka, takes its name not from hidden rocks in the water, but from an incident that occurred during the time of the Russian occupation in 1799. That year, a party of Aleut hunters on their way from Sitka to Russian headquarters at Ko-

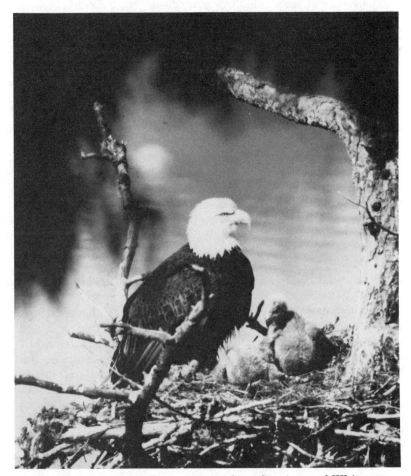

Bald eagles are especially prevalent along Sergius and Whitestone narrows approaching Sitka. (John Schoen)

diak stopped to camp on a beach, where they found quantities of mussels. More than one hundred Aleuts died from the debilitating illness that we know as paralytic shellfish poisoning. The Russians named the waterway *Pogibshii,* meaning deadly, which has come down to us in English as Peril Strait. The passage narrows at Poison Cove, where the fateful mussels were collected, and Deadman Reach, where the hunters ate their last meal.

From there Peril Strait closes to almost a ditch in a series of zigzagging passages leading to Sitka. The first is Sergius Narrows. There are only 300 feet from buoys to shore, and the tide rushes through at speeds close to 9½ miles an hour. Large ships can pass only at slack tide. Now you pass through Kakul Narrows and emerge into Salisbury Sound, which is open to the Pacific. Beyond some jewel-like islands in the distance you can see the ocean, and you probably can feel the Pacific swell. The passage narrows again into Neva Strait and constricts still further to Whitestone Narrows before opening again to Olga Strait and Sitka Sound.

Bald eagles often concentrate along the 30-mile stretch encompassing Sergius Narrows and Whitestone Narrows. As your ship glides between the forested islands, the eagles virtually line up in the treetops to greet you. You might also see deer at the water's edge. Most of the big cruise ships do not take the Sergius Narrows route, but all sorts of other vessels, including state ferries, use these waterways. You could even share the tight passage with tugboats and log rafts on their way to the pulp mill at Sitka.

AN INTERNATIONAL BOUNDARY

The boundary between the United States and Canada extends from the southern point of Prince of Wales Island to the mainland at the entrance to the Portland Canal. Traveling northbound by ship, you pass over the line while crossing Dixon Entrance en route to Ketchikan. The border follows the Portland Canal inland to the Coast Mountains and continues along the range from peak to peak to the vicinity of Skagway. From Skagway the line turns abruptly westward and stretches almost to the sea again but stops at Mount Fairweather, parallels the Saint Elias Mountains to Mount St. Elias, and then jumps onto the 141st meridian for a straight run northward to the Arctic Ocean.

The boundary was fixed in a treaty between Britain and Russia in 1825. The southern line was established at latitude 54°40'

N., but Britain's Hudson's Bay Company retained the right to use navigable rivers in Russian Alaska to reach their inland posts in Canada. When the United States purchased Alaska from Russia in 1867, the old boundaries were retained with only minor adjustments.

PART II:
Exploring
Alaska's Southeast

Chapter 8
Main-Line Ports of the Inside Passage

The towns and villages that border the Inside Passage are as ruggedly individualistic as Alaskans themselves. Some, like Juneau and Skagway, were born out of the gold rush while others, Sitka and Wrangell for example, date from earlier periods in Alaska's history. Petersburg has retained the atmosphere of a busy fishing depot, while Ketchikan balances fishing, timber, and tourism and Juneau is a white-collar government town.

Despite substantial differences in character, all Southeast communities have this in common: a working waterfront. No matter where you visit, you will find docks and harbors busy with fishing boats, tugboats, pleasure craft, ferries, floatplanes, tour boats, and cruise ships. In this islanded land of few roads, you will find a lot of the action down at the docks.

OF SPECIAL INTEREST

Southeast communities share a deep appreciation for their roots, even though the roots may extend back fewer than 100 years. All the larger towns have excellent *local history museums*. History buffs will discover relics from the gold rush, the steamship era, or the heyday of the salmon canneries. Local museums also contain fine displays of Tlingit and Haida artifacts.

Several communities mount *summer theatrical productions*. Usually these lighthearted melodramas spoof the town's history or gold rush events or play heavily on familiar verses of the Bard of the Yukon, Robert Service. Some of the plays have been running for years with periodic variations in the script. They're quite well done and provide good family fun. In some communities — Haines and Ketchikan for sure — you may have the opportunity to attend a *Tlingit or Haida dance performance*. Don't miss this opportunity. The dance brings to life the language, colorful blan-

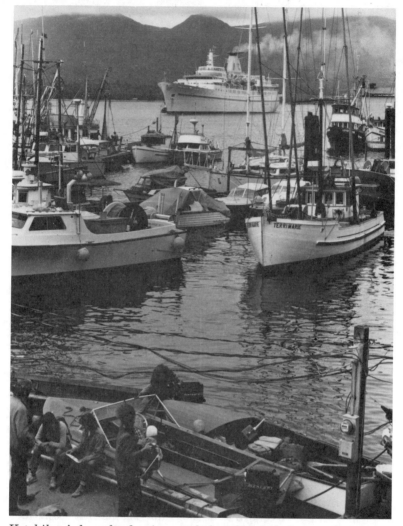

Ketchikan's busy harbor is crowded with fishing boats, pleasure craft, and exotic cruise ships.

kets, and elaborate masks and headdresses otherwise relegated to museums.

If you want to see Alaska, it's not enough to visit the towns and communities—you have to get out in the wilderness. Touring activities are available from every major community to accomplish this. *Flightseeing* by plane or helicopter, though costly (around

$100 to $130 per person for a forty-five-minute tour) is a rewarding and uniquely Alaskan experience. Popular excursions include tours over the ice fields straddling the Coast Mountains, trips to nearby glaciers (helicopter glacier tours land you right on the ice), and flights into Misty Fiords and Glacier Bay national monuments.

Likewise, it is important to experience Southeast from the water. *Cruise options* abound. Depending on the community, you can make a day or overnight cruise to glacier-filled fjords, travel up mainland rivers, or take wildlife viewing excursions among coastal islands. Any of these options will give you the opportunity to observe the Southeast inhabited not by humans but by whales, porpoise, bears, and other wild creatures. The ferries of the Alaska Marine Highway System offer many alternatives for inexpensive day cruises. You can also get out on the water by arranging a *fishing charter*. Consult local visitor information centers for a list of excursions and charter operators.

You will find developed trail systems in every town. Consult the local visitors' center and U.S. Forest Service office for brochures and other information about nearby trails. Advance reading for serious trekkers might include Margaret Piggott's *Discover Southeast Alaska with Pack and Paddle* (The Mountaineers), which outlines trails in all of the major towns (including the historic Chilkoot Trail from Dyea to Lake Bennett).

SHOPPING FOR LOCAL ART

If the heart of Southeast is down at the docks, the soul can be found in the many galleries displaying the work of local artists. One of the singular aspects of Southeast Alaska is the high caliber of local artwork, which includes traditional Native crafts such as wood and silver carving as well as graphic arts, painting, sculpture, pottery, and weaving. You will find Southeast artwork on sale in galleries, bookshops, and private studios in all of the larger communities and featured aboard Alaska state ferries. You can find a lot of high-quality local art for less than $100 that will remind you of your trip and give you pleasure for years to come.

Several Southeast artists have achieved national repute. For example, the colorful, folksy prints by Juneau artist Rie Muñoz sell in galleries across the United States. A frequent traveler to "bush" regions of Alaska, Muñoz has made a concerted effort to record Alaska Native cultural traditions and scenes from daily

*Art items for sale in a Sitka shop are contemporary versions of
Southeast Native themes.*

Alaska life. Original Muñoz paintings, should you find one, sell for
thousands of dollars. But a signed Muñoz print, framed notecard,
or poster makes an affordable souvenir.

Another well-known artist, Dale DeArmond of Sitka, produces
very small editions of handmade woodblock prints and fine wood
engravings of a variety of local subjects, such as animals, birds,
and figures from Alaska Native legend. Her exquisite, bold prints
are very reasonably priced.

William Spear's enameled art pins—collected, worn, and
traded throughout Alaska—can also be spotted in classy museum
shops from Seattle to New York City. Most of the wearable treasures designed by this Juneau artist retail for less than $15. And
anglers from one end of the Pacific coast to the other delight in the
humorous fish-art T-shirts created by Ketchikan artist Ray Troll.

KETCHIKAN
Population 14,100

Ketchikan has a habit of collecting nicknames: "Alaska's First City," because it is the first stop for ferries and cruise ships threading north through the Inside Passage; "Salmon Capital of the World," for the tremendous fishing industry that founded the town; and, more dubiously, the "Rain Capital." Technically, Ketchikan is not the rainiest place in Southeast (that distinction goes to the community of Little Port Walter on the southern tip of Baranof Island, where there is measurable precipitation approximately 239 days of the year), but the average yearly rainfall of 162 inches has led local wags to comment: "If you can't see Deer Mountain, it's raining; and if you can see it, it's about to rain."

The rain does not dampen spirits, though. Ketchikan is a robust, fun-filled town with a restless energy that is almost palpable. On a given summer day, there might be two or three cruise ships moored along the wharf, the seine fleet getting ready to put to sea, and salmon milling below the Ketchikan Street Bridge. The scene in Tongass Narrows will include floatplanes departing for Misty Fiords flightseeing, Alaska state ferries, airport ferries, tugs and barges and fishing boats all maneuvering for space—with a few dozen kayaks and skiffs thrown in for good measure.

On land, too, there's a sense of activity and purpose. The town is growing in all directions: a new civic center going up on Cape Fox Hill (adjacent to the recently completed hotel); a U.S. Forest Service SEAVIC (Southeast Alaska Visitor Information Center) complex taking shape on the site of a former lumber mill; an $8 million pier expansion; a planned "seaport village" and new museum.

In years past, Ketchikan projected something of a rough-and-tumble mill town image. But the rough edges are wearing away. Ketchikan today offers first-class lodging, fine galleries, trendy cafes, and such grace notes as Whale Park, a small downtown oasis of lush gardens, hanging flower baskets, and a newly commissioned totem pole. You'll enjoy your stay in this lively waterfront city.

BACKGROUND

Ketchikan lies on the western coast of Revillagigedo Island, 90 miles north of Prince Rupert, British Columbia, via the Marine Highway. Revillagigedo is a Spanish name, the island having been named in honor of the Count of Revilla Gigedo who was

KETCHIKAN

N

DEER MOUNTAIN TRAIL →

TOTEM HERITAGE CENTER

SAXMAN TOTEM PARK → (2.5 MI.)

S. TONGASS HWY.

FAIR ST.

DEER MOUNTAIN HATCHERY

DERMOUNT ST.

WOODLAND AVE.

WALKER FIELD

THOMAS ST.

THOMAS BASIN

KETCHIKAN CREEK

PARK AVE.

VENETIA AVE.

CIVIC CENTER

DOLLY'S HOUSE

STEDMAN ST.

CITY OVERLOOK

CREEK ST.

TRAM

KETCHIKAN CREEK

WHALE PARK

SEAVIC U.S. FOREST SERVICE

HARRIS ST.

PARK AVE.

TONGASS MUSEUM

MILL ST.

MISSION ST.

DOCK ST.

POST OFFICE

* VISITORS INFORMATION

CRUISE SHIP DOCKS

EDMOND ST.

DOCK ST.

MAIN ST.

FRONT ST.

GRANT ST.

BAWDEN ST.

PINE ST.

HARBOR VIEW PARK

TUNNEL

WATER ST.

CITY FLOAT

TONGASS NARROWS

← TONGASS AVE./N. TONGASS HWY. (0.2 MI.)
← AIRPORT FERRY (2.2 MI.)
← STATE FERRY (2.2 MI.)
← WARD COVE (5.5 MI.)
← TOTEM BIGHT (9.4 MI.)

viceroy of Mexico in the late 1700s. The correct Spanish pronunci-
ation is Rheh-bee-ya-hee-*hay*-tho. Local residents, however,
shorten the name to Revilla, which, Anglicized, or "Alaskacized,"
then becomes Ruh-*vil*-la. The name Ketchikan is thought to have
been derived from a Tlingit word meaning "the thundering wings
of an eagle," or the sound of the eagle's wings in flight.

A Tlingit fishing camp—"Kitschkhin" or "Kitskan"—had been
well established in the area when settlers built a small saltery at
the mouth of Ketchikan Creek in 1883. Within two years, canneries had sprouted at the nearby communities of Quadra on the
mainland and Loring on Revillagigedo Island. In 1887, the
Quadra cannery was moved to Ketchikan and the present-day settlement was born. The Tongass Packing Company packed 5,500
cases of salmon that first year, the beginning of an industry that
grew to more than a dozen canneries producing more than two
million cases of salmon a year, earning Ketchikan the title
Salmon Capital of the World.

Mining contributed to the growth of the settlement when gold
was discovered in the area in 1897. Prospectors located good copper deposits on Prince of Wales Island the same year, and the
community was launched on another tack. Lumber production
started at about the same time. The Ketchikan Spruce Mill was
moved from its first location on Prince of Wales Island to
Ketchikan in 1903 to provide lumber to manufacture packing
boxes for the canneries. The mill remained the focal point of
downtown Ketchikan for several decades, in more recent years
producing cants (sawed logs) for export to Japan. The local economy was dealt a blow when the mill—now owned by Louisiana-
Pacific—was relocated to Annette Island. Louisiana-Pacific's pulp
mill, built at Ward Cove in 1954, produces a dissolving pulp used
to manufacture plastics and other synthetics, and a new small-log
sawmill cuts dimensional lumber. The Cape Fox Native Corporation logs corporate lands around Ketchikan as well.

The salmon fisheries declined in the 1940s and nearly col-
lapsed in the 1970s, mostly from overfishing, but the industry
gradually recovered. Commercial fishing and fish processing remain a vital part of the economy and life-style of the community.
Like all Southeast towns, Ketchikan relies on both tourism and
government to flesh out the economy.

GETTING THERE

You can reach Ketchikan by air or by water. Alaska Airlines
provides daily jet service from Seattle and Juneau. The airport is

Flower baskets grace tiny Whale Park in the heart of busy Ketchikan. (Sarah Eppenbach)

located on Gravina Island, across Tongass Narrows from the city of Ketchikan. A small ferry shuttles passengers and automobiles between the airport and the airport ferry terminal, a little more than 2 miles north of the Ketchikan city center, near the Alaska state ferry terminal. Ketchikan is a port of call for both mainline ferries traveling north and south along the Inside Passage and for smaller vessels serving Metlakatla, Prince of Wales Island, and Hyder. The many cruise ships that visit the port tie up at the city dock on the downtown waterfront or anchor just offshore.

To See and Do

Like other communities along the Inside Passage, Ketchikan is squeezed onto a narrow ribbon of land between the mountains and the sea. Much of the business district hangs over the water on pilings. A number of attractions near the city center can be reached on foot, while others require a bus or automobile trip "out the road." A two-hour *waterfront cruise*, available from Outdoor Alaska (907–225–6044) is a good way to get your bearings.

The central sights can be viewed on the *walking tour* that has been outlined by the Ketchikan Visitors' Bureau—pick up a map at the dockside visitors' center. The full tour requires about two hours walking time and takes in the major attractions of Creek Street, the Totem Heritage Center, Deer Mountain Hatchery, and the Tongass Museum: all relatively flat terrain. Along the way you will glimpse some of Ketchikan's famous staircases leading to residential neighborhoods high in the clouds. If you can muster the strength to climb the stairs to the *overlooks* above Upland Way and Front Street, you will be rewarded with spectacular views of the waterfront and ship activity on Tongass Narrows.

Front Street, where cruise ships dock, bustles with hotels, eating establishments, and gift and souvenir shops. *Annabelle's Keg & Chowder House* in the historic Gilmore Hotel (326 Front Street) and the top-floor *Ketchikan Cafe* (314 Front Street) do a nice job, especially with local seafood. Mission Street offers targets for gallery shopping: try *Scanlon Gallery* (310/318 Mission Street) and *Artists Cove* (633 Mission). *Alaska Country Workbasket* (619 Mission) carries original Alaska design cross-stitch patterns, Alaskan dolls, and quilts.

Front Street turns inland just past the visitors' center and becomes Mill Street. On the right, the U.S. Forest Service Southeast Alaska Visitor Information Center, SEAVIC, rises from the site of a former spruce mill. When completed in the summer of 1995, the 22,000-square-foot center will include elaborate interpretive ex-

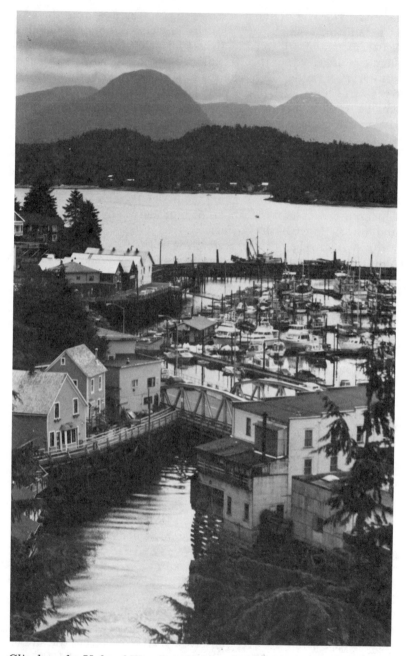

Climb to the Upland Way Overlook and view Creek Street and boat-filled Thomas Basin. Tongass Narrows is beyond.

hibits about public lands, resources, and recreational opportunities throughout Alaska, particularly the Tongass National Forest.

Few sights in Southeast Alaska so delight the eye as Creek Street, built on pilings above Ketchikan Creek. The wooden boardwalk, rimmed now with galleries and shops, was the red-light district of Ketchikan during the rowdier days when loggers and fishermen came to town looking for entertainment. The city closed the twenty-odd houses in 1953. Creek Street, local wags used to say, was the spot where "both fish and fishermen went upstream to spawn," a concept that greatly influences the plot of Ketchikan's own rip-roaring, home grown summer musical melodrama, *The Fish Pirate's Daughter*.

At number 24 on the right, painted peppermint green with a red door, you'll find *Dolly's House*. Big Dolly Arthur arrived in Alaska in 1914 at age twenty-six and exercised her considerable charms until Creek Street closed. Dolly continued to live in her house, however, until she moved into a nursing home at age seventy-three, and many of her personal furnishings are still there. Dolly's House has been restored as a small museum that offers a glimpse into her life and times. A photo of Dolly in the front room shows a spirited "Big Blonde" type of generous proportions. At five-foot-eight she was not called Big Dolly for nothing, and her weight ballooned to 240 pounds in later years. The dining room table is set for company and the bottle of bootleg whiskey stands at the ready in a tiny wet bar positioned strategically over the creek. A quick toss through the trapdoor took care of any incriminating evidence. Dolly's clothes hang in the upstairs boudoir and her chunky pink and red costume jewelry sprawls on the dressing table. Next door, at *Parnassus* (28 Creek Street), you will meet Lillian Ference, who presides over this delightful two-story bookstore (new and used), giftshop, and espresso bar. Highly recommended: the *Five Star Cafe* (5 Creek Street), for homemade soups, vegetarian specials, baked goodies, and the now-ubiquitous espresso; and, just upstairs from that, Ray Troll's *Soho Coho* art gallery, featuring his own and other artists' work.

From Creek Street, a red funicular climbs to the attractive seventy-two-room Westmark *Cape Fox Lodge/Heen Kahidi Restaurant and Lounge* and adjacent *Ted Ferry Civic Center*, 130 feet above the city center and Tongass Narrows. Hotel guests ride free to this great view; other visitors pay a nominal fee.

The *Totem Heritage Center* at 601 Deermount Street is a repository for original, unrestored totem poles that have been retrieved from the deserted Tlingit communities of Tongass and Village islands and the Haida village of Old Kasaan. There is a central gallery where five of the massive poles are displayed, plus exhibit cases of Native art and artifacts, including a beautiful set of traditional woodcarving tools made by Tsimshian carver Jack Hudson. Each implement, decorated and shaped to fit the carver's hand, is itself a work of art. The Totem Heritage Center is also used for workshops in Native crafts such as wood carving, beading, basketry, and silver engraving. You may see young artists sorting and stringing beads or working on dance blankets or other projects. In the beading room, notice the handsome copper and wood screen depicting Raven with the sun and moon.

Outside the Totem Heritage Center stands a contemporary totem pole carved by Tlingit master carver Nathan Jackson. This pole, *Raven-Fog Woman,* recalls the story of the mythical hero Raven and Fog Woman, his wife, who created the first salmon. According to this legend, Raven went fishing with his two slaves to gather the winter's food supply, but managed to catch nothing but bullheads. As they were returning to camp, a heavy fog engulfed their canoe and they lost their way. Suddenly, a woman appeared in the canoe. She asked Raven for his spruce root hat, which she took in her left hand. All the fog disappeared into the hat and Raven was able to find the way home. Fog Woman became Raven's wife and produced sockeye salmon for him out of baskets of spring water like rabbits out of a hat. When she had produced

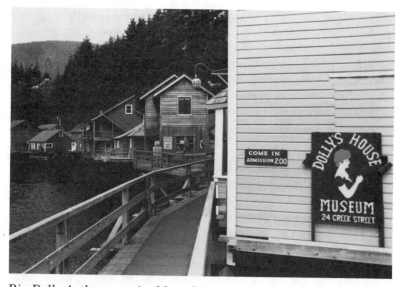

Big Dolly Arthur exercised her charms at Number 24 until Creek Street was closed in 1953.

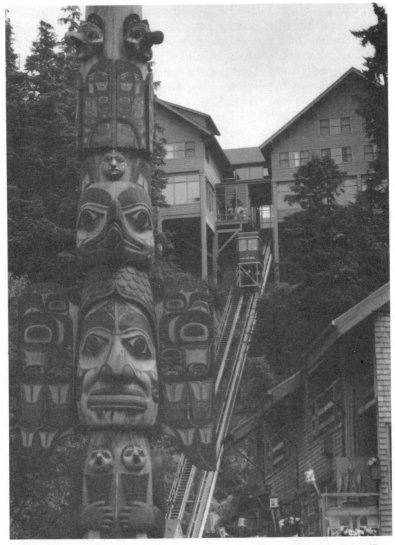

Funicular climbs from famous Creek Street to Westmark Cape Fox Lodge and Ted Ferry Civic Center in Ketchikan. (Sarah Eppenbach)

enough salmon to fill many smokehouses, Raven forgot his former hunger and began to mistreat her. She left him to return to her father's house, and as she walked into the sea, all of the salmon followed, leaving Raven nothing to eat but the bullhead.

The pole depicts Raven at the top, easily recognized by his

wings and straight beak. He is holding a bullhead on a line. Beneath him, his two slaves, Gitsanuk and Gitsanqeq, also hold bullheads. At the bottom of the pole, Fog Woman holds the spruce root hat in her left hand and a salmon in her right.

From the Totem Heritage Center, cross the footbridge over Ketchikan Creek to reach the *Deer Mountain Hatchery*. This facility can produce 400,000 salmon and 35,000 steelhead annually. Released into Ketchikan Creek, they migrate downstream into Thomas Basin and salt water. After a hazardous life at sea, the surviving adults return to the hatchery to spawn. Depending upon the month, you may see young fish in rearing pens or adult fish returning to the hatchery. The kings normally spawn from the end of July through August, and coho the end of November through December. The adjacent *City Park* has creekside picnic tables.

The *Tongass Historical Society Museum* at 629 Dock Street occupies one of the nicest sites in the city. The building, which also houses the public library, practically straddles Ketchikan Creek. Inside, you can hear the sound of water rushing beneath your feet. The museum embraces all the themes that thread through Ketchikan's history: Native cultures, mining, timber, and fishing, with permanent and changing exhibits. You can walk through the exhibits in an hour.

"This Is Our Life," focuses on the changing cultures of Southeast Native peoples. Showcases reveal a life-style rich with creativity. You will see beautiful and functional spruce root and cedar bark baskets, bentwood boxes and elaborate feast dishes, a shaman's necklace and rattle, and a large Chilkat blanket. A carved wooden crest hat in the shape of a salmon comes from the Dog Salmon clan on Prince of Wales Island. Elders of the Tlingit, Haida, and Tsimshian peoples guided the preparation of the display and explained how the artifacts were made and used.

The museum also exhibits the original lens from the Tree Point light station at Dixon Entrance. Originally illuminated by a kerosene vapor lamp, the light was replaced by a rotating beacon in 1963.

The totem pole outside the museum, *Raven Stealing the Sun,* was commissioned by the City of Ketchikan to honor the Tongass Tlingit who originally inhabited the area. The figures recall the story of Raven, who brought light to the world by stealing the box of daylight from a chief on the Nass River (see page 63). The pole was designed and carved by Tlingit artist Dempsey Bob and raised in 1983. Chief Johnson's Pole, at Mission and Stedman streets across from Whale Park, portrays the mythical bird Kad-

Ketchikan carver Nathan Jackson (right) works on a new totem pole with Steve Brown (left foreground) and Ernest Smeltzer.

juk, the crest of the Johnson clan. Israel Shotridge carved this replica of the 1901 original. The same artist created the *Chief Kyan totem* raised in Whale Park in 1993.

Two and one-half miles south of Ketchikan on the South Tongass Highway, another vast collection of totem poles stands sentry duty at *Saxman Totem Park.* Tlingit from Cape Fox and Tongass villages formed the village of Saxman in the late 1800s. It is named for Samuel Saxman, a schoolteacher lost with two other men in the winter of 1886 while they were hunting for a new village site. The twenty-four totems were brought to the site from abandoned villages on Tongass, Cat, Pennock, and Village islands and from the old Cape Fox Village at Kirk Point under a U.S. Forest Service and Civilian Conservation Corps project in the 1930s. Some were repaired and restored and others completely replicated—a process that continues today.

The park is on the uphill, or left, side of the highway as you proceed south. *Sun and Raven* stands at the entrance. Originally carved in 1902 as a memorial column, the pole recalls several Raven myths. You can identify Raven at the top, with his characteristic straight beak. The corona around his head represents the Sun, who entertained Raven during the Deluge. The eye-shaped designs on his wings, with small faces inside, symbolize the power

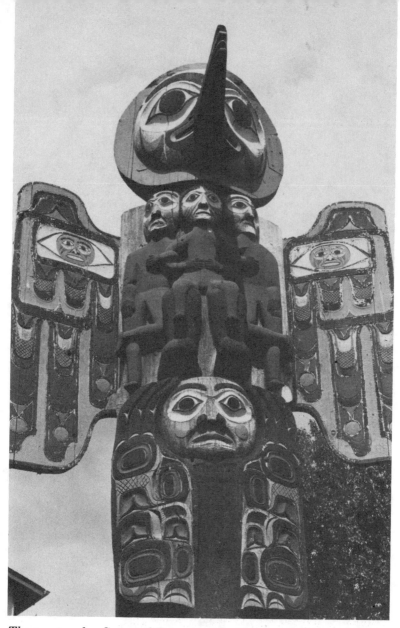

The spectacular Sun and Raven, at the entrance to Saxman Totem Park, recalls several Raven adventures.

of flight and Raven's ability to change form. The three small figures between Raven's wings represent the Children of the Sun. Below them is Fog Woman, Raven's wife, who produced salmon out of springwater. Next is Raven again, diving after Frog to the bottom of the ocean to visit the creatures of the sea.

The *Tired Wolf houseposts*, uphill from Sun and Raven, were carved in approximately 1827 for members of the Wolf phratry who had once crossed paths with a particular wolf. According to their story, the men of Forest Island House were out fishing one day in their canoe when they came upon a wolf swimming for shore. He was so exhausted that his tongue lolled out of his mouth. They rescued the wolf and took him to live with them, and the animal became a faithful companion and helped them to hunt. In the carvings, the wolves' tongues are hanging out of their mouths. The long tail up the back of each post distinguishes Wolf from Bear. Notice the small face that forms the pupil of the eye in one of the wolves, a carver's device to symbolize the life-force.

The majority of the totem poles are arranged in a wide grassy area at the top of the street. Look to the right to see the *Lincoln pole*. This is a replica. You can see the original pole in the Alaska State Museum in Juneau. The precise history of this famous totem has been lost to the past, but the carving was erected on Tongass Island in 1883 to commemorate the clan's first sighting of a white man many years previously. The carver evidently used a picture of President Lincoln as a model for the figure wearing a stovepipe hat at the top of the column. Raven, the clan crest, appeared at the base and the pole was known as the Proud Raven pole.

The plain shaft with the single lonely figure at the top wearing a potlatch hat is the *Seward pole,* which was carved about 1885 to commemorate Secretary of State William Seward's tour of Tongass Island in 1869. During his visit, Seward was entertained by the clan chief. He was given a ceremonial spruce root hat, furs, and a carved and painted chest. On the pole the secretary is shown seated on the chest and wearing the potlatch hat. Some say the Seward pole is actually a ridicule pole that was erected because Seward did not reciprocate the hospitality shown him by the people of Tongass Village.

There are several Frog totems in the park. Besides the Frog figure on the Sun and Raven pole, there is a mortuary column showing Raven poised for flight on top and Frog midway down the shaft, and *Frog Tree,* with two Frog totems atop a crosspiece on an upright support. The latter pole was erected in memory of a woman whose name was Two Frogs on a Drifting Log. The legend tells of a young Tlingit woman, a chief's daughter, who went to live with a tribe of frogs in a lake near their village. The father was eventually able to rescue her and bring her home, but she was unable to eat human food and soon died.

Many visitors photograph *Loon Tree,* the pole with the three bear cubs. The top figure, Loon, represents the crest figure of a par-

Some say the Seward pole, carved about 1885 to commemorate Secretary of State William Seward's visit, is actually a ridicule pole.

ticular Tlingit clan. Below Loon three bear cubs make their way headfirst to the base of the pole. The cubs represent the story of Kats, who married a she-bear that appeared to him in human form and was ultimately killed by their cub-children. Kats's bear wife is at the bottom of the pole, holding the human figure of Kats between her front paws. You will see many other carvings representing the popular legend of Kats, his wife, and their cub-children.

For more information about the poles in Saxman and other totem collections, the standard reference book is *The Wolf and the Raven* (University of Washington Press) by Dr. Viola Garfield of the University of Washington Department of Anthropology, and

Linn Forrest, who was the U.S. Forest Service architect in charge of the Civilian Conservation Corps totem restoration project. The authors were actively involved in the restoration project and have tried to document the history of each totem at Saxman as well as those at Totem Bight and Klawock totem parks. The book is available in most Southeast bookstores.

Saxman Native Village includes a gift shop, carving shed where you may see new poles being carved, and *Beaver Tribal House* with a beautiful carved house screen and house posts. In summer the community hosts scheduled performances of the *Cape Fox Dancers,* Saxman's traditional Tlingit dance group.

The road northward from the city center takes you to the terminals for the airport ferry and the Alaska state ferry. Just north of the downtown tunnel, you'll find small, flower-hung *Harbor View Park,* with tables and benches overlooking the commercial fishing float, and *Coffee Connections*, a small cafe and gift shop. At Ward Cove, midway along the 18.4-mile North Tongass Highway, the Louisiana-Pacific pulp mill produces a high-grade dissolving pulp for industrial use. Roads lead inland to the *Ward Lake Recreation Area* with several attractive national forest campgrounds and picnic shelters. An easy mile-long trail circles the lake.

At mile 10 you reach *Totem Bight State Historic Park.* A broad path leads through the forest to fourteen totem poles and an elaborately decorated clan house on a point overlooking Tongass Narrows. The site, with its gentle beach and salmon stream, was formerly used by the Tlingit as a summer campsite. Two Haida mortuary columns, Eagle and Thunderbird, guard the trail head.

The community house was constructed by the Civilian Conservation Corps as a replication of an early nineteenth-century clan house with painted housefront, carved corner posts, and a tall totem pole at the entrance. An oval hole in the bottom of the pole frames the doorway into the house. The interior is fashioned in typical style with a central fire pit for cooking and heating and a wooden platform around the perimeter where the inhabitants sat, slept, and stowed their belongings.

The other totems in the park are arranged along a path overlooking the water. Some are Haida in origin; others are Tlingit. You can pick up a brochure explaining the history and significance of each pole at the park entrance.

No fires, food, or camping are allowed at Totem Bight, but you can enjoy a picnic at the U.S. Forest Service campground at *Settlers' Cove* at the northern end of the road system. You will find a boat launch, campsites, and picnic tables. A path leads along the beach to the right. You duck into the mossy forest, following the

The community house at Totem Bight overlooks Tongass Narrows. The spot was formerly a Tlingit campsite.

trail and the sound of rushing water, and come to a bridge that fords the stream.

Other "out-the-road" opportunities include two full-service fishing resorts: locally popular *Clover Pass Resort* (mile 15), a casual complex with cabins, rental boats and a good restaurant lounge; and the tonier *Salmon Falls Resort* on Behm Canal (mile 17). The restaurants of both resorts are open to the public.

Ketchikan is the nearest departure point for plane or boat excursions into *Misty Fiords National Monument,* a 2.2 million-acre coastal ecosystem encompassing the east side of Revillagigedo Island and a portion of the mainland between Behm and Portland canals. "Misty" was designated a national monument in 1978 and given wilderness status in 1980. Within the monument the deep fjords of Walker Cove and Rudyerd Bay penetrate the wilderness with sheer rock walls rising to 3,000 feet. As the name implies, it's a moody and immensely beautiful environment of veiled peaks and waterfalls nourished by 150 inches of rain and snow annually. Wildlife is prevalent, and the bays and coves offer good fishing, camping, photography, and wilderness exploration. The Forest Service maintains fourteen recreational cabins within the monument (available for $20 per night), several mooring buoys, and hiking trails.

The untouched wilderness of Misty Fiords can be accessed by floatplane or boat only. Several air taxi services offer Misty Fiords flightseeing from Ketchikan. On a typical flight, the pilot will set down in the upper reaches of the monument and shut off the engine so that you can enjoy the peace and solitude of the setting. *Outdoor Alaska (P.O. Box 7814, Ketchikan, Alaska 99901; telephone 907–225–6044* offers combination cruise/fly tours into Misty Fiords plus kayak drop-offs. Kayaking in Misty Fiords is increasingly popular. *Southeast Exposure (P.O. Box 9143, Ketchikan, Alaska 99901; telephone 907–225–8829)* provides kayak instruction and rental and guided kayak trips into the monument. For more information about Misty Fiords contact *U.S. Forest Service, 3031 Tongass Avenue, Ketchikan, Alaska 99901;* telephone *(907) 225–2148.*

The 2.2-million-acre Misty Fiords National Monument is a brief floatplane ride from Ketchikan. (U.S. Forest Service)

The ripsnorting Ketchikan Logging Carnival draws an enthusiastic Fourth of July crowd.

SPECIAL EVENTS

In addition to the usual parade, Ketchikan puts on a ripsnorting *Logging Carnival* on the Fourth of July with such events as ax throwing, choker setting, powersaw bucking, ax chopping, and pole climbing. The contests are held on Walker Field off Park Avenue in town, and they guarantee splendid entertainment for everyone. The combination of parade, Logging Carnival, and evening fireworks display over Tongass Narrows recommends Ketchikan as a destination over the Fourth. Other annual Ketchikan celebrations include the *Festival of the North,* a winter arts and music gala; the *Great Alaska Sportfishing Championship,* a one-day fish-off between disc jockeys from radio stations across America (August); and the *Blueberry Festival* and street fair in August. Ketchikan's *King Salmon Derby* takes place over Memorial Day weekend and the two following weekends.

WRANGELL
Population 2,500

Wrangell is a solid frontier town with a strong spirit of independence. The false-fronted buildings on Front Street all exhibit different shapes and designs. Each stands alone, aloof from the next. The streets are broad and paved. There are wide sidewalks—room to pass without jostling your neighbor and room to grow. Some of the spaciousness is due to the two devastating fires that have rampaged through the downtown business center. The more recent, in 1952, destroyed all of the waterfront side of Main Street, which was built on pilings over the water. The burned-over area was subsequently closed with fill, but the devastation left a permanent gap along the waterfront.

Although Wrangell boasts a number of major-league visitor attractions—a beach scattered with petroglyphs, an important Tlingit clan house and totem poles, the magnificent scenery of the Stikine River—the tourism industry is still in the formative stages. On the one hand, you'll see a "real" Alaskan town—before the prettying up (hanging flower baskets, colorful banners, strategically placed benches . . .) that an aggressive tourism industry usually brings. On the other hand, facilities such as the museum and visitors' center operate on limited hours and with limited

Tugboats in Wrangell Harbor await the next assignment.

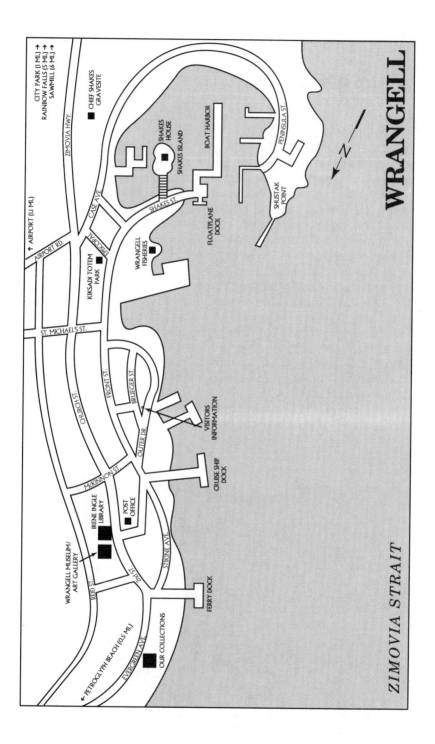

WRANGELL

ZIMOVIA STRAIT

CITY PARK (1 MI.) →
RAINBOW FALLS (5 MI.) →
SAWMILL (6 MI.) →

ZIMOVIA HWY.

CHIEF SHAKES
GRAVESITE

← AIRPORT (1.1 MI.)

AIRPORT RD.

CASE AVE.

PRINCIPAL

SHAKES
HOUSE

SHAKES ISLAND

BOAT HARBOR

PENINSULA ST.

SHAKES ST.

KIKSADI TOTEM
PARK

WRANGELL
FISHERIES

FLOATPLANE
DOCK

SHUSTAK
POINT

N

ST. MICHAEL'S ST.

CHURCH ST.

FRONT ST.

BRUEGER ST.

VISITORS
INFORMATION

OUTER DR.

McKINNON ST.

IRENE INGLE
LIBRARY

POST
OFFICE

CRUISE SHIP
DOCK

WRANGELL MUSEUM/
ART GALLERY

REID ST.

2ND ST.

STIKINE AVE.

FERRY DOCK

PETROGLYPH BEACH (0.5 MI.) →

EVERGREEN AVE.

OUR COLLECTIONS

staff. Visitors need to show some initiative and independence: Walk around, ask questions, and enjoy the frontier spirit that still exists in Wrangell.

BACKGROUND

Wrangell's multinational history has been the direct result of the town's proximity to the swift-flowing Stikine River that reaches 330 miles from the Southeast mainland into British Columbia. Located on the northern tip of Wrangell Island, just 7 miles from the river delta, Wrangell has been a terminus for river activity since the Tlingit Indians first used the Stikine to trade with the Athapaskans in the Interior.

At the time of the Russian occupation of Alaska, the Stikine delta and neighboring islands were the home of a powerful group of Tlingit Indian clans that came to be known as the Stikines. The chief of the Stikines was Shakes, the fourth in a succession of chiefs of that name. (The seventh and last Chief Shakes to assume the title died in 1944.) His village, known as Kots-lit-na, was situated on Wrangell Island, approximately 20 miles to the south of the present town of Wrangell. About 1811, the Russians began trading with the Tlingit for the valuable furs such as beaver and land otter that were obtained up the Stikine.

The story of the modern settlement of Wrangell begins not with the Russians, however, but the British. In the early 1800s when the Russians were busy relocating their headquarters from Kodiak to Sitka, the British Hudson's Bay Company controlled the fur trade in Canada. The British moved their posts farther and farther west until they reached the Pacific, where they ran smack up against the Russian-American Company in their bid for the Native fur trade. In 1825, the two countries signed treaties fixing the boundaries between Russian-America and Canada. The agreements gave the Hudson's Bay Company the right to use navigable Southeast streams to reach its posts in Canada, providing no Russian settlement stood in the way. Increasingly desirous of reaching the fur supply on the mainland just beyond the Russian coast, the Hudson's Bay Company decided to establish a post on the Stikine, which would give them easy access to the Interior and an easy exit to move the furs to market.

Before the British could set this plan in motion, the Russian-American Company got wind of the scheme. The Russians sent their own expedition, commanded by Captain-Lieutenant Dionysius Zarembo, to cut off the British from the Stikine trade by establishing their own fort at the river mouth. In 1833 they began building Redoubt Saint Dionysius (*redoubt* meaning "fort") on the shore of a sheltered bay (now Wrangell Harbor) on the northern tip of Wrangell Island. The fort, the second non-Native settlement in Southeast Alaska, was named for Zarembo's patron saint. When the British arrived—too late—to build their own fort, they were met with a show of force and made to back down. The Russian flag was raised over Redoubt Saint Dionysius on 26 August 1834.

Once the crisis had passed, the British managed to get what they wanted anyway. In 1839 the Russian-American Company agreed to lease to the Hudson's Bay Company all of the mainland coast from Portland Canal at the southern border of Russian territory to Cape Spencer west of Glacier Bay for a period of ten years. The price was 2,000 land otter skins annually, plus a quantity of provisions such as wheat and salt beef that were always in short supply. Under this arrangement, Redoubt Saint Dionysius passed into British hands and assumed the name Fort Stikine.

Under the British flag, the Stikine settlement became a major trading center for the neighboring Tlingit Indians. Chief Shakes had already moved his community from Kots-lit-na to the small harbor area now known as Shakes Island. Other clans lived nearby on Wrangell Island and on the mainland. In exchange for valuable furs, the Indians were given manufactured items that they wanted such as cloth and the rich wool Hudson's Bay Point blankets.

Fort Stikine was abandoned in 1849. When Alaska was sold to the United States in 1867, the trading settlement was received by the U.S. Army. Once again the name was changed, this time to Fort Wrangell for Baron Ferdinand von Wrangell, who had been the chief manager for the Russian-American Company from 1830 to 1836 when Redoubt Saint Dionysius was founded. The Army built new quarters on a rise near the site of the old fort. Fort Wrangell closed in the 1870s with all of the other army posts in Alaska except Sitka. Some of the buildings were purchased by a retired army supply officer who opened a trading post.

Wrangell was the jumping-off point for three different gold rushes to the Interior. In 1861 the Stikine strike, the first gold strike to affect Alaska, took prospectors upriver to a spot called Buck's Bar. Captain William Moore transported the prospectors from Wrangell to Buck's Bar aboard his steamer the *Flying Dutchman*. By the time the second wave of prospectors arrived in 1873 on their way to the new strikes in the Canadian Cassiar district, the non-Native population of Wrangell had dwindled to three. Once again the quiet outpost was transformed into a boom-

The false-fronted buildings along Front Street in Wrangell reflect a spirit of independence.

town as fortune seekers geared for the trip into the wilderness, then spent their hard-won diggings on the way back out again. Wrangell was suddenly the busiest spot in the territory. An estimated 3,000 people went up the Stikine and packed into the Cassiar in 1874. Three years later, the first mission school in Alaska was opened at Wrangell. By 1880, steamers ran directly to Wrangell from Portland and Victoria, British Columbia.

When the Cassiar rush ended, Wrangell subsided into inactivity once more. Historian Hubert Howe Bancroft reported in 1886 that the fort was deserted and the town "nearly so, except by Indians.... The main street is choked with decaying logs and stumps, and is passable only by a narrow plank sidewalk."

The town rebounded with the rush to the Klondike in 1898, as prospectors scrambled to get to Dawson in the shortest possible time. Some of them elected to follow the Stikine to Telegraph Creek and hike 160 miles overland to the headwaters of the Yukon. But by the time this strike had run its course, Wrangell had gained an economic toehold with two canneries and a sawmill.

These industries continue to dominate the economy. The number one industry in Wrangell today is lumber, produced by the dimensional lumber sawmill operated by Alaska Pulp Corporation of Sitka 6 miles south of town. The downtown harbor houses a sizable fleet of trollers, gill-netters, and seiners, plus a large cannery and cold storage plant and several smaller seafood processors. Besides salmon, they package halibut, crab, and the prized local shrimp, from salad size to beefy prawns. The recent development of major mines across the border in Canada finds Wrangell once again serving as a gold-rush depot as well. Enormous Hovercraft transport gold concentrate down the Stikine while supplies and crews move in the other direction. The surge of activity has turned the Wrangell airport into the second-busiest in Alaska (after Anchorage) for international traffic.

Wrangell is a scrappy town. The community has stuck it out for more than a century, through good times and bad. Consider the *Wrangell Sentinel.* The newspaper started publication on November 2, 1902 and continues today—the oldest continuously published newspaper in Alaska.

GETTING THERE

So far, Wrangell has not been a regular stop on most cruise ship itineraries. This may change, though, as cruise companies search for undiscovered destinations and less crowded ports. Alaska state ferries call at Wrangell on their normal route between Bellingham/Prince Rupert and Skagway, and the ferry terminal is right in the center of town. The airport, with daily jet service to cities along the Seattle-to-Juneau route, is 1.5 miles north of town.

You can find comfortable accommodations both in town and out the road, including an increasing number of bed and breakfasts. The waterfront *Stikine Inn* remains unmatched for convenience and its spectacular view out to Zimovia Strait, but bring your earplugs to block the beat of the rock band that plays in the lounge at night and ask for a room away from the noise. *Harding's Old Sourdough Lodge* and *Roadhouse Lodge* (mile 4 Zimovia Highway) are good alternatives. (See Lodging Directory, page 311, for others.)

TO SEE AND DO

Wrangell is so small that you can walk to all the major attractions. Since the state ferry docks downtown, you view much of the community even if you are in port for only an hour or two. Whether you arrive at the state ferry terminal or the city dock, angle off to your right to Outer Drive and Brueger Street, where you will find the *Visitors' Information Center* in a small A-frame hut. There you can get a visitors' guide, brochures, and other in-

Totem pole in Wrangell's Kiksadi Totem Park depicts Raven, who manufactured the earth from mud and stones and brightened the sky with the sun, moon, and stars. (Sarah Eppenbach)

formation you need. The area toward the water is what is known as the "downtown fill area." This is the part of town that was filled in after the 1952 fire destroyed the waterfront side of Front Street that had been built on wooden pilings.

Front Street continues southward toward the boat harbor. You will pass old false-fronted wooden buildings, each painted a different color and design. Some show the founding date: "Biehl's, 1898," for example. At the intersection with Episcopal Street, you come to Wrangell's latest addition, pocket-sized *Kiksadi Totem Park.* Four new totem poles, replicas of historic Wrangell-area carvings, stand in the park surrounded by plantings of shrubs and trees. The *One-Legged Fisherman pole,* at the upper left of the park, represents a Tlingit myth about a supernatural being of the Eagle clan known as the one-legged fisherman (in the pole, however, he is given two legs). The one-legged fisherman used a magic harpoon to catch salmon, which he strung up on ropes, as shown in the carving. The original version of the tall pole at the front, the *Kiksadi pole,* was carved in the 1890s to honor a chief of the Kiksadi clan, whose crest figure, the Frog, appears near the top.

When you reach the end of Front Street, Shakes Street continues around to *Shakes Island,* a grassy compound with a replica of the Shakes community house and several totem poles, and the *boat harbor* with its seafood processing plants and berths of commercial fishing boats and tugs. There are few signs—you have to proceed on faith. On the way you pass the Marine Lounge, which is the site of the original Russian fort, Saint Dionysius.

Shakes House, like the community house at Ketchikan's Totem Bight, was constructed as part of the Civilian Conservation Corps's totem restoration project in the 1930s. The building was meant to be a replica of the house where the various Chiefs Shakes lived after the clan moved from Kots-lit-na. All the lumber and support poles were hand-adzed to give the house an authentic look and, like the original dwellings, no nails were used in the construction. The green and black Bear totem framing the entrance was painted and carved on the interior screen in the original Shakes House.

The interior of the house is generally open to view only when tour ships are in port or by appointment. (Ask at the visitors' center or museum.) It is arranged in the traditional style with a central fire pit for cooking surrounded by two tiers of wooden platforms for sitting, sleeping, and storage, and has a smoke hole in the roof. A carved and painted wooden screen separates the chief's private quarters from the common room. Instead of the original Bear design, the screen is decorated with the design from a Chilkat blanket that belonged to the Shakes family. The interior houseposts were originals brought from the old village in the 1800s. Now more than 200 years old, they have been removed for protection and display in the Wrangell Museum. Carved replicas replace the originals in Shakes House. The Shakes Island house was dedicated at a great potlatch in 1940 that was attended by Indian leaders and other dignitaries from Southeast Alaska. On this occasion the next chief in the Shakes line, Kudanake, age seventy-six, formally assumed the title of Shakes VII.

Shakes Island houses several totem poles from the Wrangell area. Some of the poles belonged to the Shakes clan, while others were copied from poles owned by neighboring clans. The two short poles directly in front of the house at the left are replicas of memorial poles. If you go around behind them, you can see the carved niches where the ashes of the deceased would have been placed.

Shakes House is a replicated Tlingit community house of hand-adzed lumber and no nails. (John Schoen)

The *Bear-up-the-Mountain pole* with bear prints leading to the Bear figure at the top, is similar to the Kats pole at Totem Bight but recalls a different story. This pole commemorates the ancestors of the Shakes family who were led up the highest peak in the area by a grizzly bear to escape the great flood. The clan took Bear as their crest, and the pole symbolizes their tracks up the mountain to safety. The original version of this pole was a memorial to the younger brother of Chief Shakes VI.

To the left of the Bear-up-the-Mountain pole stands the *Double Whale Crest Hat,* or *Gonakadet pole.* The original version of this pole contained the ashes of Chief Shakes VI's father and mother. The carving recalls the story of a young man who slew a legendary lake monster called Gonakadet. The youth found that by putting on the monster's skin he could swim under the lake waters indefinitely and catch salmon and halibut for his family to eat. He had to return each morning, however, before the ravens called. One morning he failed to come home and his wife found him dead on the beach, still inside the monster's skin. From that day on, the village people called the youth by the name of Gonakadet. One night Gonakadet's wife heard him calling out to her to climb onto his back and hold on tight! She did as he bid and he took her to his home beneath the water. Gonakadet and his wife are seen only occasionally, but the sighting is always considered good luck.

Stories of some of the other poles on Shakes Island are contained in a pamphlet entitled *The Authentic History of Shakes Island and Clan,* by E. L. Keithahn (Wrangell Historical Society). You can obtain a copy at the Wrangell Museum.

Chief Shakes's gravesite is across the boat harbor from Shakes Island on the uphill side of Case Avenue. The plot is enclosed within a Russian-style picket fence with two Killer Whale totems on top. This is the gravesite of Shakes V, who was head of the clan when the British occupied Wrangell and at the time of the American purchase.

Back in the center of town, the First Presbyterian Church on *Church Street* is known for the large, red, neon cross that shines for miles out to sea at night. Local mariners use the cross, erected in 1939, as a navigational light. The church is the oldest American protestant church in Alaska, dating from the time of the first mission school in Wrangell. The building was founded in 1879, but was severely damaged by fire on two occasions and has been extensively renovated. The Saint Rose of Lima Catholic Church next door is the oldest Roman Catholic parish in Alaska.

In a few more yards along Church Street you'll come to the

Rock carvings have been found in many locations in Southeast Alaska. They may have been used as boundary markers.

Irene Ingle Public Library and the *Wrangell Museum.* The collection starts with some petroglyphs displayed on the grounds outside. These mysterious rock carvings, of undetermined age, have been found on several beaches in Southeast Alaska. Archaeologists do not know their significance; some speculate they were a type of boundary marker. Some of the etched designs are clearly shaped like animals, others like human faces. Some just look like abstract scribbles. The most extensive known collection of petroglyphs in Southeast Alaska is at Wrangell's Petroglyph Beach north of town.

The *Wrangell Museum* is housed in the city's first schoolhouse, erected in 1906. The building has proved versatile through the years, hosting at various times the library, the morgue, a doctor's office, and city hall. The museum, operated by the City of Wrangell, is devoted to local Wrangell history. Of the Native artifacts, one of the most interesting pieces is a ceremonial Tlingit dance blanket depicting a Bear design sewn by a Wrangell woman more than thirty years ago. The Bear totem is outlined in abalone shell buttons and thousands of tiny beads. There are 232 buttons in the border alone. The collection includes carved wooden halibut hooks, cedar bark and spruce root baskets, and a small Tlingit canoe from the local area.

The main exhibit room contains an assortment of items connected with Wrangell's rich and varied past: for example, small,

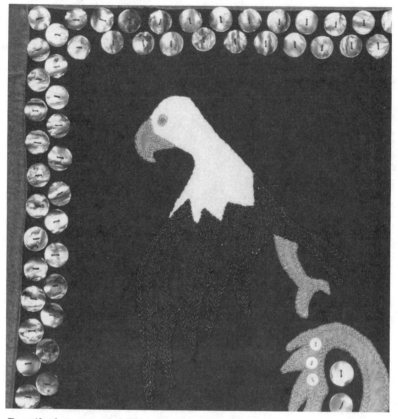

*Detail of ceremonial Tlingit dance blanket in Wrangell Museum
shows beads and abalone shell buttons.*

lidded copper kettles of a type that the Hudson's Bay Company
first sent to Canada around 1782, a Russian iron float used to suspend fishing nets, old cameras, and a collapsible wooden crate
from Chas. Benjamin's store in Wrangell.

Equipment buffs will enjoy the communications room containing the old Campbell press that printed the *Wrangell Sentinel*
until more modern equipment was installed in 1965. There is also
a late-1800s linotype, an old letter press, and other pieces of machinery.

A lobby shop carries a small selection of local history and art
books, cards, and gifts. The museum shares a roof with the
Wrangell Art Gallery, which sells works by local artists.

To get to *Petroglyph Beach*, a fifteen-minute walk from the ferry terminal or city dock, walk north on Evergreen Avenue. After a few minutes you will come to a barnlike building on your left with a sign that reads OUR COLLECTIONS. Our Collections is a hodgepodge of miscellanea that was lovingly gathered and protected over a lifetime in Wrangell by Elva Bigelow and her late husband, Bolly. Whether you should visit Elva's private museum is a matter of personal inclination. Some people find the Bigelow barn distressingly reminiscent of a garage in need of a cleaning. Others—the types who enjoy rooting around at garage sales—will wax poetic over the treadle and hand-crank sewing machines, old trapping gear, lanterns and binnacles, waffle irons, copper wash kettles or cooperage tools. You may get a charge out of the old costume jewelry or the valve off the *Matanuska*. Our Collections is memorabilia, curiosities, old things—in no particular rhyme or order. Much of the pleasure in viewing them comes from meeting the collector and hearing her stories about her things.

Petroglyph Beach lies another .3 mile beyond the Bigelow House. Start looking for the trail marker and sign just after you have passed a mobile home park on your right. A wooden boardwalk leads from the road to the beach. There are perhaps forty different petroglyphs (no one knows precisely how many) carved onto the rocks at this important site. You need a tide below the twelve-foot level to find them. There are no directional signs, so locating them is something like an Easter egg hunt. Here are some hints: Turn right at the end of the boardwalk and walk along the beach, keeping your eyes on the rocks between you and the water. You will see strange images looking back at you. When you come to a large rock outcropping in front of a small building, walk straight toward the water. You will see a spiral on a nearby rock. Look to your right and you will see a big face.

Hunting for petroglyphs makes a pleasurable family expedition. The mysterious images appear and disappear according to the light and whether the rocks are wet or dry. In years past it has been something of a Wrangell tradition to make souvenir rubbings from the petroglyphs using rice paper and crayon. Archaeologists now frown on rubbings, however, for fear the carvings will be damaged. They recommend photographing the images instead. This is tricky business. Local experts recommend using a polarizing filter to reduce glare and shooting in the late afternoon or evening when maximum shadows enhance the design. Wetting the surface will help provide definition. The Forest Service markets souvenir rubber stamps with rock art designs, including some from Wrangell glyphs.

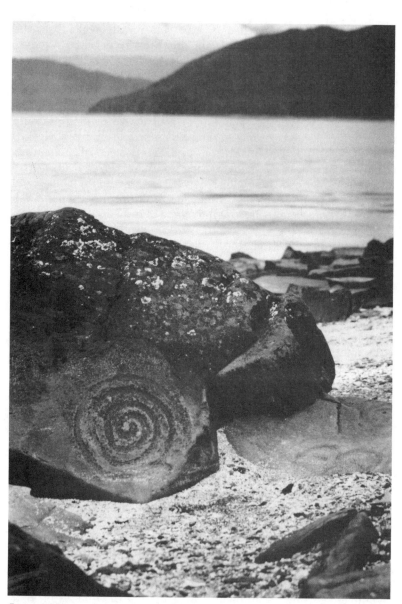

Low tide reveals mysterious rock carvings at Wrangell's Petro-glyph Beach. (Sarah Eppenbach)

Wrangell offers the usual complement of hiking trails, picnic spots, and other opportunities "out the road." *City Park*, about 1 mile south of town on Zimovia Highway, has waterfront picnic tables and shelters. At approximately mile 4.5, across from Shoemaker Harbor and Shoemaker Bay Recreational and RV Park, a short, easy trail leads through the rainforest to *Rainbow Falls*, a local favorite. For other destinations contact the Forest Service (907–874–2323) for its pamphlet on hiking trails and recreational facilities.

The Stikine River is the backyard playground for Wrangell residents. Since 1980 the waterway has been protected as part of the 443,000-acre *Stikine–Le Conte Wilderness* that encompasses much of the mainland territory between Wrangell and Petersburg. The internationally navigable and historic waterway offers something for everyone: river and mountain scenery, glaciers, wildlife, fishing, boating, and camping. The broad, braided delta serves as a stopover for several hundred thousand migrating shorebirds, such as the western sandpiper. Snow geese rest and feed on the river flats as well. During the April run of eulachon (a type of smelt), the delta hosts more than 1,500 bald eagles—the second-largest known concentration of bald eagles in the world (after the Chilkat River near Haines).

The arms and side sloughs of the Stikine nurture all five species of salmon and provide habitat for moose, brown bears, wolves, and many other creatures. The upper reaches of the river include some very enticing spots, such as Shakes Glacier and Chief Shakes Hot Springs, a Forest Service recreation facility with an enclosed wooden bathhouse in a forest glade and an outdoor tub overlooking a meadow of lupine and a distant mountain range (heavily, and sometimes rowdily, used by locals, especially on summer weekends). The mosquitoes can be fierce, but oh, the setting . . .

A garnet ledge on the river delta produces semiprecious stones. The ledge was deeded to the children of Wrangell and the Boy Scouts of America by one of Wrangell's civic leaders many years ago. Others wishing to dig for garnets must pay a small fee. (Permits are sold at the Wrangell Museum.) Digging your own garnets is not necessary, though, as they are sold in local shops and by Wrangell children who greet ferry and cruise ship passengers with muffin tins full of purple stones. Priced at $1.00 to $5.00 each, they make inexpensive and unusual souvenirs.

Several local charter operators provide jet-boat service up the Stikine and will tailor the trip to your interests. Todd Harding of *T.H. Charters (P.O. Box 934, Wrangell, Alaska 99929; telephone*

907–874–3613 or 874–2285) operates a variety of vessels, including the 50-foot, twenty-three-passenger *Stikine Princess* built expressly to sightsee the Stikine. The visitor center can provide a complete list of charter companies.

Boat and floatplane charter operators can also take you to *Le Conte Glacier*, 25 miles north of Wrangell, and to *Anan Creek Bear Observatory*, 30 miles south on the mainland. During July and August, the abundant salmon in Anan Creek attracts a high concentration of bears—primarily black bears but also brown—as well as bald eagles and harbor seals. The Forest Service has constructed a roofed observatory on a bluff overlooking a set of falls on Anan Creek where bears habitually fish. You reach the observatory by an easy .5-mile trail from the boat or floatplane anchorage. There is also a Forest Service recreation cabin on Anan Bay, a mile from the observatory via a planked trail, but it is heavily used—you need to reserve well in advance.

Anan offers a unique opportunity to view and photograph bears in their natural habitat. It is not a game park or a zoo—the bears are not contained or restrained, and certain rules must be followed to maximize safety to both animals and humans. They include not bringing in food or pets and not straying from the observatory or trail. There is a Forest Service interpreter on site every day during the viewing season. Please follow the instructions given by your guide or Forest Service personnel.

Due to increasingly heavy visitation, the Forest Service may eventually impose a permit system or other measures to limit access at Anan Creek. For more information contact *U.S. Forest Service, Wrangell Ranger District, P.O. Box 51, Wrangell, Alaska 99929; telephone (907) 874–2323.*

Special Events

Like other small towns, Wrangell puts on a rousing down-home *Fourth of July celebration* with fireworks, loggers' rodeo, and parade. Local residents contend that Wrangell's loggers' contests are better than those of other communities because *real* loggers compete instead of professional contestants drawn by the prize money offered elsewhere. Wrangellites also host the *Tent City Winter Festival* on the first weekend in February to celebrate the role that Wrangell played in three gold rushes and give residents some relief from the winter wearies. There is a food and craft fair and lighthearted contests such as beard-growing and tall tales. The Wrangell *King Salmon Derby* takes place in May.

PETERSBURG
Population 3,600

Petersburg stands out from the other Southeast communities by virtue of a deeply felt Norwegian heritage. The townspeople celebrate their Scandinavian origins during the renowned Little Norway Festival that takes place annually on Norwegian Independence Day (the third weekend in May) and in the attractive *rosemaling* (traditional Norwegian tole painting in floral design) that garnishes shopfronts and homes. It is a neat community with prim houses and careful yards.

Colorful rosemaling, *a form of Norwegian tole painting, decorates a Petersburg door.*

PETERSBURG

FALLS CREEK FISH LADDER (9 MI.) →
PAPKE'S LANDING (9 MI.) →
CRYSTAL LAKE HATCHERY (16.5 MI.) →
THREE LAKES LOOP ROAD (19 MI.) →

N

FERRY DOCK

MITKOF HWY.

SOUTH BOAT HARBOR

FLOATPLANE DOCK

MIDDLE BOAT HARBOR

SONS OF NORWAY

CHATHOM STRAIT SEAFOODS

HAMMER'S SLOUGH

NORTH BOAT HARBOR

POST OFFICE

HARBOR WAY

VISITORS INFORMATION

ALASKA GLACIER SEAFOODS

HAUGEN DR.

PETERSBURG FISHERIES

1st ST.

NORDIC DR.

← AIRPORT (1 MI.)

GJOA ST.

2nd ST.

1st ST.

FRAM ST.

EAGLE'S ROOST PARK

EXCEL ST.

CLAUSEN MUSEUM

WRANGELL AVE.

← SANDY BEACH (2.2 MI.)

WRANGELL NARROWS

Along with the Norwegian heritage comes fishing. This is a cannery town. With four seafood processing plants and the largest home-based halibut fleet in Southeast, fish and fishing are the dominant themes. Even the streets are named for famous old boats of the commercial fishing fleet.

Except for the Little Norway Festival, there is little organized activity planned around tourists in Petersburg. The streets are refreshingly bare of curio and T-shirt shops. But there is plenty to see and do in this town of friendly, hardworking Norwegians.

BACKGROUND

Petersburg is situated on the extreme northern tip of Mitkof Island. It is the last stop for most northbound ferries before reaching Juneau, and the prize that awaits mariners who have navigated the 21-mile Wrangell Narrows.

The town was founded by Peter Buschmann, who emigrated from Norway to Tacoma, Washington, with his wife and eight children in 1891. Six years later, he was homesteading a site along Wrangell Narrows that showed potential for a year-round fish-processing industry. Not only were both salmon and halibut in abundance, but there was a natural harbor, timber to build with, and a ready supply of ice from the Le Conte Glacier just 25 miles away.

Other Norwegians followed Buschmann to his spot on Wrangell Narrows, and they set to work developing a neat, well-planned, Scandinavian-style community. By 1900 the Icy Straits Packing Company, with Buschmann as manager, had constructed a sawmill, wharf, warehouses, bunkhouses, and store, and packed 32,750 cases of salmon. The fishermen brought in salmon for the cannery in summer and fall and harvested halibut in winter. Peter Buschmann's new community, called Petersburg, grew into a stable, year-round enterprise, in contrast to the mining towns that were subject to cycles of boom-and-bust.

The salmon industry proved successful, but it was halibut that put Petersburg on the map. Packed in glacier ice, the fine white fish was shipped by steamer to Seattle and forwarded directly to eager East Coast markets. Petersburg emerged as the halibut capital of Alaska and remains so today.

At the height of the cannery era, as many as eight seafood-processing plants operated simultaneously in Petersburg. The town remains the major fish-processing community in Southeast, with four processing plants and a reduction plant that produces fish meal from scraps. Petersburg Fisheries, Buschmann's old com-

Commercial fishing boats dwarf pedestrians in Petersburg harbor. (Sarah Eppenbach)

pany (now a subsidiary of Icicle Seafoods), has operated continuously since its founding. Besides salmon and halibut, the town processes crab, herring, prawns, and the tiny, delectable Petersburg shrimp that are fished within a 25-mile radius of town. Petersburg ships 150,000 pounds of shrimp to market annually.

GETTING THERE

As with all Inside Passage communities except Haines, Skagway, and Hyder, access is by water or air only. The trip between Wrangell and Petersburg via the 21-mile Wrangell Narrows (see pages 146–47) is among the most exciting legs of the Marine Highway. Alaska state ferries make the trip on the regular north/south run. The ferry terminal is about 1 mile south of town. Few cruise ships currently include Petersburg in the Southeast itinerary. Those that do—mostly the smaller "exploration class" vessels—dock right downtown at one of the boat harbors. There is daily jet service on Alaska Airlines between Petersburg and other Southeast communities with connections to the rest of Alaska and the Lower 48, and scheduled commuter airline service to Juneau on Wings of Alaska.

TO SEE AND DO

Petersburg is an artist's delight, whether the medium is oils, watercolors, or color film. So many images leap to the eye, from kerchiefed cannery workers in tall rubber boots to old wooden buildings reflected in Hammer's Slough. A walk around town rewards you with scenes of three boat harbors and the halibut fleet, canneries, rosemalinged store- and housefronts, and the natural scenery of Wrangell Narrows. Make your first stop the *Chamber of Commerce Information Center* at First and Fram streets to acquire a town map and Mitkof Island Road Guide.

The *seafood plants* of Petersburg Fisheries (Buschmann's old company) and Alaska Glacier Seafoods lie at the north end of town. You can take a half-hour tour of the latter with lifelong Petersburg resident Patti Norheim, whose father started the shrimp

A boatload of Dungeness crab arrives at the Petersburg Fisheries dock. Petersburg is still a major fish-processing community.

cannery in 1916. Call Tongass Traveler Tours, (907) 772–4837. Depending on the season, you'll see shrimp, crab, salmon, or halibut being processed. No tours of the other canneries are available, but there's plenty of activity visible from the docks.

Continuing past Petersburg Fisheries on Nordic Drive, you'll round a bend to the north and see Wrangell Narrows opening up into Frederick Sound. *Eagle's Roost Park* on the left captures the view with a hilltop garden, picnic tables, benches, and stairs leading down to the beach. Bald eagles perch in the trees at this site overlooking their prime fishing grounds. The road continues about a mile north of town to *Sandy Beach Recreation Area,* where you can see petroglyphs at low tide. The *Frederick Point Boardwalk,* a wheelchair-accessible boardwalk trail, leads about a mile through woods and muskeg bordering Frederick Sound. Eventually the trail will be extended another mile to a water overlook and picnic site. Back in town on Nordic Drive, look in at *Berthiel's Gallery* (No. 223) for silver jewelry and paintings by local and regional artists; and *Lee's Clothing* (No. 212) for imported Icelandic and Norwegian sweaters.

At the south end of town, stilthouses line the narrow, wood-planked street above *Hammer's Slough.* The barnlike *Sons of Norway Hall,* begun by founder Peter Buschmann in 1897 and completed in 1912, stands on pilings at the entrance to the saltwater inlet. The oft-photographed hall, painted white with red rosemalinged shutters, still hosts the local chapter of the International Sons of Norway who work to preserve the town's Norwegian heritage.

An upstairs shop, *Husfliden,* carries Norwegian imports and local arts and crafts, including rosemaling and hand-knit Norwegian-style sweaters. Also in the vicinity: *Sing Lee Alley Books* and *Helse* restaurant and natural foods store, patronized for home-made soup and bread, muffins, sandwiches and brownies—which disappear fast.

The *Clausen Memorial Museum* (Second and Fram streets) focuses on local history and community life, especially commercial fishing. Exhibits include the world's largest king salmon (estimated weight 126.5 pounds), captured in a fish trap off Prince of Wales Island in 1939, and the record chum salmon (36 pounds). Interesting displays illustrate the operation of different types of commercial fishing gear. You will also find a model fish trap, old cotton and linen fishing nets, early canning equipment and outboard engines, the lens from the Cape Decision lighthouse, and relics from fox farming and whaling.

Exhibits pertaining to early Petersburg include photos and be-

Weathered houses on stilts line the shore of Hammer's Slough,
where the street is still planked with wood.

longings of founder Peter Buschmann and his wife, Petra, and
household objects of the period, such as a wooden hat stretcher
and high-top shoes. Those familiar with Norwegian custom will
know of the traditional dress, the bunad, which differs from region to region. The museum has on display the bright blue Petersburg bunad, embroidered with Alaskan wildflowers.

Outside the museum stands the *Fisk* (Norwegian for "fish"), a
bronze fountain sculpture of halibut, salmon, and herring. Former
Petersburg artist Carson Boysen created the work for the 1967
Alaska Centennial as a celebration of all Southeast fish. A similar
theme inspired the wood and copper mural on the outside wall of
the museum, a community project organized by the Petersburg
Arts and Crafts Guild in 1977.

With a free afternoon in Petersburg, you might rent a bicycle
or car and explore *Mitkof Highway.* The road passes the Alaska
state ferry terminal and extends southward along Wrangell Narrows to mile 34. At 806 Nordic Drive, you come to *Jewell's by the
Sea,* a waterfront bed-and-breakfast lodging and gallery. In the
course of her career, owner-artist Jewell Dean Herbrandson has
hand-painted more than 6,000 gold pans with Alaskan scenes.

At approximately mile 10 you come to the *Falls Creek Fish Ladder.* Stairs lead from the parking area to a bridge from which you can watch migrating coho and pink salmon maneuver upstream in late summer and fall. Just past the sign to the fish ladder, look for another road on the right to *Papke's Landing,* a favorite recreation spot overlooking Wrangell Narrows. There is a state float and boat launch ramp and the entrance road is a riot of fireweed and other wild flowers in July. *Kupreanof Island* is only a few yards away. The site is named for Herman Papke who homesteaded the site in 1903. "Ol' Man Papke" lived alone in his log cabin, raised a bountiful garden, and observed the happenings around him, which he recorded every day in his diary for some sixty years. He died in 1964—among the most beloved of area residents and definitely not forgotten.

At approximately mile 14, a planked forest service trail takes you a third of a mile across the muskeg to *Blind River Rapids,* a beautiful spot with excellent king salmon fishing in July, coho in late August and September, and cutthroat and Dolly Varden in late summer and fall. Two miles farther south, a sign points to the *Trumpeter Swan Observatory,* a simple blind positioned to overlook Blind Slough. One of the northernmost wintering areas for

A weathered storage shed overlooks Wrangell Narrows not far outside of Petersburg.

The Beachcomber Inn is the site of a former cannery. Its restaurant specializes in fresh local seafood.

trumpeter swans, Blind Slough attracts fifty to one hundred birds between late October and April. Several hundred additional swans stop over during their southward migration to other wintering grounds along the northwest coast. The *Crystal Lake Hatchery* at mile 17.5 produces over a million king salmon and hundreds of thousands of coho and steelhead annually in the outdoor rearing pens. Visitors are welcome. The adjacent *Blind Slough Recreation Area* has picnic shelters and grills.

The *Three Lakes Loop Road,* an old logging road, leaves Mitkof Highway to the north at mile 20 and loops through hills and forest to rejoin the highway near Papke's Landing. The road winds through some beautiful country with vistas of trees, wildflowers, and water. Short trails (less than .5 mile) give access to three large freshwater lakes (Sand, Hill, and Crane) that harbor small populations of cutthroat trout. The Three Lakes area was once the site of considerable logging activity but is used primarily for recreation now. Enjoy a picnic or hike; take some photographs and watch the wildlife. In winter, Petersburg residents frequent the area for ice fishing, snowmobiling, and Nordic skiing. The *Beachcomber Inn* complex at mile 4 offers possibilities for a local seafood dinner on the way back to town. The waterfront hotel/restaurant is the site of the former Scow Bay Packing Company cannery that closed in 1953. There is a boat and seaplane dock, and plenty to watch from the restaurant windows.

Excursions from Petersburg center around the *Le Conte Glacier* 25 miles to the east. The southernmost tidewater glacier in North America, the Le Conte flows into Frederick Sound from the Stikine Ice Field in the Coast Mountains. This glacier has remained relatively stable since the mid-1960s, showing neither significant advance nor retreat. The terminus, though, is very active and produces a continuous crop of icebergs along the mile-wide face. Some 2,000 harbor seals live in Le Conte Bay and rear their pups on the glacier icebergs. Boat, floatplane, and helicopter excursions to the glacier are readily available from Petersburg.

SPECIAL EVENTS

The full glory of Petersburg's Norwegian heritage erupts the third weekend of May during the *Little Norway Festival.* Folk dancing, costumes, halibut filleting contests, and Viking raids characterize this annual celebration of Norwegian Independence Day. Tables groan under the weight of fish cakes and puddings, gravadlox, lutefisk, and an array of Norwegian desserts—all prepared by the good Norwegian cooks in town. There is also a salmon bake at Sandy Beach. The *Petersburg salmon derby* takes place on Memorial Day Weekend, and the community salutes U.S. *Independence Day* with an old-fashioned Fourth of July. Other annual festivities: *Devil's Thumb Days,* a winter festival of family games and activities in February; and *Octoberfest,* featuring an arts and crafts fair.

SITKA
Population 8,800

As a visitor destination Sitka enjoys an unfair advantage over other Southeast cities. The setting is unbelievably spectacular, from the countless forested islands that bob and weave upon Sitka Sound to the perfectly symmetrical cone of Mount Edgecumbe that rises to the west. Add to that the exotic Russian heritage, the fabulous totem park, and the attractive city center that corrals all the important sights within easy walking distance of the harbor. Even the lodgings have a touch of the extraordinary. Where else

The New Archangel Russian Dancers put on an authentic performance for Sitka visitors. (Alaska Division of Tourism)

but Sitka can you book a stay in an operational lighthouse on a private island?

The Sitkans have put their Russian pedigree to good advantage, from their widely acclaimed Russian dance troupe to tunicked bus drivers who meet the ferries. Saint Michael's Russian Orthodox Cathedral dominates the heart of town. Orthodox crosses in the old Russian graveyard and blackened cannons on Castle Hill are other relics of a foreign heritage.

Sitka takes pride in being a cultural center and college town. The community supports two colleges, two libraries, two museums, and a national historic park containing one of the largest exhibitions of Tlingit and Haida totem poles in existence. The annual summer music festival unites outstanding musicians from all corners of the United States and abroad, while the Sitka Symposium, held concurrently, draws guest writers of an equally high caliber.

Big changes are on the horizon for Sitka, though. Even with all the visitor attractions and amenities, tourism has played a minor role in Sitka compared with the timber industry. The scheduled closure of the Sitka pulp mill, the city's largest private employer, may not be obvious to visitors but will be felt in every corner of town.

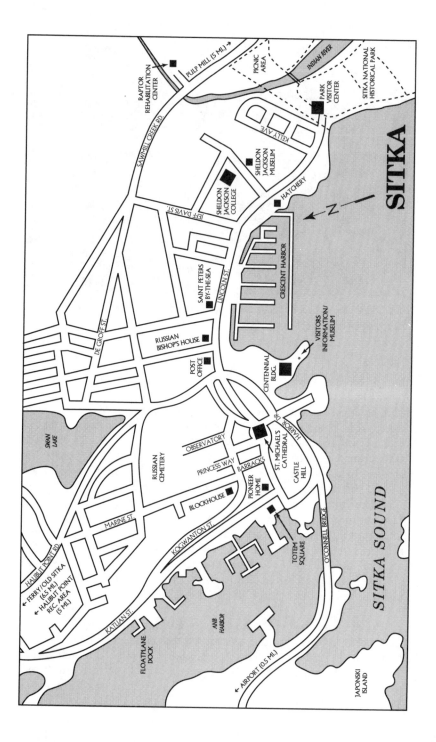

SITKA

N

SITKA SOUND

JAPONSKI ISLAND

SITKA NATIONAL HISTORICAL PARK

PICNIC AREA

INDIAN RIVER

PARK VISITOR CENTER

KELLY AVE

SHELDON JACKSON MUSEUM

SHELDON JACKSON COLLEGE

JEFF DAVIS ST.

PULP MILL (5 MI.) →

RAPTOR REHABILITATION CENTER

SAWMILL CREEK RD.

HATCHERY

CRESCENT HARBOR

SAINT PETERS BY-THE-SEA

LINCOLN ST.

DE GROFF ST.

RUSSIAN BISHOP'S HOUSE

POST OFFICE

SWAN LAKE

RUSSIAN CEMETERY

OBSERVATORY

PRINCESS WAY

BARRACKS

BLOCKHOUSE

MARINE ST.

CENTENNIAL BLDG.

VISITORS INFORMATION/ MUSEUM

HARBOR DR.

ST. MICHAEL'S CATHEDRAL

CASTLE HILL

PIONEER HOME

KOGWANTON ST.

TOTEM SQUARE

O'CONNELL BRIDGE

HALIBUT POINT RD.

← FERRY/OLD SITKA (6.5 MI.)

← HALIBUT POINT REC. AREA (5 MI.)

KATLIAN ST.

FLOATPLANE DOCK

ANB HARBOR

← AIRPORT (0.5 MI.)

BACKGROUND

Sitka is situated on the west coast of Baranof Island on Sitka Sound, a body of water that faces the open Pacific. The site of the Russian capital after 1804, the town is the oldest non-Native settlement in Southeast. Sitka was home to a community of Tlingit Indians prior to the Russian arrival. When Alexander Baranof, chief manager of the Russian-American Company, decided to move the Russian headquarters from Kodiak in 1799, he bargained with the local Tlingit chief for ground for a fort. The completed post, consisting of various outbuildings enclosed within a wooden stockade, was located 6 miles north of the present town and called Saint Archangel Michael.

The Tlingit grew increasingly hostile toward the Russians and the Aleut hunters they brought with them from Kodiak. Armed with guns and ammunition received from English and American traders in the area, they attacked the fort on a Sunday in June of 1802, burned the buildings, and killed all of the occupants except the few who managed to escape into the woods to take refuge aboard foreign trading vessels in Sitka Sound.

Baranof, who was away at Kodiak at the time of the massacre, immediately began making plans to retake Saint Archangel Michael. The battle was joined in September 1804, the Tlingit making their stand from a wooden stronghold near the beach at Indian River (the site of the present-day historical park), and the Russians bombarding with cannons. After several days of negotiations, interspersed with shelling, the Tlingit abandoned the site and retreated northward to Chichagof Island. The Russians built a new settlement where Sitka is located today, calling it New Archangel. By the following spring they had completed eight buildings within a wooden stockade and cleared land for gardens and livestock. Shipyards were established two years later.

The Sitka Indians were allowed to return to Baranof Island in 1821. They rebuilt their homes around the Russian encampment, outnumbering the colonists about three to one. The Russians were in constant fear of another uprising, but their food supplies were low, and they depended upon the Tlingit to exercise their superior hunting skills and provide meat to be purchased for the table.

New Archangel reached the height of activity and stability in the 1840s and 1850s. Besides the fur business, the settlement bustled with shipbuilding and repair facilities, sawmills, a forge and foundry, a salmon saltery, and even an ice industry that shipped blocks of lake ice to California markets. The colony expanded to include schools, hospital, library, clubhouse, and Saint

Michael's Cathedral. The crowning jewel was the governor's residence built at the top of a hill overlooking the harbor. A seal oil beacon was kept burning in the cupola window, and a three-foot diameter reflector projected the light 6 miles out to sea to guide mariners into the harbor. This was the first lighthouse on the Alaska coast. The interior, furnished with fine European furniture, rugs, paintings and a library, was considered a haven of culture and enlightenment for European traders who plied the lonely waters of the North Pacific coast. Although rebuilt many times, the structure came to be known as Baranof's Castle and the hilltop site as Castle Hill. Today, Castle Hill remains a monument to the Russian colony, but the last castle burned down in 1894.

When the fur trade declined, the Alaska colonies became expensive to maintain. With both British and American traders threatening the Russian prerogative, the political situation was uncomfortable and renewal of the Russian-American company charter was in question besides. Russia decided to give up Alaska, and in October of 1867 the Russian flag was lowered from Castle Hill and the American flag raised in its place. The Americans changed the name of the community to Sitka, a derivation of the Tlingit word for their forested island by the sea.

The years following the Russian departure were lean ones for Sitka. Employment centered around the sawmill, which operated intermittently, and fishing. Sitka was the site of one of the first two salmon canneries built in Alaska in 1878 (the other was at Klawock on Prince of Wales Island). The plant folded after two years, however, and Sitka did not become a successful fish-processing center until after the turn of the century.

The gold rush caught up to the community at about the same time. Prospectors had been poking around Baranof Island, like other places, and there were attempts at lode mining in the vicinity as early as 1871. A rush to Sitka followed the discovery of gold-bearing quartz at Stewart Ledge on Silver Bay, slightly southeast of Sitka. In 1879, George Pilz built Alaska's first stamp mill on the Stewart claim. (Pilz would also finance the two vagabond prospectors who located the Juneau lode the following year.) In the years that followed, other mining efforts were made on nearby Chichagof Island. The two biggest Chichagof gold mines produced consistently until World War II closed them down. Gypsum was also mined on Chichagof for a seventeen-year period beginning in 1906.

A mission school opened in 1878 under the auspices of the United Presbyterian church and evolved into an industrial trade school for Native students. The school continues today as Sheldon

Jackson College, a private two-year institution specializing in fisheries management, forestry, wildlife management, and other Alaska fields of interest. The college is named for Dr. Sheldon Jackson who, as general agent for education in Alaska's infancy, is credited with establishing the state's school system. With the founding of Sheldon Jackson College, Sitka was on the way to reestablishing itself as a cultural center, but in 1906 the capital of Alaska was transferred to Juneau, where the predominant gold-mining activity had centered.

The whaling industry moved onto Baranof Island in 1912 when the U.S. Whaling Company established a shore station at Port Armstrong on the south end of the island. Using a fleet of three modern "killing boats" with bow-mounted harpoons, the company harvested 314 whales the first year. The station processed the entire carcass, extracting oil and turning leftovers into fertilizer. When the whaling operation ceased in 1923, the Port Armstrong facility continued as a herring reduction plant.

The next surge of development came with the military in the late 1930s, when a U.S. naval air station was built on Japonski Island, across Sitka Harbor from the city. World War II brought an army fort as well, and suddenly Sitka was host to 30,000 military personnel and 7,000 civilians. After the war the naval station was converted to the Bureau of Indian Affairs's Mount Edgecumbe boarding school to accommodate Native high school students from all over Alaska. Since 1972, the facilities on Japonski Island (which also include the Sitka airport), have been brought within easy reach by the 1,225-foot O'Connell Bridge from Sitka. Mount Edgecumbe boarding school continues as a unique high school that attracts students from all ethnic groups and all corners of Alaska to pursue a curriculum focused on Pacific Rim studies. An entrepreneurial program provides hands-on experience on the import-export trade, and language requirements specify competence in Japanese or Mandarin Chinese.

Today Sitka's economy is supported by two colleges (Sheldon Jackson College and the University of Alaska-Southeast), tourism, commercial fishing and fish processing, and timber. Besides housing a sizable commercial fishing fleet, the town has two fish-processing plants, the newest a cold storage facility built in 1980 to process salmon, black cod, herring, and halibut. The Alaska Pulp Corporation mill, built 6 miles east of town in 1960 to produce a high-grade dissolving pulp for industrial use, fueled the local economy through the 1980s as the town's largest private employer. In recent years, however, the mill has operated in a climate of uncertainty due to a number of factors, including continued controversy over timber harvest in the Tongass National Forest, stiffer environmental regulations, and a depressed pulp market. Mill officials forecast permanent closure of the mill.

GETTING THERE

Sitka figures in most cruise ship itineraries. The vessels usually run down the outside coast of Baranof Island after visiting Glacier Bay and anchor in Sitka harbor opposite town. Alaska state ferries dock at the Marine Highway terminal 7 miles north of town near Old Sitka, the site of the first Russian settlement. Buses meet every ferry in summer offering shuttle service to downtown lodgings and ferry stopover tours of Sitka sights—available twenty-four hours a day and guaranteed to get you back before sailing. Sitka is also serviced by Alaska Airlines on the Seattle to Juneau route. The airport is located on Japonski Island, across O'Connell Bridge from the downtown area.

TO SEE AND DO

Your first destination should be the *Sitka Convention and Visitors' Bureau* in the Centennial Building (overlooking Sitka Sound near the cruise ship embarkation point) for maps, brochures, and other information. Check on the performance schedule of the *Sitka New Archangel Russian Dancers,* a women's dance troupe that has entranced audiences with authentic Russian folk dances since 1969. While you are in the building, take a turn through the *Isabel Miller Museum,* devoted to items from local history. An extensive scale model of Sitka shows how the community looked during the Russian era. Exhibits from the Russian tenancy include ice saws that were used to cut blocks of ice from Swan Lake for shipment to San Francisco during the gold rush.

Other displays feature enterprises of later years, including fishing, logging, and gold mining (note the mold for forming gold bricks). Of special interest: copies of documents pertaining to the Alaska Purchase agreement and a copy of the actual warrant for $7.2 million (the original is in the Smithsonian Institution in Washington, D.C.).

At the other end of the Centennial Building, members of the *Baranof Arts and Crafts Association* proffer a selection of recent work. There is also a small *wildlife display* of bald eagles, sea otters, fur seals, beaver, Arctic fox, and other fur-bearing animals and pelts.

Outside the building stands a 50-foot ceremonial canoe carved by local woodworker George Benson for the Alaska Purchase Centennial commemoration in 1967. The canoe was hollowed from a single, 70-foot red cedar log that was towed to Sitka from Port Renfrew, British Columbia, behind a fishing boat. The painted totemic designs represent Eagle and Raven, the two major phratries or social divisions, in Tlingit and Haida culture. On one side of the canoe Eagle is on the prow and Raven on the stern. The order is reversed on the opposite side.

Leaving the Centennial Building with map in hand, take a stroll through town. *Saint Michael's Russian Orthodox Cathedral,* which straddles Lincoln Street, the main thoroughfare, and dominates the skyline, is a replica of the original cathedral that was built on the site between 1844 and 1848. In 1966 the old church was destroyed by a fire that swept through the business district. The townspeople rushed in and managed to save almost all the precious icons and other furnishings that had been brought from Russia in the early days of the church. The cathedral was rebuilt in 1976 from original blueprints.

The architecture, a mixture of bulbous onion dome and delicate spire, reflects a combination of styles that was common around Saint Petersburg at the time of the Russian occupation. Natural-colored canvas (originally sailcloth) covers the interior walls. The dome is painted sky blue on the inside and the windows set around the top flood this artificial heaven with natural light.

The cathedral is a showcase of icons (sacred images or paintings) brought to Alaska from Russia. The two most prized are Our Lady of Sitka, familiarly known as the Sitka Madonna, and Christ Pantocrator (Christ the Judge or Christ Omnipotent) that flank the doors of the altar screen. Both paintings are attributed to Vladimir Borovikovsky, a leading eighteenth-century portrait artist and one of Russia's most revered masters. The Sitka Madonna, the oldest of the icons and thought to have been the gift of the Russian-American Company employees, is regarded by many faithful as a miraculous healer and protectress. At Saturday evening services, letters are read from faithful the world over petitioning the Sitka Madonna to intercede on their behalf. The painting, of a gentle-faced madonna holding the Christ Child, is oil on canvas overlaid with a heavy silver gilt *riza.* (The riza, or metal overlay, often elaborately carved or sculpted, became common in seventeenth-century Russia as a means of honoring and protecting the sacred image.) Another cherished icon, Saint Michael the Archangel, patron saint of the cathedral, was brought to Sitka in 1816 by the first ordained priest.

Other interesting items within the cathedral: the carved and

Sitka's Saint Michael's Cathedral is a prominent reminder of the Russian influence.

The carved doors of the altar screen are part of the original furnishings brought from Russia.

painted doors in the altar screen, saved from the original church; silver gilt wedding crowns dating from 1866; Bishop Innocent Veniaminov's pearl-encrusted miter; and a 13-inch silver gilt tabernacle with cloisonné cupola and steeple modeled after the cathedral.

Saint Michael's Cathedral is the seat of the Russian Orthodox church in Alaska; the bishop travels from Sitka to parish churches throughout the state. The cathedral is a working church with an active congregation and regular services, to which visitors are always welcome.

Lincoln Street is lined with enticing shops and galleries. *Impressions, Artists' Cove Gallery,* and *Old Harbor Books* are especially worth your while. Behind the bookshop, the inviting *Backdoor Cafe* draws an artsy crowd for espresso, pastries, and sandwiches. *Calico Cross Stitch* (223 Lincoln) sells original Alaskan cross-stitch and needlepoint patterns developed by Sitka residents Gail Sohornak and Sandy Greba and locally made quilts. At *Three Guys by the Church* (235 Lincoln), you'll find unique necklaces of rare beads and polished ivory created by Sitka artist Phil Slattery, and at *Fairweather Prints* (301 Lincoln) you'll drool over colorful hand-silkscreened and hand-painted garments of "wearable art" (lots of fish art) produced in a Sitka studio.

Also check out the *Russian-American Company* in the Bayview Trading Company (407 Lincoln) for Russian imports such as carved wooden toys, wool shawls, and lacquerware. Then backtrack to *The Coffee Express* (104 Lake Street, across from the Shee Atika Hotel) for a restorative espresso brew and a muffin (blueberry peach, rhubarb . . .). For more substantial fare, go to *Staton's,* a block from the Centennial Building, for halibut fish-and-chips.

A short path leads to the top of *Castle Hill.* Castle Hill was the site of a Tlingit Indian village when Alexander Baranof reestablished the Russian fort in 1804. The Russians destroyed the Indian houses and built their own quarters with the manager's residence at the top. In time the residence came to be known as Baranof's Castle and the hilltop site as Castle Hill. The castle was rebuilt twice before fire destroyed the structure completely in 1894.

On 18 October 1867, Castle Hill was the site of transfer ceremonies between Russia and the United States as the Russian flag came down and the Stars and Stripes was raised in its place. The transfer is reenacted at the site every October 18 as part of the Alaska Day celebration. Several Russian cannons still guard the

Residents of the red-roofed Sitka Pioneer Home, the first of Alaska's state-supported care facilities, take pride in their gardens devoted to native plants. (Sarah Eppenbach)

hilltop (note the double-eagle insignia) and historic markers explain the significance of Castle Hill. The site offers a sweeping view over Sitka Sound.

The large red-roofed building across Lincoln Street is the *Pioneer Home,* a state-supported residence and medical care facility for Alaska's longtime residents. There are several Pioneer Homes in the state. Sitka's, built in 1934, was the first. The 13½-foot bronze statue of a prospector in front of the home was created by Alonzo Victor Lewis in 1949. The residents and staff of the Pioneer Home welcome visitors. They are especially proud of their gardens planted with native Alaska species and a basement shop, which sells handicrafts made by residents. *Totem Square,* across Katlian Street from the Pioneer Home, contains a Russian cannon and three anchors recovered from the Sitka vicinity, probably lost by early British or American explorers. The totem pole, designed by local carver George Benson in 1940, displays the double-headed eagle of Sitka's Russian heritage.

Uphill from the Pioneer Home, you'll see the *Russian blockhouse*—a replica of the type the Russians built to guard their stockade. Three such structures stood sentry along the wall separating the Indian village from the Russian community. Old headstones and Orthodox crosses mark the adjacent *Russian cemetery.* The only original Russian building still standing in Sitka is the *Russian Bishop's House* on Lincoln Street at the opposite end of town from Totem Square. The Bishop's House—the oldest building in Alaska that has not been significantly altered and one of the few remaining Russian log structures in Alaska—was built in 1842 by the Russian-American Company to house Bishop Innocent Veniaminov, the first bishop of the Russian Orthodox Church. The church continued to use the facility until 1972. Now owned by the National Park Service, the Bishop's House received a $4.5 million restoration as part of Sitka National Historical Park. Visitors can view the bishop's study, private apartments, and chapel, restored to their 1850s appearance. All the icons in the chapel except one were original to the house.

A grassy esplanade takes you the short distance along Crescent Boat Harbor to Sheldon Jackson College and the main portion of Sitka National Historical Park. Just past the Russian Bishop's House you will come to the stone and brown-shingled *Saint Peters-by-the-Sea Episcopal Church* built in 1899. A few more steps bring you to the state-owned *Sheldon Jackson Museum.* The octagonal structure was built in 1895 as a repository for the articles that Dr. Sheldon Jackson collected in remote areas of Alaska during his travels as general agent for education. The collection of Alaskan Indian, Eskimo, and Aleut artifacts is one of the most important in the world.

When you walk through the door, look up: On top of the display cases and suspended from the ceiling are examples of all the traditional kinds of sled and boat used in Alaska, from dog and reindeer sleds to kayaks, umiaks, and canoes. Start with the Eskimo and Aleut exhibits. Intriguing items include ceremonial masks, including finger masks that the women used for dancing; fishing flies made of stone, bone, and sinew or baleen; bentwood sunshades for kayaking; waterproof clothing of walrus intestine and salmon skin; and a man's ivory-decorated workbox with a set of tools for making nets.

The Tlingit and Haida exhibits include a collection of argillite carved by the Haida, Tlingit feast dishes, beautiful bentwood boxes, baskets, and a historic Chilkat blanket and pattern board. Don't miss the Raven's head helmet worn by Sitka Chief Katlean during the battle with the Russians in 1804. If you have time left, open some of the special display drawers, which contain some of the little charmers from this extensive collection, such as ivory sewing implements, jewelry, pipes, and lip labrets.

The *Sheldon Jackson College Salmon Hatchery,* located across Lincoln Street from the museum, was established in 1975 as part of the college aquaculture technology program. The nonprofit facility releases up to fifteen million pink and chum and 200,000 coho and chinook salmon a year to the surrounding waters (tours available).

The fifteen totem poles in *Sitka National Historical Park,* are spaced along a forested path beside the sea. The 107-acre park is the site of the Tlingit and Russian battle of 1804. The original collection of totem poles was gathered at the instigation of District of Alaska Governor John Brady, who had a deep and abiding interest in preserving Alaska Native culture. The poles—most from Prince of Wales Island near Ketchikan—were displayed at the 1904 Louisiana Purchase Exposition in Saint Louis. After the fair they were returned to Alaska for placement in the Sitka park. During the 1930s, the poles were repaired by the Civilian Conservation Corps as part of their totem restoration project, and most have since been replicated.

The park visitors' center has exhibits on Tlingit culture, including old houseposts from the Sitka area, Chilkat blankets, and a brief slide-tape presentation on the history of Sitka and the battle of 1804. One wing is devoted to workshops and demonstrations of Native woodcarving, silverwork, bead- and buttonwork, and other crafts. An excellent booklet, *Carved History, The Totem Poles and House Posts of Sitka National Historical Park* by Mari-

*The Sheldon Jackson Museum has a rich collection of Native arti-
facts, including carved wooden masks.*

lyn Knapp (Alaska Natural History Association and National Park Service), sold at the visitor center, describes all of the totem poles in the park. There are more than 2 miles of established trails within the park, although you do not have to walk that far to see the totem poles. If it is a nice day, bring a picnic lunch with you. There is a picnic shelter across Indian River from the totems; a path follows along the riverbank to a Russian memorial.

One of the totem poles in front of the visitors' center is a relatively new pole that was created for the nation's Bicentennial celebration in 1976. The Bicentennial pole, carved by Duane Pasco, depicts new concepts in a traditional style. The topmost figure represents the Northwest Coast Indian of today holding two staffs, one symbolizing the rich heritage of the past and the other the unknown future. The second figure recalls the arrival of the white man (note beard and dress) with his rifle, religion, and paper treaties. Raven and Eagle are below him, and on the bottom the Coast Indian in pre-contact days, holding a wooden halibut hook and rattle.

Slightly farther afield but still within walking distance (or take a cab), the volunteer-operated *Alaska Raptor Rehabilitation Center* (1101 Sawmill Creek Road; telephone 907–747–8662) treats injured bald eagles and other birds of prey and rehabilitates them for release back to the wild. During a tour of the nonprofit medical clinic and education center (available as a walk-in or with Sitka tour operators), you see several recuperating eagles close at hand and meet Buddy, a resident bald eagle unable to live in the wild. Buddy stars in the center's educational presentations and occasionally goes on tour.

With such a variety of interesting sights convenient to town, one tends to overlook opportunities for enjoying Sitka's abundant natural scenery. Two special places "out the road" are *Halibut Point State Recreation Site* (approximately mile 5, Halibut Point Road, north of Sitka), a beautiful meeting of forest and sea, with

Eskimos commonly engraved hunting scenes on their ivory pipes. This pipe is on display in the Sheldon Jackson Museum.

The middle figure of the Bicentennial pole depicts the arrival of the white man with his rifle and religion.

picnic areas, views, and beachcombing; and *Whale Park,* a high overlook off Sawmill Creek Road from which migrating humpback whales can often be seen, especially in fall. The facilities are still being developed, but plans call for a large viewing deck with picnic area and interpretive signs. Check with the visitors' center about the many hiking trails in the Sitka area.

Buddy, a bald eagle trained for educational presentations, and one of his handlers greet visitors at the Alaska Raptor Rehabilitation Center. (Sarah Eppenbach)

Several charter operators offer *sightseeing and naturalist cruises* from Sitka, including trips to the tubs at nearby Goddard Hot Springs. *Sea Otter & Wildlife Quest (P.O. Box 1049, Sitka, Alaska 99835;* telephone *907–747–7474)* offers an unusual guarantee with a half-day wildlife cruise to Salisbury Sound, 25 miles north of Sitka: If you don't see an otter, whale, or bear, you receive a partial refund. The same company operates *evening harbor cruises* aboard the blue-and-white Saint Nicholas or Saint Aquilina. The ships depart from Crescent Harbor by the Centennial Building.

SPECIAL EVENTS

The annual *Sitka Summer Music Festival* is held during three weeks in June. Performing artists from all over the world gather in this seaside setting for daily instructional workshops and twice-weekly evening concerts in the Centennial Building. The festival dates from 1972 when protégés of Jascha Heifetz and Gregor Piatigorsky put together an informal concert in Sitka. The event has proved so popular that there are standing room-only crowds for the Tuesday and Friday evening performances (there may be some special Saturday concerts, too). Write ahead for reserved seats to *Sitka Summer Music Festival, P.O. Box 3333, Sitka, Alaska 99835;* telephone *(907) 277–4852* (July 1 to May 14) or *747–6774* (May 15 to June 30). Rehearsals are open to the public without charge. Concurrently with the music festival, the Island Institute hosts the annual *Sitka Symposium on Human Values and the Written Word,* featuring guest writers and lecturers (examples from past symposiums: Terry Tempest Williams, William Kittredge). For information write: *P.O. Box 2420, Sitka, Alaska 99835;* telephone *(907) 747–3794.*

Other local events include the two-day *All-Alaska Logging Championships* over the last weekend in June, in which loggers from all over the Pacific Northwest compete in traditional loggers' contests such as ax throwing and powersaw bucking. *Independence Day* celebrations feature a parade, dance, food booths, and fireworks. The *Alaska Day Festival,* scheduled for five days around October 18, commemorates the Alaska Purchase with a reenactment of the transfer ceremonies on Castle Hill. A costume ball and parade mark the event. *Russian Christmas and Starring* are just some of the festivities that take place during *Holiday Fest,* from November through January. The month-long *Mayfest* heralds spring with special exhibits and events, and a *salmon derby* over Memorial Day and the following weekends.

JUNEAU

← FISH HATCHERY (3 MI.)
← AIRPORT (9 MI.)
← MENDENHALL GLACIER (13 MI.)
← AUKE BAY FERRY TERMINAL (14 MI.)
← SHRINE OF SAINT THERESE (23 MI.)

GLACIER AVE.
EGAN DR.

AURORA BASIN

HARRIS HARBOR

DOUGLAS BRIDGE

EVERGREEN CEMETERY

GOVERNOR'S MANSION

JUNEAU/DOUGLAS CITY MUSEUM

HOUSE OF WICKERSHAM

COPE PARK

CALHOUN AVE.

GOLD CREEK

BASIN RD.

RUSSIAN CHURCH

← LAST CHANCE BASIN (1.5 MI.)
← MT. ROBERTS TRAIL

STARR HILL

EAST ST.

5TH ST.

4TH ST.

3RD ST.

2ND ST.

N. FRANKLIN ST.

GOLD ST.

MAIN ST.

SEWARD ST.

FRONT ST.

S. FRANKLIN ST.

CAPITOL

COURT BLDG.

DAVIS LOG CABIN/VISITORS INFORMATION

POST OFFICE

STATE OFFICE BLDG.

WHITTIER ST.

WILLOUGHBY AVE.

CENTENNIAL HALL

ALASKA STATE MUSEUM

EGAN DR.

SEALASKA PLAZA

MERCHANT'S WHARF

FLOATPLANE DOCK

MARINE PARK
VISITOR INFORMATION KIOSK

N ←

JUNEAU LIBRARY
CRUISE SHIP DOCKS

CRUISE SHIP TERMINAL/VISITORS INFORMATION

THANE RD.

POST OFFICE

WILLOUGHBY AVE.

DOUGLAS HWY.

← EAGLECREST SKI AREA (12 MI.)

DOUGLAS (2 MI.) →

GASTINEAU CHANNEL

JUNEAU
Population 29,300

After visiting the other ports of call along the Inside Passage, Juneau seems like a big city. It is not simply the imposing physical plant associated with the state capital that gives this impression, but the cosmopolitan atmosphere that comes with an affluent, well-educated, well-traveled population. For those of us who make this city our home, though, the small-town traits are the most endearing. We still recognize many of the people we pass on the narrow, hilly streets; know shopkeepers by their first names; and leave cookies in the mailbox for the mail carrier.

As Alaska's state capital, Juneau bustles twelve months of the year, but especially during the winter legislative session when the town fairly explodes with elected officials and their staffs, concerned citizens, lobbyists, and the usual political hangers-on. By the time that lot retreats to their own districts in May, the big tour ships come steaming into port—on some days five and six at a time—to unload thousands of eager tourists into the city streets.

Until a few years ago, visitors spilled out of the cruise ships onto uneven sidewalks bordered by sagging buildings seemingly held in place by a rat's maze of overhead wires. Today, after a massive multiyear face-lift, the downtown historic district boasts broad pedestrian walkways outlined with brilliant banners and twin-globe streetlamps, buried utilities, renovated shopfronts, and flowers, flowers, flowers. While portions of South Franklin Street still suffer the ill effects of too many bars, the new old-Juneau is a very pleasant place.

Visitors to Juneau will find first-class galleries and shops, a choice of small and large hotels, a selection of passable but expensive restaurants, solid professional theater, and on any given night—summer or winter—a menu of activities from which to choose. The beautiful outdoors, remarkably accessible everywhere in Southeast, calls loudly in Juneau. Anglers, skiers, kayakers—all find their bits of paradise here, but none more so than hikers. Dozens of trails give access to mountains, glaciers, beaches, and river valleys around Juneau. Whatever your interests, Juneau can keep you busy for several days.

BACKGROUND

What we commonly refer to as Juneau is in reality a number of geographically and historically distinct communities interconnected by highway and bridge. Juneau proper is snuggled up against the flanks of 3,600-foot Mount Juneau on the Southeast mainland, 900 air miles north of Seattle. The residential communities of Thane, the Mendenhall Valley, Auke Bay, and others stretch north and south of Juneau along the coast. Across Gastineau Channel by bridge lies the small city of Douglas and neighboring developments on Douglas Island. Together these communities and surrounding lands make up the 3,108-square-mile city and borough of Juneau.

The story of Juneau and the surrounding communities begins with the discovery of a vast treasure of gold-bearing quartz. The Gastineau Channel area was a fishing ground for local Auk Tlingit in the late 1800s when prospectors began scouring the hills and gullies of Southeast Alaska and Canada for signs of gold. One man set about locating potential gold-bearing properties more efficiently than the rest. George Pilz, a German-born mining engineer in charge of the Stewart Mine near Sitka, offered a substantial reward ("100 pair of Hudson's Bay blankets and work for the tribe at one dollar per day," he later recalled) to any local Indian chief who could lead him to gold-bearing ore in minable quantities. When samples began coming in from up and down the coast, Pilz sent his men out in teams with Indian guides to investigate the prospects.

Galleries and shops entice visitors to Juneau's downtown historic district.

Constructed in 1894, Juneau's Saint Nicholas Orthodox Church is the oldest original Russian church in Southeast Alaska.

Chief Kowee of the Auks brought samples of ore from Gastineau Channel to Pilz in 1879. To investigate the body of ore, Pilz selected Richard T. Harris and Joseph Juneau, a pair of down-and-out prospectors recently returned from the Cassiar. Harris and Juneau left Sitka in July 1880 and explored several likely looking sites before reaching Gastineau Channel in mid-August. They followed Gold Creek inland, getting good color in their pans and deciding the place was the best prospect so far (which is why they named it Gold Creek), but went back to Sitka without tracing the gold to its source. Pilz was not terribly impressed with their results and Kowee was extremely put out. The chief carried more samples to Sitka and insisted that Harris and Juneau would have found what Pilz was looking for had they only continued up Gold Creek. When Pilz sent the pair back again, Kowee made sure they reached the mother lode.

On October 3 Harris and Juneau climbed Snow Slide Gulch, where they had stopped the first time, and looked down over Silver Bow Basin and Quartz Gulch which, Harris later recalled, "I named from the fact that it contained the most gold-bearing quartz I had ever seen in one gulch." The quartz outcroppings were shot through with streaks of gold, and "little lumps as large as peas or beans." Inspired by this splendid sight, Harris and Juneau fell to work. Harris wrote out a code of local laws governing the staking of claims in the Harris Mining District (this his legal prerogative according to the Mining Act of 10 May 1872, which allowed miners to make regulations concerning claims in their district), and they set out claims throughout Gold Creek Valley for themselves, Pilz, and several creditors and friends. On October 18 they staked a 160-acre townsite on the beach along Gastineau Channel, naming it Harrisburgh.

In November, the first shiploads of prospectors left Sitka for the new strike location on Gastineau Channel. Forty or so miners spent an uncomfortable winter in Harrisburgh, clearing land to build rough cabins, hacking a pack road to the diggings, and sawing planks to build flumes when the ground thawed in the spring. In February 1881, the miners voted to change the name of the mining camp to Rockwell, for Lieutenant Commander Charles H. Rockwell who had been sent with a party of men from the naval vessel USS *Jamestown* to keep an eye on developments.

When spring came, the banks of Gold Creek crawled with prospectors working their claims while others, recently arrived by steamer from the south, looked for places to drive in their stakes. In May, Lieutenant Commander Rockwell returned to Rockwell with a detachment of marines. His instructions were to establish a military post and preserve order, especially between the miners and the estimated 450 Auk and Taku Tlingit who had taken up residence in the town. The marines put up some small buildings on a ridge overlooking the town, but by December things had simmered down to the extent that the post was closed. Rockwell turned the buildings over to the postmaster and eventually a federal courthouse was built on the site. Meanwhile, the town residents decided to change the name of their community again—to Juneau City after Joe Juneau. The post office dropped the city part and the miners had to be satisfied with just Juneau.

Across the channel on Douglas Island, the ground proved equally rich. The first gold taken out of the entire Gastineau region came from the "Ready Bullion boys," who recovered $1,200 of gold by the spring of 1881 from their claim on Ready Bullion Creek at the southern end of the island. In September 1881 a piece of property close to the Ready Bullion claim passed auspiciously into the hands of John Treadwell, a carpenter-cum-miner who had been sent into the area by a group of San Francisco investors to check out the new strike. After ore samples from Treadwell's claim were tested, Treadwell hastened back to Juneau to acquire more property for the newly established Alaska Mill and Mining Company. Their 5-stamp mill, established in May 1882 and replaced by a 120-stamp mill the following year, was the beginning of the great Treadwell mining complex that would produce more than $70 million in gold.

In the ensuing years, Gastineau Channel would become a center for large-scale, hard-rock gold mining. Initially, lone prospectors took what they could from their claims with shovel and sluice box and drifted on to other strikes. (Among them was Joe Juneau, who went on to the Klondike and died at Dawson in 1899. Richard Harris mined in Juneau for several years until he lost his claims in a suit brought by one of his original backers. He died in a sanitarium in Oregon in 1907. Both are buried in Evergreen Cemetery in Juneau.) Harvesting the Juneau lode, however, was really a job for organized mining companies with the resources to tunnel deep within the earth and mill thousands of tons of ore per day. Companies formed, consolidated claims, and grew larger. On the Juneau side of the channel there were the Perseverance and Alaska Juneau mines in Silver Bow Basin, Jualpa at Last Chance Basin, and Ebner Mine on Gold Creek. Across the way were the Ready Bullion, the Mexican, the Seven Hundred Foot Mine, and the Treadwell. Around the mine and mill sites grew the stable communities of Juneau, Douglas, Treadwell, and Thane, peopled by mine and mill employees and their families. The mines and the businesses that serviced them functioned twenty-four hours a day.

The Treadwell mines reached the peak of production in 1915 with 960 stamps crushing 5,000 tons of ore daily, a world record. Two years later, a cave-in at the edge of Gastineau Channel flooded all the Treadwell workings except the Ready Bullion. That mine shut, too, in 1922 for lack of quality ore, bringing to a close one of the greatest mining efforts ever. Over in Juneau, the revolutionary Alaska-Gastineau mill at Sheep Creek, patterned after a dry-ore copper mill in Utah, surpassed the Treadwell record by grinding 12,000 tons of ore per day until 1921 when costs became prohibitive. The last of the big mills, the Alaska Juneau, constructed in 1916, was closed down by the war in 1944, but not before producing $80.8 million in gold. Together these three industrial giants produced $158 million worth of gold at values of $20 to $35 per ounce.

The visible remains of the three great plants are awesomely insignificant. The burned-out shell of the Alaska-Juneau mill is little more than a scar above Gastineau Channel on the approach into town. The Gastineau mill was dismantled and shipped south when the company folded. As for the Treadwell—that wondrous complex of mills, mines, wharves, piers, shops, warehouses, trams, and a town full of people—nothing remains except a few ghostly pilings in the channel and the occasional crumbled foundation that has been spared the advance of the undergrowth.

But by the time the last mine had closed, the surviving communities of Douglas and Juneau had managed to diversify their interests. The governor's office had been transferred from Sitka to the thriving mining town of Juneau in 1906, establishing Juneau as the capital city. The governor's mansion was built in 1912 and the capitol building in 1930. When statehood was awarded in 1959, Juneau remained the focal point of state government activity and continues so today, despite repeated campaigns to relocate the capital of Alaska nearer the northern population centers of Anchorage and Fairbanks.

Government—federal, state, or local—employs one out of every two workers in Juneau today. Tourism plays an integral role in the local economy, the capital city being a destination or transfer point for most cruise ships plying the Inside Passage, and commercial fishing is a significant factor here as elsewhere in Southeast Alaska. The arrival of major merchandisers such as Fred Meyer, J.C. Penney, K mart, and Costco has turned Juneau into an important regional retail shopping center in recent years. And a return to large-scale gold mining may be in the offing as Echo Bay Mines pursues the possibility of reopening the Alaska Juneau Mine.

GETTING THERE

Access to Juneau is by air and water only. Several flights a day from Seattle, Anchorage, and the communities between land at

Juneau International Airport, 9 miles north of the city center. As of this writing Alaska Airlines services Juneau year-round while Delta provides summer service only. Alaska state ferries dock at the Auke Bay Terminal, 14 miles north of Juneau. The more than twenty cruise ships regularly calling at Juneau during the May through September cruise season tie up at one of the downtown docks or anchor in the Juneau Harbor. If the latter, passengers are lightered ashore, disembarking at Marine Park on the downtown waterfront or at the Intermediate Vessel Float by the Cruiseship Terminal.

TO SEE AND DO

Cruise ship passengers never fail to be awed by their first glimpse of Alaska's capital city. Gliding slowly up the narrow reaches of Gastineau Channel, your ship will pass the remnants of the Treadwell wharves off Douglas Island to your left, while ahead looms the towering profile of Mount Juneau. At the bottom and insignificant in comparison, the buildings of Juneau cling to their shelf between mountains and sea.

Juneau's extensively renovated waterfront facilities extend in one unbroken, flower-festooned walk. At the north end you'll see

The Juneau waterfront encompasses cruise ships, fishing boats, and government office buildings.

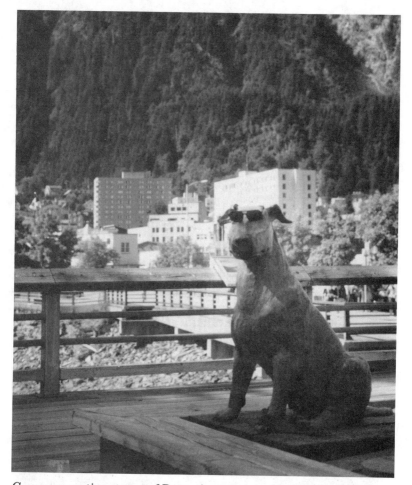

Commemorative statue of Patsy Ann, Juneau's official canine greeter, awaits cruise ship passengers alighting at Marine Park wharf.

Merchant's Wharf, a former seaplane hangar that now houses restaurants and shops, and the *seaplane float* where flightseeing excursions depart for the Juneau Ice Cap. Brightly colored banners mark the location of *Marine Park,* a popular gathering spot and focal point of wharf activity. On sunny days, Juneau residents spill out of adjacent office buildings and enjoy their lunch at the outside tables and benches or sprawled on the grass. There is an *information kiosk* staffed by volunteers who dispense maps, brochures, and answers to questions.

Toward the south end of the waterfront, the wharf continues past the award-winning *Juneau Public Library*. Built on top of the Marine Park Garage, the library affords the best views in town of Mount Juneau, Douglas Island, and the cruise ships parked in Gastineau Channel. Cruise ship passengers disembarking at the Marine Park wharf near the library will be greeted by a commemorative statue of Juneau's beloved *Patsy Ann*, an English bull terrier and canine-about-town. Patsy Ann gained her page in local history by her habit of greeting incoming steamships at the Juneau dock. At the south end the wharf terminates at the Cruiseship Terminal and Intermediate Vessel Float.

The *Davis Log Cabin Visitor Information Center* (Third and Seward streets) is housed in a replica of the Presbyterian log church that stood in Juneau in early days. The visitors' center contains a reading and video area as well as brochures from Juneau and other Southeast communities. Pick up a Juneau Walking Tour map to guide you to the many attractions around town.

Many downtown buildings have retained their original facades, due to the fact that Juneau has been spared the sort of major fire that ravaged Douglas and Wrangell. A stroll along South Franklin, Front, and Seward streets will carry you back to the turn of the century. South Franklin (all the way to the Cruiseship Terminal) brims with gift and curio shops—and taverns, including the landmark *Red Dog Saloon,* an old-fashioned, sawdust-on-the-floor establishment that draws both residents and visitors. The turreted *Alaska Steam Laundry Building* dates from 1901. Today the building connects with the Emporium Mall on Shattuck Way. The interior walls are hung with very interesting photo murals of early day Juneau. You will find several specialty shops within the mall, including the studio outlet for *William Spear Design* enameled pins. The ground floor *Heritage Coffee Co.,* a specialty coffee roaster and cafe, serves great sandwiches and desserts.

Recommended art galleries on Franklin Street include the *Decker Gallery,* which carries Rie Muñoz prints; *Objects of Bright Pride, Artists Cove,* and *Artwork Unlimited* (a co-op of local artists). Also try *Kaill Fine Crafts* on Front Street near Franklin), for unusual gift items with or without an Alaska theme. The restored *Senate Building* houses several shops (Christmas ornaments, Irish and Russian imports), as does *Marine View Center* (check out *Taku Smokeries* for local smoked salmon to eat here or ship).

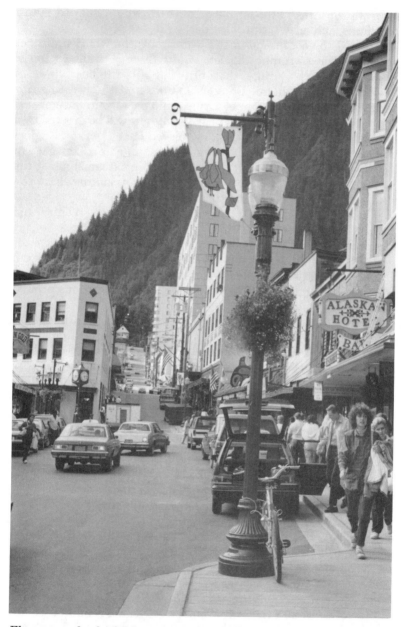

Flowers and colorful banners decorate the downtown historic district in Juneau. (Sarah Eppenbach)

At Fifth Street between Franklin and Gold you'll come upon the tiny, octagonal *Saint Nicholas Russian Orthodox Church.* Although constructed in 1894, nearly thirty years after Russia sold the Alaska colony, Saint Nicholas is the oldest original Russian church in Southeast Alaska. The postage-stamp-sized Cathedral Park next door offers a comfortable bench for resting your feet. Continue on Fifth two blocks toward the mountains, and you will find yourself looking up at a long set of stairs. They lead to *Starr Hill,* one of the oldest and most picturesque residential neighborhoods in Juneau. Many of the houses were built for employees of the nearby mines. Behind Starr Hill, Mount Roberts rises 3,819 feet. A steep but excellent trail to the top departs from Sixth Street—see local trail guides. The flight of steps from Fourth Street is even more of a challenge.

The state government complex is centered at Fourth and Main. The six-story Capitol was built as the Federal and Territorial Building in 1930, when Alaska was not yet a state. Local marble from Tokeen, near Prince of Wales Island, was quarried for the front columns and interior paneling. The Alaska Senate and House of Representatives meet in the building, which houses the governor's office as well. Tours of the Capitol are available in summer (check at the tour desk in the lobby or contact the Legislative

Rare sunny days find Juneau office workers at Marine Park during the lunch hour.

Information Office, 907-465-4648, to find the time of the next tour departure). During the legislative session (approximately January to May), you can request a special tour by contacting the House of Representatives sergeant-at-arms at (907) 465-3869. Or just look around by yourself. The front doors of the Capitol remain open during weekday office hours (8:00 A.M. to 4:30 P.M.). The ground floor lobby has been restored to the original blue and gilt decoration.

The governor has only a short walk from office to home. The *governor's mansion* is a couple of blocks away from the Capitol on Calhoun Avenue. The white-pillared colonial, completed in 1912, could just as easily be situated in Massachusetts or Vermont, were it not for the dramatic totem pole in front. The Governor's totem, carved in 1940 by Tlingit Indians from Klukwan and Saxman, represents several Tlingit legends, among them the origin of the mosquito, pictured as the fourth figure from the top. The mansion is not usually open to view. Contact the governor's office in advance (write *P.O. Box 110001, Juneau, Alaska 99811-0001*) if yours is a special request, such as for a group of visiting schoolchildren.

More recent additions to the state government complex include the bunkerlike *State Office Building* (which Alaskans quickly dubbed the "S.O.B.") completed in 1974 and the high-rise Alaska *Court Building* built in 1975. The vast open foyer of the S.O.B. stretches four stories above the lobby floor, and the surrounding tiled terraces offer a marvelous view of Gastineau Channel and Douglas Island. The *Old Witch totem pole* displayed in the foyer came from a Haida village on Prince of Wales Island and was carved in the 1880s. The pole recalls the Haida version of the "old witch" or mother-in-law story of Gonakadet, who assumes the identity of a lake monster in order to provide fish for his abusive mother-in-law. A *brown-baggers' concert* takes place every Friday noon on the 1928 Kimball theater organ housed on the lobby floor. There is a small snack bar where you can buy sandwiches and beverages.

The *Friendship pole* displayed in the lobby of the nearby Court Building is one of several large-scale copies of a 28-inch totem pole that has special significance for Chilkat Tlingit of Klukwan, near Haines. In the late 1920s, the Indians presented the original pole to Steve Sheldon of Haines, a U.S. deputy marshal who was instrumental in restoring goodwill between conflicting clans. The Friendship totem symbolizes peace by representing both Eagle and Raven moieties on the same pole. From top to bottom the primary figures represent: Eagle, Raven, Hawk, Bear, Frog, Wolf, and (very small) Eagle. This pole was carved by Alaska Indian Arts, in Haines.

Juneau has many treasures tucked here and there about town. The 45-foot *Four-Story totem* at the top of Seward Street was carved in Hydaburg in 1940 and represents four Haida legends. Another pole, outside the *Juneau–Douglas City Museum* (Fourth and Main), was carved for Alaska's Centennial celebration in 1967 by Amos Wallace. This small museum houses a fascinating and artfully displayed collection of equipment and curiosities from Juneau's gold-mining era, such as miners' helmets, carbide lamps, and surveying gadgets plus a hands-on children's exhibit.

Uphill from the city museum, the *Wickersham State Historic Site* overlooks the city and downchannel view from a part of town known locally as Chicken Ridge. This fine house was built around 1899 for one of the early mine owners. The residence was later owned by Judge James Wickersham, who came to Alaska in 1900 and played a prominent role in shaping Alaska's body politic. As Alaska's voteless delegate to Congress, Judge Wickersham worked tirelessly to achieve territorial status and followed that victory of 1912 with the first statehood bill four years later. He died twenty years before that goal was finally achieved in 1959. Recently acquired by the State of Alaska, the Wickersham House is undergoing renovation and restoration. Visitors can view the main-floor rooms, which are furnished as Judge Wickersham enjoyed them, with his 1904 gramophone and Chickering concert square grand piano that the Russian government installed in Sitka in the 1850s. Some of Wickersham's vast collection of Alaskan artifacts and mementos spanning his thirty-nine years in Alaska also are on display.

Plan to spend a minimum of one hour at the *Alaska State Museum*. To get there on foot, walk along Egan Drive to Whittier or take a shortcut through the State Office Building: Pass through the foyer and bear right to the rear bank of elevators leading to the parking garage and exit at P2. You will emerge onto Willoughby Avenue, a long block from the museum. (Willoughby follows the original shoreline of Gastineau Channel. The waterfront was extended by tailings from the Alaska-Juneau Mine.)

The ground floor of the museum contains a strong collection of Alaska Native artifacts, for example: Eskimo masks, Aleut waterproof clothing, and carved wooden feast dishes of the Tlingit and Haida. There is a Thunderbird house screen from the northern Panhandle village of Yakutat dating from 1905. The painted and carved screen depicts the mythological Thunderbird, creator of thunder and lightning, emerging from the storm clouds (repre-

Among the Aleut items in the Alaska State Museum is this water-proof gut parka. (Alaska State Museum, Alfred A. Blaker)

sented by small faces). The story that inspired the screen concerns a small boy who became lost on a canoe trip down the Alsek River and was subsequently found by Thunderbird. The parents located the boy as he was about to be changed into a bird. Thunderbird agreed to return the child if the family put up a screen in a Yakutat house. Of special interest: the famous Lincoln Totem pole carved in the late 1800s to commemorate the clan's first contact with a white man. Needing a model from which to work, the carver apparently used a photograph of Lincoln obtained from an army post that was located on Tongass Island from 1868 to 1870.

Children will enjoy the museum's eagle nesting tree. This unusual exhibit replicates a bald eagle nest in a tall Sitka spruce tree. As you follow the gently spiraling ramp to the museum's second floor, you circle the tree to look down upon the nest and its occupants.

The second floor is devoted to post-Contact Alaska. The Russian heritage corner displays a brass double-headed eagle of the Russian imperial crest. Russian explorers used such crests as territorial markers along the North American coast; this is one of the few known to have been recovered. Another exhibit focuses on gold mining. The museum contains the original French-made lens (circa 1900) from the Cape Spencer lighthouse.

One block from the museum on Egan Drive, the *U.S. Forest Service Information Center* operates out of Centennial Hall, the Juneau convention center. You will find exhibits about the Tongass National Forest, films, books, maps . . . and plenty of soft chairs. Rest your feet awhile! During summer artists may be demonstrating Native heritage crafts.

All through the year "Juneauites" pile children, dogs, lunches, and—depending upon the season—fishing rods, berry pails, or cross-country skis into the car and drive "out the road." The destination can be just about anywhere that is pretty to look at and possesses the desired habitat: Twin Lakes for swimming, fishing, or ice-skating, Fritz Cove for blueberry picking, or Eagle Beach for picknicking. Consider renting a car for a day or two to explore the local haunts.

Outside of downtown Juneau, Egan Expressway extends northward along Gastineau Channel past two boat harbors and the bridge to Douglas Island. About 3 miles from downtown, you'll spot the red roof of the Douglas Island Pink and Chum *salmon hatchery* adjacent to Gastineau Channel. The hatchery raises four species of salmon. You can see the returning adults ascending the fish ladder outside the hatchery throughout the summer. Inside, interpretive displays explain the life cycle of the salmon, and a small salt-water aquarium showcases local species of marine life. As you drive out the expressway near the airport, look for Canada geese on the *Mendenhall Wetlands State Game Refuge,* the salt-water marsh area that borders Gastineau Channel. These tide-lands—green in summer and straw gold in fall—are a feeding station for migrating waterfowl. There is a turnout and viewing platform on the channel side of the highway at mile 6. The Canada geese are present year-round in the Juneau area, but you will see large flocks of them in early summer and fall.

Turn right at Lemon Creek to tour the *Alaskan Brewing Company* (5429 Shaune Drive; 907–780–5866), makers of Juneau's award-winning amber beer and pale ale. The tour includes a visit to their hospitality/tasting room and gift shop. Dozens of service enterprises and food outlets are clustered around the airport and nearby shopping malls of the Mendenhall Valley. One shop of note: the *Rie Muñoz Gallery* (211 Jordan Avenue), the headquarters outlet for Rie Muñoz prints, cards, and books.

Thirteen miles north of the city center via the expressway and Mendenhall Loop Road, you come to Juneau's major natural attraction, the *Mendenhall Glacier.* This 12-mile river of ice descends to sea level from a 1,500-square-mile ice field in the Coast Mountains behind Juneau. The glacier was formed during the Little Ice Age that peaked in the seventeenth and eighteenth centuries, and has retreated 2.5 miles in the last 230 years. The glacier terminates in Mendenhall Lake, which reaches depths of 200 feet. Chunks of ice are continually falling from the glacier with a resounding crack!—leaving a deep blue rent in the 1.5-mile-wide face. There is a visitors' center and overlook located about .5 mile from the face of the glacier where you'll find books, brochures, films, and exhibits pertaining to the glacier and the Juneau Ice Field. Forest Service personnel are on hand to answer questions and conduct guided walks. A path leads from the visitors' center to an observation point overlooking the glacier and lake. A brochure outlines a self-guided exploration along the "trail of the glacier." You need about forty-five minutes to walk the path and observe the telltale signs of a receding glacier, such as grooved bedrock, kettles or depressions in the soil made by blocks of melting ice, and a glacial moraine. More rigorous trails are mapped out for serious hikers seeking a closer look at the terrain. There is good cross-country skiing near the glacier in winter.

You may be able to see red sockeye salmon in *Steep Creek,* not far from the glacier parking lot. From July through December, sockeye, coho, and chum salmon enter the creek from salt water and swim upstream to spawn near Mendenhall Lake. A roadside

Just 13 miles from Juneau is the Mendenhall Glacier, a 12-mile river of ice that originates in the Coast Mountains.

exhibit on the Mendenhall Loop Road points you in the right direction to observe these spawning salmon.

When you leave the glacier, continue north on the expressway (it becomes Glacier Highway at this point) for *Brotherhood Bridge* over the Mendenhall River, which affords a stupendous view over fields of wild flowers (especially lupine, wild iris, and Alaska cotton) and the glacier beyond. There is a turnout from the highway. The *Mendenhall River Trail* starts at this turnout and winds gently along the river for several miles. This level trail makes a good, nonstrenuous family outing. There are several good picnic spots on the river. Another scenic wayside 1.5 miles farther along gives you a view of *Auke Lake*. In summer the lake suggests a quiet paddle in a canoe or kayak, and you will see sockeye salmon there late in the season. In winter the scene turns to ice and glittering snow.

Past a small lily pond at the edge of Auke Lake there is a turnoff for the lakeside campus of the *University of Alaska–Southeast,* which offers associate, bachelor's, and master's degree programs in education, fisheries management, business administration, and several other fields of study. You would be hard put to find a more dramatic setting for a college campus. Two sights of interest on or near the campus: The *William A. Egan Library,* at the far end of the drive, contains an impressive collection of Northwest Coast Native art commissioned as part of the percent-for-art public building program. The individual pieces range from cedar bark paper masks to carved houseposts. As you leave the campus, stop at the log-and-shingled *Chapel by the Lake*. The simple, varnished spruce logs are a perfect foil for the grandeur framed by the front window. The Presbyterian chapel was completed in 1958.

From Auke Lake, Glacier Highway stretches northward for another 30 miles to terminate at Echo Cove at mile 40. If you have time, by all means make the entire drive. The road is good and offers exceptional views of water, mountains, forest, and wildflower-strewn fields. Side roads lead from the highway to waterfront residential neighborhoods such as *Fritz Cove* and *Point Lena* and *Amalga Harbor*. *Auke Bay,* 12 miles from town, is a small commercial community and boat harbor with a convenience store. In summer you can count on good burgers and shakes at the *Hot Bite* stand in the harbor parking lot. Lots of bald eagle activity here, too.

The *Auke Village Recreation Area,* a short distance beyond the boat harbor, was for centuries the site of a winter village of the Auk Tlingit. Mining activity in Juneau drew the Indians into town where the jobs were, and the village was mostly deserted by 1900. Today the site is again populated—with picnickers, campers, anglers, and boaters who revel in the gentle beach and glorious view. Covered shelters guarantee a pleasurable outing even on liquid-sunshine days, and there is a campground nearby. An unusual totem pole normally stands opposite the site on the highway. The *Yax-te pole* was raised in 1941 to commemorate the old village site. The Yax-te—what we call Ursa Major or the Big Dipper—was a crest of a clan of Indians near Klawock on Prince of Wales Island. After a battle, the crest was given to one of the Auk chiefs, who adopted it for his clan. The top figure on the pole is Raven. Below him several tiny faces peer out from the wood. They represent different birds that assisted Raven in his adventures, except for the bottom face which represents an Auk princess. The last figure on the pole, resembling a bear, is Yax-te. Regrettably, the pole was damaged by fire in 1993 and has been removed for repair.

At mile 23 you arrive at another scenic chapel, the Roman Catholic *Shrine of Saint Therese*. A gravel causeway extends to a small island with a stone church tucked into a wooded path on the sea. The shrine was built in 1938 and, like Chapel by the Lake, is in great demand for weddings. Eagle Beach (mile 28) has picnic facilities and wonderful beach walking and views.

South out of Juneau, *Thane Road* begins at South Franklin Street and continues for 5 miles beyond the Cruiseship Terminal. Uphill on the left, you will pass the shell of the Alaska-Juneau mill and, on your right, the tailings from the A-J Mine. Several years ago, Juneau residents played a form of golf on this "million-dollar golf course" now under development as a marina and industrial park. Thane is residential today, but in former years quite a community of warehouses, shops, offices, boardinghouses, and even a school grew up around the great Alaska-Gastineau mill at Sheep Creek. There is a small *fish hatchery* at Sheep Creek. The nearby *Thane Ore House* (mile 4) serves grilled salmon, deep fried halibut, and barbecued ribs at its "Miner's Cookhouse" on the beach, with entertainment from the Gold Nugget Revue.

Across the Douglas Bridge you turn left for a 2-mile drive to the small town of Douglas. (You will pass an old Tlingit cemetery on the left.) Primarily residential, Douglas has its own library (attached to the fire hall), post office, cafe, and professional theater. The award-winning *Perseverance Theatre* presents a full season of theater (September through May) at its Third Street home. At the end of town the road angles left to the boat harbor and *Sandy Beach* in Savikko Park. Bring the family here for a picnic (covered shelters with fireplaces), softball game, tennis match, or walk on the beach. A trail to the Treadwell mining ruins starts from Sandy Beach—you can obtain a *walking tour map* of historic Treadwell at the Juneau Douglas City Museum.

In the other direction, Douglas Highway extends a dozen miles to the north end of Douglas Island and *Eaglecrest* municipal

This is not Soapy Smith's gang down from Skagway, but a makeup class at Douglas's Perseverance Theatre.

TEMSCO Helicopters' Glacier Tour sets you on top of Mendenhall Glacier to walk on the ice with a glacier guide. (Mark Kelley)

Ice Field to see the amazing expanse of ice and snow that feeds over thirty glaciers. Wings of Alaska (907–586–8258) takes off right from the seaplane float at Merchants Wharf downtown as well as from the airport. Or, take a *helicopter glacier tour.* Several companies now offer the opportunity to land and walk on a glacier. TEMSCO Helicopters (907–789–9501), which developed the original tours, flies to the Mendenhall Glacier. You see some very dramatic formations of the Juneau Ice Field, including a number of other glaciers, and look down into deep, blue pools and crevasses. Then you land on the Mendenhall Glacier and explore the surface features with a guide. An excursion to *Taku Glacier Lodge* (907–586–8258) combines floatplane flightseeing over part of the Ice Field with a salmon bake at a picturesque log wilderness lodge on the Taku River, a stone's throw from two spectacular glaciers.

Cruise excursions from Juneau include day and overnight trips to beautiful *Tracy Arm,* a deep fjord about 50 miles south of Juneau, where two glaciers descend to the sea (good place to see killer whales, seals, porpoises, and bears). Inquire about different day-cruise options to Tracy Arm at the visitors' center. Alaska Sightseeing/Cruise West offers overnight cruises to Tracy Arm and Glacier Bay aboard the fifty-eight-passenger *Spirit of Glacier Bay* (see page 297).

Juneau is also the departure point for visiting the *Stan Price Bear Sanctuary* at Pack Creek on Admiralty Island. This wilderness sanctuary, managed jointly by the U.S. Forest Service and Alaska Department of Fish and Game, provides an amazing opportunity to observe and photograph brown bears as they fish for spawning pink and chum salmon at the stream mouth. July and August are the prime viewing months. During this period a number of bears can often be seen on the tide flats or from an observation tower on the stream. As many as thirty bears are believed to use the site over the course of a summer.

Pack Creek is located in a wilderness area; facilities for humans are limited and access is restricted in order to preserve the bears and the integrity of the area. Forest Service or Fish and Game personnel are on site to answer questions and brief you on rules of conduct regarding food and access to the area. Camping is not permitted at the bear sanctuary but is allowed at a small island nearby.

You must obtain a permit before visiting Pack Creek. The number of permits per day is limited and allocated among professional guide services and individuals. You will have to charter with one of several local flying services (or charter boats) to get to Pack Creek, or go with a guided group. (The Forest Service will provide a list of approved guides and air charter companies.) Despite the regulations, expense, and possible discomfort from a damp day, Pack Creek is the sort of experience you will remember for a long, long time. For additional information or to request a permit, contact *U.S. Forest Service, 101 Egan Drive, Juneau, Alaska 99801;* telephone *(907) 586–8751.*

Anchored on a grassy bluff above the Taku River, Taku Glacier Lodge commands one of the most impressive views in wilderness Alaska.

Juneau has a large number of cafes and restaurants, including the familiar fast-food franchises, both in town and in the Mendenhall Valley. Mexican and pizza restaurants seem to be the perennial favorites. *Armadillo Tex-Mex Cafe* (431 South Franklin Street) packs in a local clientele, as does the *Fiddlehead Restaurant and Bakery* (429 W. Willoughby Avenue), close to the Alaska State Museum. I also like *Olivia's de Mexico* (222 Seward Street), a modest basement cafe with simple, well-prepared dishes. On weekdays in summer, downtown streets sprout food carts to serve the noontime office crowd. The "hot dog ladies" and taco salad stand on Seward Street, and Mickey's Bagel Bistro on Seward and Front are reliable favorites. (Mickey's "veggie bagel" still has to be Juneau's best lunch buy.) For fancier dining try the Fiddlehead's second floor Fireweed Room or one of the many hotel restaurants.

Summer entertainment options include *Lady Lou Revue,* a musical comedy about the Klondike Gold Rush staged by Perseverance Theatre at Merchants Wharf (907–586–3686). Also in summer, the Juneau Arts and Humanities Council sponsors *free concerts* every Friday evening in Marine Park.

SPECIAL EVENTS

Annual celebrations in the Juneau vicinity include the *Alaska Folk Festival* in April (a free, weeklong series of concerts and workshops); the *Juneau Jazz & Classics Festival* (May); parades and fireworks on the Fourth of July; and the three-day *Golden North Salmon Derby,* usually held in August. The *Juneau Public Market* kicks off the holiday shopping season over Thanksgiving weekend, and downtown merchants host an evening *Gallery Walk* on a Friday evening in early December. In February the University of Alaska stages *Winterfest,* with a variety of family outdoor activities.

HAINES
Population 2,200

It is hard to imagine a setting more stereotypically Alaskan than that of Haines. The jagged Cathedral Peaks of the Chilkat Mountains are massed behind the town, raw-edged reminders that an ungentle spirit is abroad in this far-northern land. Salt water is also close to hand in frigid, salmon-filled Chilkoot Inlet on the upper reaches of Lynn Canal.

Haines was the only town north of Hyder with highway connections to the outside until 1978 when the Skagway-Carcross leg of the Klondike Highway opened the way to Whitehorse and the Alaska road system. A steady stream of traffic and freight still passes through the community en route between the Alaska state ferry terminal and the Haines Highway.

Too many highway travelers look upon Haines simply as a ferry transit point. I recommend staying at least a couple of days. There is plenty of good lodging, and three state campgrounds from which to choose, each more beautiful and isolated than the last. Plenty of RV parking, too. There are interesting sights, a flourishing art community, good hikes, and great fishing. All these things can be found to a greater or lesser degree in any community along the Inside Passage, but Haines has a come-hither quality that reaches out to the visitor and says, "Welcome."

If you spend one day in Haines you will enjoy the sightseeing opportunities presented by Port Chilkoot, Alaska Indian Arts, and the Sheldon Museum. At night there is the salmon bake at the Totem Village Tribal House. If you spend two days you can take in some of the spectacular wilderness scenery along the way to wilderness, but Young was looking for a site to establish a mission. The two had journeyed from Wrangell in an open canoe in late October, which is a feat few would attempt today. The Tlingit chiefs offered Hall a site on Portage Cove, on a well-used portage trail between the Chilkat River and Chilkoot Inlet. The Tlingit name for the place was Dei-shu, or "End of the Trail." The mission school opened the following year. The settlement was named Haines for Mrs. F. E. Haines, secretary of the Presbyterian home mission board that had raised funds for the mission.

Hard on the heels of Haines Mission came the canneries. Several operated in Chilkat and Chilkoot inlets starting in 1882, but only one, Haines Packing Company at Letnikof Cove, was a long-term success. Haines Packing Company continued operations as a cannery until 1972.

Haines next found itself caught up in the gold rush. In 1897, Jack Dalton, a shrewd businessman and sawed-off-shotgun-toting Wild West type who had come to Alaska in 1890, began driving livestock and pack horses over a trail to the Interior to stock the mining camps that had sprung up in Yukon Territory. The price was $2.00 a head for cattle and $2.50 a head for horses. The Dalton Trail, in reality a toll road, led from Pyramid Harbor on Chilkat Inlet to the vicinity of Whitehorse, some 300 miles distant. Today's Haines Highway follows the route of the trail quite closely.

The Dalton Trail was heavily used as a pack route into the Klondike, a longer but easier alternative to the Chilkoot and White Pass trails, until the White Pass and Yukon railroad out of Skagway was completed in 1900. In 1898 a stop on the trail about 35 miles from Haines turned into a bonanza itself: Porcupine became the center of a rich mining district that produced gold until the mid-1930s, and Haines was the supply depot.

In 1903 the army stepped in with the construction of Fort William H. Seward at Port Chilkoot, .5 mile south of Haines Mission. Fort Seward housed two companies of soldiers. By 1904 Haines counted three hotels, two restaurants, several stores, and more than 400 residents. Between 1922 and 1939, Chilkoot Barracks, which the post had been renamed in 1922 in commemoration of the famous trail to the Klondike and to avoid confusion with the town of Seward, was the only army post in Alaska. The post served as an induction and rest camp during World War II but closed in 1946 in favor of other military installations that had been built in Alaska. The property was purchased by a group of World War II veterans who established the community of Port Chilkoot, later merged with the city of Haines. The handsome white frame buildings of the old army post, ringing the grass parade grounds, are a serene sight today. Most have been restored for use as private residences or commercial enterprises. The post was designated a National Historic Site in 1972, reverting to the original name Fort William H. Seward.

Two great transportation links were forged out of Haines in the 1940s. The 159-mile Haines Highway was built by the military during World War II to provide access from the Interior to tidewater. Approximating the route of the old Dalton Trail, the all-weather road extends from Haines to Haines Junction to link with the Alaska Highway, giving access to Anchorage, Fairbanks, and the Yukon Territory in Canada. The present Alaska Marine Highway System also had its birth in Haines as the brainchild of Steve Homer, one of the purchasers of the Port Chilkoot post. Homer envisioned a ferry system that would transport both passengers and freight between Southeast ports and connect them with the Alaska Highway through Haines. He purchased a landing craft, named it the *Chilkoot,* and in 1948 initiated the first ferry service between Haines, Skagway, and Juneau. After three successful years, Homer sold the Chilkoot to the territory of Alaska. The system proved so popular that a special ship, the 100-foot-long *Chilkat,* was commissioned, becoming the first vessel of the Alaska Marine High way fleet.

Today Haines relies primarily upon tourism and transportation to keep the economy fueled. Commercial fishing has always contributed to the economy, and a small lumber mill 4 miles north of town has operated intermittently. With noticeably drier weather than most parts of Southeast, striking wilderness scenery, excellent fishing, a magnificent state park, year-round highway and water access, and the world's largest gathering of bald eagles in residence October through January each year, Haines seems poised to become a significant visitor and recreational destination in Southeast.

GETTING THERE

You can reach Haines year-round by road via the 159-mile Haines Highway that links with the Alaska Highway at Haines Junction. U.S. and Canadian customs and immigration offices are located at mile 42 on the Haines Highway. Be sure to find out in advance how late they stay open (it has previously been until midnight only). Also check into Canadian regulations concerning such matters as car insurance, cash requirements, pets, and firearms before setting out for the border from Haines.

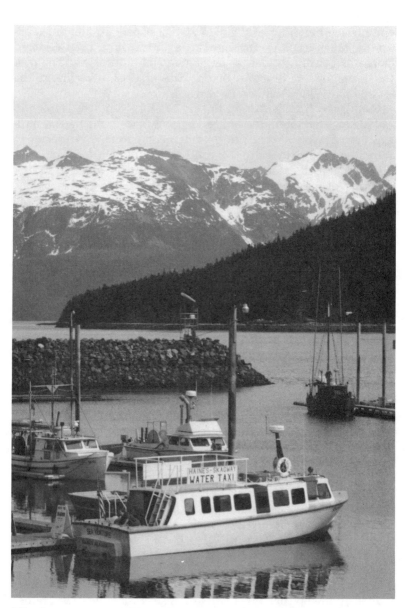

The forty-passenger Water Taxi departs from Haines harbor for the 14-mile run to Skagway. The twice-daily excursion takes seventy-five minutes each way. (Sarah Eppenbach)

There is scheduled air service into Haines from both Juneau and Skagway, but no jet service. Alaska state ferries stop at Haines en route between Juneau and Skagway, both northbound and southbound. Although the schedule varies from day to day, you can generally make the four-hour-plus passage from Juneau any day of the week at the height of the summer season. The trip from Skagway takes only one hour. The ferry terminal is located at Lutak Inlet, 4.5 miles north of Haines (shuttle transportation to town is available). There is also a privately operated Haines-Skagway Water Taxi that carries passengers and bicycles—no automobiles—between Haines and Skagway. The forty-passenger boat makes two round trips daily in summer and departs from downtown boat harbors in both ports. The one-hour-and-fifteen-minute ride past waterfalls, eagle's nests, and sea lion rocks makes a delightful and convenient excursion from either community. A few large cruise ships and several smaller ones currently call at Haines. Write the Haines Visitors' Bureau to find out which ones. (See Information Sources, page 335.)

The northward sail up Lynn Canal rewards ferry and cruise-ship passengers with some of the most beautiful and diverse scenery of the Inside Passage, from the broad shoulders of the Chilkat Mountains to commercial fishing vessels, cruise ships, and tugs with barges. You pass two picturesque lighthouses: Sentinel Light and octagonal Eldred Rock. As you near the approach into Haines, you can see Davidson Glacier flowing toward Chilkat Inlet and, a little farther on, Rainbow Glacier, a "hanging glacier" cascading over a cliff.

TO SEE AND DO

The *Haines Visitors' Information Center* is conveniently located at Second and Willard streets downtown. There is lots of parking available, even for the largest motorhomes, and the coffeepot is always on. Pick up walking tour maps for Haines and Fort Seward.

Your first destination should be historic *Fort William H. Seward* at Port Chilkoot, only a few minutes' walk from Haines center. The neat parade green ringed with white pillared houses of the former army post is an anomaly in Southeast Alaska. The buildings, now in private hands, are identified with small plaques. The large homes at the top of the parade grounds originally constituted officers' row, housing captains, lieutenants, and their families. The white-painted buildings with beautiful oval gable windows have been turned into private residences, rental condominiums, shops, and bed-and-breakfast lodgings.

Officers' quarters face the parade grounds at Fort William H. Seward. The premises now house the Hälsingland Hotel.

The bachelor officers' quarters, captains' quarters, and commanding officers' quarters were on the right side of the green as you face uphill. Today these buildings are part of the graceful *Hälsingland Hotel and restaurant.* Directly across the parade grounds from the hotel, the former post hospital now houses the workshops of Alaska Indian Arts, Inc. The shingled, barnlike building behind the old hospital dates from the 1890s but not on this site. It was built originally as a cannery warehouse at Pyramid Harbor. The army dismantled the building and moved it to the present location in 1919 as the E & R (Education and Recreation) hall. The building was renovated in 1967 as the *Chilkat Center for the Arts,* a convention hall and theater. The center also houses the Haines public radio station.

The nonprofit *Alaska Indian Arts* organization is dedicated to the preservation and furtherance of traditional Northwest Coast Indian arts. Artists work on the premises every weekday carving totem poles, masks, silver jewelry, and other art pieces. Their artisans have produced totem poles for clients all over the world, and many in Alaska. In 1970 they carved Alaska's tallest totem pole (132.5 feet) for Japan's Osaka World's Fair. The pole now stands in the village of Kake on Kupreanof Island. Visitors are welcome to tour the workshops and visit with the artists. There is a showroom where you can purchase their work.

Alaska Indian Arts was founded by the late Carl Heinmiller, a retired army major and one of the group of veterans who purchased the Port Chilkoot post. His son Lee Heinmiller is the present director. The elder Heinmiller also formed the *Chilkat Dancers* that give scheduled evening performances in the Chilkat Center for the Arts. Searching for a way to involve the local youth in constructive projects, Heinmiller drew upon the knowledge of the local Tlingit population in Haines and Klukwan to help recreate traditional Tlingit dances with authentic costumes and masks. All children were encouraged to participate—Tlingit, Caucasian, old, young, boy, or girl. Gradually the idea took shape until today, some thirty-five years later, the Chilkat Dancers of Haines are known throughout the world for their stirring performances. The group performs three evenings a week in summer. You can't help but enjoy the fantastic carved wooden masks, elaborate Chilkat blankets, ermine headdresses, beaded dance shirts, and button blankets. Take your camera (with flash), as photographs are permitted.

Totem Village, located on the parade grounds of Fort William H. Seward, is also the work of Alaska Indian Arts. A *salmon bake* takes place here at the Raven Tribal House several evenings a week in the summer with fresh salmon grilled over an alder fire. The totem poles in and around the house were some of the first ever carved by Alaska Indian Arts, and it is interesting to compare these early efforts with some of the later ones.

The two corner posts at the front were carved in the late 1960s. The top figure is Bear, with a small Frog on his chest. The center figure is Sea-Bear (with fins instead of legs), holding Halibut in his mouth. On the bottom is Bear again, holding a tinneh, a shield-shaped copper plate that was used as a form of currency by Southeast Natives in earlier days. In the carving, the tinneh symbolizes wealth.

The freestanding pole at the front and to the left of the house was one of the first carved. From top to bottom the figures are Raven, as the founder of the world, Bear holding a tinneh, and Beaver holding the traditional stick (the staff of authority of a chief of the Beaver clan) but, untraditionally, in a vertical position. The lone face is the sun, and the bottom figure is Whale, with the tail curled in front.

The back corner posts show a potlatch chief at the top, holding a staff and wearing his ringed potlatch hat. Raven is below him, easily identified by the wings and long, straight beak. The head at the bottom is Frog, known by the wide mouth with protruding tongue.

The tall center totem in back of the house is one of several copies of the small Friendship pole that can be seen in the city's

*Lee Heinmiller explains Chilkat blanket design during a perfor-
mance of the Chilkat Dancers.*

Sheldon Museum. The original pole, only 28 inches high, was presented to Steve Sheldon of Haines in the 1920s by Chilkat Tlingit
from Klukwan. Sheldon, a U.S. deputy marshal, had been instrumental in restoring goodwill between conflicting clans, and the
totem symbolizes peace by representing both Eagle and Raven
moieties on the same pole. From top to bottom the primary figures
are: Eagle (wearing hat), Raven (diving), Hawk, Bear, Frog, Wolf,
and (very small) Eagle. Alaska Indian Arts carvers have produced
two other copies of the original pole. One is displayed in Juneau in
the foyer of the Alaska Court Building. A more recent pole, completed in 1977, stands before the Main Street school in Haines.

There are carved interior houseposts, too. Inside the door to
the right, you will recognize the figure of Beaver from his crosswise stick and crosshatched tail with a small face in the tail joint.
Hawk is below him and Frog is on the bottom. Inside the door to
the left is Raven on top with a protruding beak. On the rear wall
on the right is a special pole honoring Carl Heinmiller and his
Tlingit name, Ka Woosh' Gaaw, which he translated as meaning
the "sound of the Raven's wings." The diving Raven figure is dramatic on this post. The pole on the left was raised in honor of
Heinmiller's daughter, Judy Heinmiller Clark. It is called "Look-

ing in the Water," and, according to Heinmiller, was named for her "big, blue eyes." The pole recalls the story of Raven who looks in the water, sees his own image, and fears that he represents all of the evil in the world. The top figure is Raven with a long bill, almost like a mosquito's. In the middle is an inverted figure with arms, representing imagination. On the bottom, the inverted figure of Raven represents his image reflected in the water.

A 37-foot totem pole, *Raven: Guardian Spirit of the Clans,* stands outside the Chilkat Center for the Arts. Each of the figures of this unusual pole was carved by a different artist. From top to bottom the figures include: Raven (carved by Greg Horner); Strong Man, holding Whale by the tail (by Dave Svenson); Bird figure, emerging from Whale's mouth (John Hagen); Beaver (Edwin Kasko); Man holding tinneh (Clifford Thomas); Frog (Charles Jimmie). The pole was completed in 1980.

Fort Seward galleries include the *Sea Wolf* sculpture studio of lifelong Haines resident Tresham Gregg, situated on the parade green. Also check out *The Wild Iris,* featuring handcrafted gold and silver jewelry, prints, cards, handscreened shirts and carry bags, and other items by owner-artists Fred and Madeleine Shields; and *Dejon Delights,* for smoked salmon.

From Port Chilkoot it is a short walk along Beach Road, following the shoreline to the north, to arrive at Haines proper. *Lookout Park* overlooks the Haines waterfront and small boat harbor, with benches, picnic areas, circular viewing platforms, totem pole, and a Rube Goldbergian steam-mining drill used in the Chilkat Valley around 1900. A topo sign identifies mountain peaks, glaciers, and other natural features in the vicinity. The *City Boat Harbor* is home port for the Haines fishing fleet. You might see the gill-net fishermen spreading their nets on the dock to dry, or making repairs.

Across Beach Road from the harbor, the *Sheldon Museum* houses an extensive local history collection. The museum is named for Steve Sheldon, who adventured his way through Alaska at an early age and wound up in Haines, where he and his wife operated a series of businesses. He later became a U.S. deputy marshal and a U.S. commissioner. The Sheldons were enthusiastic collectors of Indian artifacts and other items of historical or artistic significance, and it is their collection that forms the nucleus of the Sheldon Museum. One of the two Sheldon daughters, Elisabeth Hakkinen, of Haines, organized the collection into museum exhibits. You might encounter her bringing local history to life with her accounts of early-day Haines or offering a cup of Russian tea from the urn upstairs.

Corner post at Totem Village in Fort William H. Seward depicts Bear, Frog, and Halibut motifs.

The museum's collection of more than 3,000 artifacts takes up two floors. Upstairs you will find a model Chilkat clan house; exhibits on Tlingit-style fishing, basketry, beadwork, and dance; and Chinese camphorwood trunks. These colorful trunks, covered with pigskin and painted bright red, green, or blue with floral designs, were brought to Alaska by early traders. A special case houses the original lens from the Eldred Rock lighthouse (24 miles south of Haines in Lynn Canal), one of twelve manned lighthouses that once watched over the Inside Passage. The lens was in place from 1906 to 1973 when the station was automated.

Downstairs features industry, pioneer, and natural history exhibits. Missionaries, canneries, gold prospecting, pioneer life, and the military are the focus for several displays. A corner of the room is devoted to Jack Dalton, the shrewd, early businessman who operated a toll road to the Interior and later built a hotel and a saloon in Haines. You see Dalton's pack saddles, yokes, and other equipment used on the Dalton Trail and the sawed-off shotgun he kept loaded with rock salt behind the bar of his saloon.

The museum puts you in perfect position to start the *Haines Walking Tour*. The 1.6-mile route from the museum to Lookout Park is easy walking, mostly on level ground. The tour is based on a historical building survey and provides an insider's look at past and present Haines. Count on spending forty-five minutes to one and one-half hours on your walk. You might reward your effort with a slice of buttermilk pie at the *Lighthouse Restaurant* overlooking the City Boat Harbor or an apricot bearclaw from the *Chilkat Bakery and Restaurant*, off Main Street on Fifth Avenue. *Whale Rider, Northern Arts,* and *Chilkat Valley Arts* galleries, near the Visitors' Information Center, all feature Haines artists. The *Trading Post* specializes in furs and fur products from Alaska and the Yukon, including red fox and wolverine from the local Chilkat Valley, and handmade items.

A footpath leads from Main Street in Haines to Port Chilkoot. The trail crosses *Tlingit Park* beside an old tree-shaded cemetery and emerges near the Hotel Hälsingland at Fort William H. Seward. Continuing down Beach Road .5 mile in the other direction from Fort Seward, you come to the state-operated *Portage Cove State Recreation Site* with tent sites, picnic tables, rest rooms, and a view of the passing ship traffic on Lynn Canal. A gentle trail follows the shore beyond the campground for about 2.5 miles to Battery Point.

Out-the-road touring from Haines can take you in three different directions. Follow *Lutak Highway* to the north along Chilkoot Inlet to reach the state ferry terminal. You will pass the Haines

Tank Farm, southern terminus of an old oil pipeline to military installations in Fairbanks. The highway leads to the wide *Chilkoot River* that tumbles madly over stumps and boulders in its rush to the sea. You can easily imagine brown bears standing in the shallow water and scooping out the salmon that struggle upstream to spawn in *Chilkoot Lake* (mile 11 at the end of Lutak Road). There is a fish weir on the river to count the salmon as they travel upstream. The daily tally is noted on a blackboard alongside the road.

Go left at a fork in the road to reach the state campground and *Chilkoot Lake,* with good fishing for salmon and Dolly Varden. The facilities include campsites, picnic shelters, and a boat launch. Visitors have been known to drive all the way across the country and up the Alaska Highway to return to this spot. The right fork in the road leads across the river to a residential road on Lutak Inlet.

Driving south out of Haines on Mud Bay Road, you will be following the shore of Chilkat Inlet. You will be rewarded with views of the Chilkat Mountains, the Chilkat River, glaciers, wild flowers, and picturesque old cannery buildings at Letnikof Cove. A right turn off Mud Bay Road at mile 7 (follow the signs) takes you to *Chilkat State Park,* with campsites, rest rooms, and a hand-hewn ranger cabin that was built in Nenana (near Fairbanks in

A well-worn Haines gill-netter submits to a preseason overhaul at Letnikof Cove.

the Interior) of white spruce, disassembled, and trucked to the site. From the front deck of the cabin, you can practically reach out and touch the Davidson and Rainbow glaciers. A 6.5-mile trail leads to Seduction Point at the tip of the Chilkat Peninsula. Back on Mud Bay Road, continue straight to reach Mud Bay on Chilkoot Inlet. Beach peas bloom here in summer, with lupine and wild roses.

The third road out of Haines, the Haines Highway (connecting with the Alaska Highway), parallels the Chilkat River, which is wide and shallow with many islands and lined with cottonwood trees. Before you get that far, stop in at *Mountain Market* (Haines Highway at Third Avenue). Haines locals gather over morning lattes at this espresso bar, bakery-deli, and natural foods emporium. At Haines Highway and Sixth, less than a mile from the city center, you come to the entrance to the *Southeast State Fairgrounds* (see Special Events section) and *Dalton City* (907–766–2476), a gold rush theme park created from the movie set for *White Fang*. The Disney movie of the Jack London classic, filmed locally in 1990, left behind a couple dozen false-fronted buildings. State fair officials moved seventeen of them to the forty-acre fairgrounds, set them up to look like an 1890s gold rush boomtown, and refit them as shops, galleries, and restaurants. Visitors can try their hand at gold panning, watch a sled dog demonstration, chat with working artists, visit a natural resources museum, or simply retreat to the pleasures of the Klondike Saloon. Hosts and merchants wear period costume and enliven the atmosphere with dances and skits. Dalton City opened in 1993 and should get better and better as it hits its stride. The organizers have made an effort to attract quality artists and craftspeople, so you'll find more T-shirt shops here.

On the river flats near mile 19 are the famous *Eagle Council Grounds,* where an estimated 3,500 bald eagles gather in the cottonwoods along the river from October through January every year to take advantage of a late run of spawning chum salmon. In 1982 the state of Alaska set this area aside as the 49,000-acre Chilkat Bald Eagle Preserve to protect the birds and their habitat. You can observe and photograph the eagles from turnouts on the highway. *Alaska Nature Tours (P.O. Box 491, Haines, Alaska 99827;* telephone *907–766–2876)* leads fall eagle-viewing tours from Haines; there are interpretive walks, birding treks, and guided hikes in summer.

At mile 22 you will see a turnoff for the Tlingit village of Klukwan. Klukwan, on the bank of the Chilkat River, has always been the principal village of the Chilkat Tlingit. This is a residential

Costumed employee awaits opening at Dalton City, a gold-rush theme park built from a movie set in Haines. (Sarah Eppenbach)

community with two streets of homes and a log tribal house. I do not encourage you to drive into Klukwan. The community is not equipped for tourists, and there is nothing for visitors to see except private residences. While Klukwan is an acknowledged repository of fine Tlingit art, none is on public display. There are no totem poles. If you must go, proceed on foot. Klukwan residents object particularly to visitors who roar down the dirt road in their large automobiles or campers and then, deciding there is nothing to see, turn around and roar out again, leaving billowing clouds of dust in their wake. The residents also ask visitors to respect their privacy and refrain from taking photos.

Outdoors enthusiasts will find several hiking trails to their liking in Haines. A brochure, *Haines is for Hikers,* available at the visitors' information center or book stands around Haines, contains maps of principal routes. The most strenuous leads to the top of 3,610-foot Mount Ripinsky.

Among the opportunities for those who prefer their adventure by water, *Chilkat Guides (P.O. Box 170, Haines, Alaska 99827; telephone 907–766–2491)* offers float trips (no white water) down the Chilkat or Klehini rivers. The trips pass through the Chilkat Bald Eagle Preserve; you might also glimpse bears and moose. Chilkat Guides also operates multiday float trips on the spectacular Alsek and Tatshenshini rivers. In winter, *Chilkoot Sled Dog Adventures (P.O. Box 826, Haines, Alaska 99827; telephone 907–766–3242)* offers family *dogsled rides* and overnight trips in Chilkat Bald Eagle Preserve.

Evening entertainment in Haines includes two excellent family shows: the Chilkat Dancers, performing traditional Northwest Coast Indian dances (three evenings a week) and the Lynn Canal Community Players, performing their current melodrama, "The Smell of the Yukon" (two evenings a week). All performances take place in the Chilkat Center for the Arts.

SPECIAL EVENTS

The list of special events in Haines is topped by the *Southeast Alaska State Fair* held the second or third week in August. Popular features of the five-day regional fair include craft exhibits, homebaked and homecanned foods, a horse show, and a parade. Reservations for the ferry are a must for the week of the fair, even for walk-on passengers.

The *Alaska State Community Theatre Festival* occurs in April of odd-numbered years in the Chilkat Center for the Arts and brings plays from performing groups throughout the state. In

The face of Alsek Glacier looms behind rafters during a guided float trip on the Tatshenshini and Alsek rivers. (Bart Henderson; Chilkat Guides)

The Southeast Alaska State Fair, held every August in Haines, draws visitors from across the Panhandle.

summer, *Dalton Trail Days,* July 1–4, celebrated jointly with Haines Junction, segues into the community barbecue and fireworks festivities on *Independence Day.* The Haines Sportsman's Association sponsors a pre-Labor Day *Master Anglers Tournament,* and the city hosts the annual *Alcan 200 Snow Machine Race* in late January.

SKAGWAY
Population 700

Every day is show time in this tiny outpost of the gold rush (812 miles from Bellingham via the Marine Highway)—in summer. The curtain comes down when the last cruise ship leaves in the fall, and the population dwindles to nearly nothing. Other towns might offer more grandiose scenery, fancier hotels, or better fishing, but Skagway knows how to entertain. Don't let the show fool you, though. For all the period costuming and honky-tonk veneer, Skagway is not a gold rush theme park—it's the genuine article. You can stay at hotels on Broadway that opened during the gold rush, drink in saloons that served whiskey to stampeders. The ties to history are very direct. Quite a few families living in Skagway today set down their roots during that eventful era of '98.

Skagway is good fun for a day or two, especially if the weather is nice (which it probably will be since the precipitation averages only 26 inches a year—a desert compared with other parts of Southeast). You will enjoy the wooden sidewalks, meticulously restored storefronts, old-time hotels, and other trimmings of the Days of '98, topped off with an evening melodrama and a drink at the famous Red Onion Saloon.

BACKGROUND

The historic gold rush town of Skagway is tucked up into the head of Taiya Inlet at the northern extreme of Lynn Canal, 90 air miles northwest of Juneau. The town occupies the level floor of a long, narrow valley at the mouth of the Skagway River. The Coast Mountains rise on every side, a seemingly impenetrable barrier to the gold fields of the Canadian Klondike. No one knows for certain

Skagway retains a gold rush image with wooden sidewalks and carefully restored false-fronted buildings.

↑ CARCROSS (67 MI.)

↑ LAKE BENNETT (41 MI.)

KLONDIKE HWY.

GOLD RUSH CEMETERY

REID'S FALLS (0.7 MI.) ↑

WP&YR SHOPS

WHITE PASS & YUKON ROUTE

23rd AVE.

DYEA RD.

15th AVE.

12th AVE.

AIRSTRIP

SKAGWAY RIVER

ALASKA ST.

MAIN ST.

STATE ST.

BROADWAY ST.

HANOUSEK PARK

TRAIL OF '98 MUSEUM

7th AVE.

POST OFFICE

EAGLES HALL (DAYS OF '98 SHOW)

MOORE'S CABIN

5th AVE.

SPRING ST.

DEWEY LAKES TRAILS

1st AVE.

FOOT BRIDGE

WP&YR DEPOT

KLONDIKE GOLD RUSH PARK VISITORS CENTER

PULLEN CREEK PARK

← DYEA/START OF CHILKOOT TRAIL (9 MI.)

SMALL BOAT HARBOR

WP&YR ORE TERMINAL

SOAPY SMITH'S PARLOR

N

CRUISE SHIP DOCK

ARCTIC BROTHERHOOD HALL VISITORS INFORMATION

FERRY DOCK

TAIYA INLET

SKAGWAY

the origin of the town's name. A popular explanation is that the name derives from a Tlingit word, *Skagua,* meaning "windy place" or "place where the north wind blows," as indeed it does in winter. Early residents spelled the name Skaguay, but the name was changed to the present form when the post office was established.

The first recorded settler in Skagway was a prescient riverboat captain named William Moore. Moore had been in Wrangell during the first gold strike to affect Alaska in 1861. He got his share of the bonanza by transporting prospectors by steamer up the Stikine River to the diggings in Canada. He was on the Stikine again in 1873 to move prospectors into the new Cassiar gold fields. By 1887 Moore was helping a survey party determine the boundary line between Alaska and Canada. With his son, he staked a homestead on the flats at the mouth of the Skagway River and began planning a wharf to accommodate the traffic he was sure would come knocking at the back door to the Yukon.

And come they did, ten years later, at a time when the nation was suffering a severe economic depression. When word reached a moody and out-of-work populace in July 1897 that a "ton of gold" had been brought out of the Klondike, West Coast docks groaned under the weight of fortune hunters waiting for steamers to take them north. Six days after the *Portland* docked in Seattle with the first samples of Klondike gold, the *Queen* was bound for Moore's wharf at the head of Lynn Canal with a cargo of impatient prospectors. The stampeders promptly overran Moore's property and set about the business of getting into the Klondike. A tent city sprang into place on the Moore homestead. By October, the new boomtown of Skagway had streets, frame houses, dance halls, and three wharves under construction. The population passed 10,000 and more as wave upon wave of fortune seekers made their way north.

From Skagway, the way to the Klondike led over the Coast Mountains through 2,900-foot White Pass to Lake Bennett in Canada, a trip of approximately 40 miles. Lake Bennett was the beginning of a system of interconnecting lakes and rivers that would float the prospectors the rest of the 500 miles to Dawson on the Yukon River. A more popular alternative was the Chilkoot Trail that followed a parallel course through the mountains from Dyea, an old Indian village and trading post 9 miles from Skagway (by today's road) at the extreme northern tip of Taiya Inlet. This trail had long been used by the Chilkat Tlingit as a trading route to the Interior, and hundreds of prospectors had used it to traverse the mountains years before the big strike came. Both trails led to Lake Bennett, but the Chilkoot was shorter at only 32 miles.

With shorter came steeper, however; the final half-mile to the

3,550-foot summit of Chilkoot Pass was a tortuous forty-five degree climb. In the winter, steps were chopped into the snow, and the image of the long, black line of prospectors trudging single file up the "Golden Stairs" of Chilkoot Pass has come to symbolize the sacrifices made in the name of gold. Crossing the pass one time would have been plenty for anyone, but the stampeders were forced to assault the summit repeatedly, some as many as thirty times, to transport their gear and the 1,550 pounds of food, clothing and gear (enough for a year's prospecting) that the Canadian government required them to have before crossing the border. At the end of the trail, the stampeders camped beside Lake Bennett where they manufactured crude boats out of the surrounding stands of timber and waited for the spring breakup. When the lake ice broke up on 29 May 1898, more than 7,000 boats charged downriver to Dawson.

Skagway grew in reputation as a hard-bitten, lawless frontier town. Everyone was there for one reason only: to make money—big money—if not in the gold fields, then by providing services (some of them of the more reprehensible and unmentionable variety) to those who were on their way to the gold fields, or even by relieving the gold from those on their way back. The most notorious outlaw of the era was Jefferson Randolph "Soapy" Smith, a sleazy, two-bit con artist whose nickname derived from one of his better-known cons, which was to "give away" ordinary bars of soap purportedly wrapped in large-denomination bills for the price of a mere $5.00. Soapy enjoyed great success with this and other variations of the standard shell game but did not hesitate to use more direct methods to unburden prospectors of their grubstakes or their pokes of gold when appropriate.

The citizens grew increasingly outraged at Smith's brazen lawlessness, and in July 1898, Soapy's luck ran out. Two of his henchmen had robbed a prospector, J. D. Stewart, of $2,600 in gold dust, and Stewart screamed long and loudly for justice. The town citizens gathered down at the docks to discuss the situation. Frank Reid, the town surveyor, stood guard outside. When Soapy learned about the meeting, he took his rifle and set off for the dock but was halted. He struck at Reid with his rifle. Reid pushed it aside and fired his revolver but missed with the first shot. His second and third shots killed Smith instantly, but Reid took a bullet in the groin and died twelve days later. Both men are buried in Skagway's Gold Rush Cemetery.

During the first year of the rush, an estimated 20,000 to 30,000 '98ers crossed the two trails into Canada. It was not long before several enterprising individuals had built crude tramways to help transport goods to the summit. The most sophisticated on the Chilkoot Trail was an aerial tramway completed by the Chilkoot Railroad and Transportation Company in May 1898. The company charged seven and one-half cents a pound to haul supplies over the pass. In times of such fervor as the gold rush of 1898, though, big dreams are the order of the day, and the man who now stepped onto the stage had the biggest vision of all: to build a railroad over White Pass.

Michael J. Heney, an Irish railroad contractor, was sure that the railway could be built and, after an all-night meeting in Skagway, a group of English financiers agreed. Construction began 27 May 1898, with picks, shovels, and blasting powder. The rails reached to the summit of White Pass by 18 February 1899; to Lake Bennett by 6 July 1899; and to Whitehorse by 29 July 1900: a total distance of 110 miles. Many stories attend the building of the White Pass and Yukon Route (which was quickly nicknamed the "Wait Patiently and You'll Ride") and the superhuman feats of Big Mike Heney, the "Irish Prince." One of them concerns Heney's reaction when his crew reached the summit of White Pass only to be halted by a Canadian border guard. Heney sent up an ambassador with a bottle of scotch in each pocket and a box of cigars under each arm. When the guard woke up a day or so later, so the story goes, Heney's crew was laying track a mile down the other side.

With completion of the railroad, the town of Dyea, which had vied with Skagway for the title of largest town in Alaska, folded. Most of the buildings were torn down for lumber. The White Pass and Yukon Route helped things along by buying up and dismantling the Chilkoot Railroad and Transportation Company tram to eliminate any competition from that direction. Today, the most tangible reminder of the thousands of people who once passed through the town is the Slide Cemetery where victims of an avalanche on the Chilkoot Trail in April 1898 lie buried.

Although the rush to the Klondike was nearly over by the time the railroad was completed, prospectors having been diverted to the Nome strike in 1899, the White Pass and Yukon operated steadily as a connecting link for passengers and freight between the coast and the head of navigable waters in the Yukon, bringing a sense of stability to the town of Skagway. From its boomtown origins, Skagway steadied to become one of Alaska's first two incorporated cities in 1900 (Juneau was the other). The thousands of occupants turned to hundreds of residents and the population has remained at that level except for a period during World War II when the town swelled again as a supply depot for construction of the Alaska Highway.

Until 1982, the White Pass and Yukon railroad was the focal point of Skagway's economy, operating continuously, winter and summer, as an integrated ship-train-truck transportation system to bring goods into and out of the Yukon. In later years a major

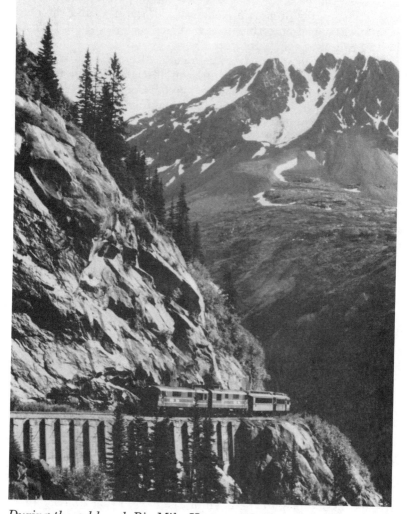

During the gold rush Big Mike Heney, an Irish contractor, pushed the White Pass and Yukon Route railroad from Skagway to White-horse in two years, two months, and two days. The railroad still operates as a popular excursion train to the 2,900-foot White Pass summit, with through service to Fraser, British Columbia. (Courtesy White Pass and Yukon Route)

portion of the freight business consisted of hauling mineral concentrates (silver, lead, zinc, copper, and asbestos—not gold) out of Interior mines and shipping them south by water. In 1982, railroad officials announced that the White Pass and Yukon would suspend operations indefinitely: Closure of the Anvil Mines near Ross River in the Yukon and the subsequent loss of freight business made the railroad uneconomical. With a majority of permanent residents employed by the railroad, closure of the White Pass and Yukon Route struck at the heart of the community, and the already meager population dwindled. The summer visitor industry continued to grow, however—currently more than 300,000 visitors arrive by cruise ship and highway each season. In 1989 the railroad reopened on an excursion basis between Skagway and Fraser, British Columbia, and the sounds of the steam whistle once again echo through the valley.

And what of Captain Moore, who was unceremoniously pushed aside while his homestead was marked off into city streets? He did not make out too badly after all. After pursuing his claims through the courts, Moore was ultimately awarded one-quarter of the assessed value of all the original town lots in Skagway, and he sold his wharf to the railroad.

GETTING THERE

Skagway is the northernmost stop on the Inside Passage for both cruise ships and Alaska state ferries. Both dock right in town. You can reach Skagway by car from Carcross via the Klondike Highway (connecting with the Alaska Highway at Whitehorse). If traveling this route, you must report to U.S. customs and immigration before entering Skagway. If you are outward-bound, you report to Canadian customs in Fraser. Check ahead for office hours and Canadian regulations concerning firearms, pets, vehicle registration, and cash requirements (and be thankful you do not have to carry a ton of food with you the way the '98ers did!).

Gray Line of Alaska operates scheduled motorcoach service between Skagway, Whitehorse, and other cities in Alaska and the Yukon; smaller shuttle services are available as well. In summer you can also travel to Skagway aboard the historic White Pass and Yukon Route railroad from Fraser (with connecting bus service from Whitehorse to Fraser). Scheduled air taxi service (not jet) into Skagway is available from Juneau and Haines. The airstrip is located alongside the Skagway River at the edge of town.

In the summer, Westours/Gray Line operates the day-cruise

vessel *Fairweather* between Skagway and Juneau. The *Fair-weather* makes one round trip a day, departing from Skagway in the early morning. The ticket includes bus transportation to and from the ship and, on the Juneau end, a visit to the Mendenhall Glacier. Southbound, you reach Juneau after your tour of the glacier in midafternoon. Northbound, you land in Skagway in time for dinner. Cruise/fly combinations are available. Another summer option: the forty-passenger Haines-Skagway Water Taxi makes two round trips daily between the two communities. The taxi carries bicycles but not automobiles, and takes one hour and fifteen minutes to complete the scenic 14-mile passage.

TO SEE AND DO

Approaching Skagway by water, you'll cruise the length of Taiya Inlet. A perfect fjord, the passage is dark and brooding but very beautiful, the walls gradually closing together while the mountains drop to the sea. Your first sight of Skagway will be the brown ore terminal owned by the White Pass and Yukon Route. Soon you will be able to pick out the gold onion dome on the Golden North Hotel, the oldest operating hotel in Alaska, dating from 1898. When the ship docks, look up at the rock walls above the wharf area. Painted there is the *registry for ships* that have called at Skagway since the town's beginning (the practice continues today). Skagway's cliffs have long served as natural billboards. The *painted advertisements* east of Fourth Avenue were the creations of gold rush shopkeepers. The clock was contributed by Kirmse's curio shop which, established in 1897, advertises today as "Alaska's oldest gift shop." (Look for the colorful totem pole in front of the store on Broadway. The store clerks still use the original cash register to ring up sales.) The hands of the clock point to 8:20, the hour Lincoln was shot, which was the conventional setting for clocks not running.

Broadway, the main street, beckons with a cornucopia of curio shops, galleries, restaurants, and saloons, many housed in buildings original to the gold rush. This commercial core of Skagway is part of *Klondike Gold Rush National Historical Park*. There are four separate units to the park: a visitors' center in Seattle's Pioneer Square (117 South Main Street) with historical exhibits and films (the '98ers departed from here on their 1,100-mile journey to Skagway); the eight-block historical district in Skagway; the townsite of Dyea and the Chilkoot Trail; and the White Pass Trail.

In the Skagway sector, state, city, federal, and private funds are at work restoring many of the historic structures in town. This is a three-step process, beginning with research and documentation, followed by "stabilization" of buildings in their present locations and conditions, and finally complete restoration to the original appearance. Some of these efforts may be taking place around you as you walk through the streets of Skagway. (One of the most recent, the *Mascot Saloon,* has been restored as a museum illustrating the role of saloons in gold rush history.) The park *visitors' center* is located in the restored White Pass and Yukon depot at Broadway and Second Avenue. The depot was hastily thrown together in 1898, of packing crates and other ready-to-hand materials. Inside you will find exhibits, films, brochures, and maps. National Park Service naturalists conduct forty-five-minute *guided walking tours* of historic Skagway several times a day. Tours leave from the visitors' center. Or you can guide yourself through the historic district with a *Skagway Walking Tour* brochure and map, obtained from the visitors' center. The basic self-guided tour takes sixty to ninety minutes.

The *Skagway Visitor Information Center* is housed in a most remarkable structure: the *Arctic Brotherhood Hall* on Broadway near Second Avenue. This building, completed in 1899, was the headquarters and first hall of the Fraternal Order of the Arctic Brotherhood, a benevolent organization that, like many others, sprang into being during the gold rush era to provide a social outlet for men who were far from home. At the height of the gold rush, the organization counted thirty chapters, or "camps," in Alaska and Canada. The facade of the building is constructed of more than 20,000 pieces of driftwood arranged in a basket-weave pattern, with the date 1899 over the door, and the brotherhood's emblem—the letters AB—in a gold pan full of gold nuggets, at the top.

Skagway has a history of moving things around. Originally, the tracks of the White Pass and Yukon railroad headed straight up Broadway toward the mountains, while the main commercial streets ran east and west. In 1908, several of the commercial proprietors decided to cluster their businesses along Broadway where they are presently located. The *Lynch and Kennedy Dry Goods* store, on Broadway near Fourth Avenue, had to be cut into three pieces before it could be moved from its former location on Sixth Avenue. The building was an army barracks prior to the construction of Fort William H. Seward in Port Chilkoot in 1904. When the barracks was installed at the new address, a false front was added to make the building blend in with surrounding facades.

Almost every building in Skagway seems to have played a part in the gold rush, from *Soapy Smith's old parlor house* (Second Avenue and Broadway; not open to the public) to the antique-filled

Golden North Hotel (one of Alaska's oldest). The *Red Onion Saloon* dates from 1898 as a saloon and house of prostitution. The saloon, which serves from the original 19-foot mahogany bar, packs in locals as well as tourists. Staff members dress in authentic 1890s attire, and a small collection of bawdy-house miscellany is on display. When the Red Onion was moved to the present location, the building was installed backwards; evidently it fit better front-to-back. Farther up Broadway, the *Skagway Inn Bed & Breakfast* (Broadway and Seventh) dates from 1897, first as a brothel, then as a boardinghouse and inn. (With twelve cozy rooms, all different and full of character, it's a great place to stay if you don't mind a bath down the hall.)

The oldest building of all is *Moore's Cabin* (Fifth Avenue, off Broadway), which was built by Captain Moore and his son Ben as part of the Moore homestead in 1888. The tiny house has been stabilized with new exterior logs—but the interior newspaper-lined walls remain unchanged. You can peer through the small window in the front door but will be able to make out little in the gloom. The gray frame house beside the cabin is the *Moore House,* later built by Ben Moore to house his family.

A National Park Service naturalist shows visitors Skagway's first cabin, built in 1888.

Another historical structure houses the Skagway city offices and *Trail of '98 Museum* on Seventh Avenue. The building was constructed in 1899 as McCabe Methodist College, Alaska's first institute of higher learning, but it stayed open for only two terms. The building then housed U.S. District Court Number One. In fact, you will see the judge's bench, counsel tables, and jury chairs in the museum upstairs.

The Trail of '98 Museum is packed with wonderful relics of the gold rush, from wagon wheels and a pilot's hand-drawn chart of the Yukon River from the stern-wheeler *Klondike,* to games of chance, gold scales, rocker boxes, and an early 1900s menu board offering "plain steak" for 25 cents, rib steak for 35 cents, and sirloin for 40 cents. Every corner offers up treasures: a rusty stove and kettle that crossed the Chilkoot Trail, a small organ lovingly carried to Skagway in 1898. A model room depicts "Victorian Life in Skagway."

The museum devotes quite a bit of space to those famous Skagway characters, Jefferson Randolph Smith and Frank Reid, and you can purchase copies of the 15 July 1898 edition of the *Skagway News* reporting the events leading up to their deaths. The paper makes interesting reading, not just for the details of the story but for the steamer ads: "Quick Time. First-Class Accommodations. The Fast and Commodious Steamer 'Farallon,' Makes Regular Trips Between Skaguay, Dyea, Haines' Mission, Juneau, Wrangel and all Puget Sound Ports."

The museum has records of persons crossing the Canadian border in either direction during the critical stampede years, including information that appeared in the original logbooks kept by the Royal Canadian Mounted Police, plus passenger lists from White Pass Steamships and other records. When time permits, the staff will check the records for information about your ancestors who might have helped make gold rush history.

Serious walkers with a couple of hours at their disposal can easily make their way to the *Gold Rush Cemetery,* about 2 level miles from downtown Skagway. The route lies straight up State Street from the waterfront. At Twenty-Third Avenue, State Street curves around to the left to cross the Skagway River for the road to Dyea and the Klondike Highway. Your way lies straight ahead, following the sign to the Gold Rush Cemetery.

Most of the graves in the Gold Rush Cemetery date from 1898 to 1904. The two most famous are those of Frank Reid and Jefferson Randolph Smith. Soapy's grave is enclosed within four plain wooden posts with iron pipes strung between and the simple inscription "Jefferson R. Smith, died July 8, 1898, age 38 years."

This is not the original tombstone, which disappeared long ago. Reid has been given a massive monument and the words, "He gave his life for the honor of Skagway." The National Park Service publishes a brief "Gold Rush Cemetery Guide" containing biographies of some of the individuals buried there (available at the park visitors' center). For additional information look in bookshops for *Gold Rush Cemetery* by local historian Glenda Choate (Lynn Canal Publishing). From the cemetery, a short trail (five-minute climb) leads to *Reid's Falls,* a cascading froth of water deep within the forest.

Although Skagway, more than other Southeast destinations, lends itself to walking, there are interesting options for seeing the sights. For example, the *Skagway Street Car Company* (907–983–2908) conducts Skagway historical tours (including the Gold Rush Cemetery), in a fleet of vintage 1936–37 black-and-buttercup-yellow White Motor Company national park sightseeing vehicles. Costumed chauffeurs breathe life into the cast of Skagway pioneers with polished vignettes from gold rush history. The two-hour tour concludes with a slide show/performance, "The Skagway Story," at the Arctic Brotherhood Hall.

Vintage sightseeing vehicles contribute to the historical flavor of Skagway, at the head of Taiya Inlet. The landmark Golden North Hotel dates from the 1898 gold rush. (Sarah Eppenbach)

The host of shops along Broadway offer every imaginable trinket and souvenir, from the tacky to the sublime. The venerable *Kirmse's* and *Corrington's Alaskan Ivory* are emporiums of gold, jade, ivory, and soapstone. The wonderfully bizarre Corrington Museum of Alaskan History, in the back of the store, sketches periods and themes of Alaskan history—aviation, World War II, the Iditarod Race—through artifacts, photographs, and carved ivory models. Thirty-two scrimshawed walrus tusks, commissioned by proprietor Dennis Corrington to commemorate events in Alaska's past, form the core of the collection.

Dedman's Photo specializes in books pertaining to Skagway and the Chilkoot Trail. Some of the paintings in the upstairs art gallery are by Dedman's owner, third-generation Skagway resident Barbara Kalen, who specializes in scenes of the White Pass and Yukon railroad. *Inside Passage Arts, David Present Gallery,* and *The Cabbage Rose* all deserve a browse.

All that shopping builds up an appetite, and selection of cafes, restaurants, and snack shops stand ready to oblige. The *Sweet Tooth Cafe,* a Skagway institution, opens at 6:00 A.M. with fresh donuts and cinnamon rolls. A more recent addition, *Mabel G. Smith's* (Fifth Avenue off Broadway), serves espresso and desserts. Two other suggestions: pizza from the wood-burning oven at the *Sourdough Cafe,* and Greek specialties at *Portland House.*

Entertainment options include the long-running "Days of '98" show, a lively melodrama based on the town's early history that features Soapy Smith and the other Skagway characters. Some strictly-for-fun gambling (for kids, too—bring the whole family) precedes the evening show, which plays in the Eagles Hall at Broadway and Sixth. (There's a daytime version as well.) The Skagway Street Car Company presents nightly performances of "The Cremation of Sam McGee" and other *Robert Service ballads* in the Arctic Brotherhood Hall.

Check with the Skagway Visitor Center or the Red Onion Saloon about the schedule of shows for *Madame Jan's Goldpanning Camp,* located about 3 miles from Skagway at a spot called "Liarsville." The lighthearted gold-camp experience begins with a warm welcome from the luscious Miss Lil. Gathered around the campfire you'll hear some yarns, drink hot cider, meet a musher and team of dogs, and learn how to pan for gold. The show lasts about one hour.

From Skagway you can embark on many interesting excursions. From May through September, the *White Pass and Yukon Route railroad* operates twice-daily, three-hour excursion trains to the White Pass summit, as well as through-service to Fraser, British Columbia, with connecting motorcoach service to Whitehorse. You travel in the original dark green coaches, each named for a Yukon lake. The train climbs from sea level to 2,885 feet in 21 miles, one of the steepest railroad grades in the world. (Sit on the left leaving Skagway for the best view.) For schedules and information, write *The White Pass and Yukon Route, P.O. Box 435, Skagway, Alaska 99840;* telephone *(800) 343-7373* or *(907) 983-2217.* The railroad also provides a daily shuttle for Chilkoot Trail hikers (see below).

TEMSCO Helicopters (907-983-2900) will take you *helicopter flightseeing* to area glaciers. You fly over Dyea and part of the Chilkoot Trail, investigate a remote glacier-hung valley, then land on the surface of a glacier. You disembark onto the "river of ice," where a guide escorts you to view crevasses, moulins, and other features of the glacier terrain—pretty amazing. Sourdough Shuttle (907-983-2523) runs one-and-one-half-hour van tours to the *White Pass summit* and provides year-round shuttle service to Whitehorse. Also, the *Haines-Skagway water taxi* makes a fine excursion cruise (or cruise one way and fly the other).

Hikers will want to pick up a Skagway trail map from visitor centers. The *Dewey Lakes trail system* starts across the railroad tracks between Third and Fourth avenues. Signs point the way to several different lakes and falls on trails varying from .5 to 5 miles in length. A suspension footbridge over the Skagway River at First Avenue gives access to an easy 1-mile trail to picnic areas at Yakutania Point and Smugglers Cove.

The trail of trails, of course, is the historic *Chilkoot Trail* that leaves from Dyea, 9 miles from Skagway via a dirt road (take a cab or scheduled bus). Largely abandoned after the opening of the White Pass railroad, the Chilkoot was reopened for hikers in the 1960s. Today's trail, much improved over the original with footbridges and occasional shelters, measures 33 miles from Dyea to Lake Bennett with an elevation gain of 3,739 feet. At Bennett you can catch a White Pass & Yukon Chilkoot Hikers Shuttle back to Skagway; it leaves daily.

Although you will be passing through untamed country, the Chilkoot Trail is more of a walk through history than a wilderness adventure. You will encounter many other people along the trail—in recent years some 3,000 people have hiked the route every season. Camping is allowed in designated areas only; open fires are not allowed. Shelters must be shared and are for drying out only and not overnight use.

All along the trail you will see objects left behind by the thousands of prospectors who traveled the route in 1897 and 1898 and the remains of the sizable communities that sprang up along the way. For example, Sheep Camp at mile 13 at one time had a population of 6,000 to 8,000 people waiting out winter storms so they could cross over the pass. There were hotels, saloons, and restaurants to serve them. Lindeman City, over the border almost to Bennett, was a tent town of 10,000 transients in the spring of 1898, but little remains today. At trail's end at Lake Bennett, you pass the weathered log facade of Saint Andrews Church, which prospectors built during the winter of 1898–1899 while waiting to journey down to the Yukon. The interior furnishings have been lost to time and souvenir hunters.

I hiked the trail in 1975 with five other women and three dogs. It was quite far along in the season, late September or early October, and the trail saw considerably less traffic then, so we met only one or two other parties along the entire route. The rain pummeled us unpityingly, and we holed up at Lake Lindeman for two or three days to dry ourselves out. When the sun finally emerged, we went out and filled our packs with the largest, roundest, sweetest blueberries I have ever seen. Hiking the Chilkoot was one of the most memorable—and best—outdoor experiences of my life. I vividly recall the moment the clouds lifted from The Scales and we got our first look at the pass. I assumed there had been an avalanche or earthquake because the way seemed completely blocked by a mountain of enormous boulders. I had not cottoned to the fact that the photographs showing stampeders ascending the steep but steady slope to the top of the pass were taken in *winter*. We were crossing Chilkoot Pass in *summer*, without the leveling cloak of snow.

If you contemplate hiking the Chilkoot Trail, plan well in advance. You need three to five days for a hike as opposed to a forced march. Before setting out for the trail you will need to obtain a backcountry permit from the National Park Service visitor center. As of this writing, permits are free and are not limited, but daily use limits may be imposed at some future date. For additional information about hiking the trail contact *Klondike Gold Rush National Historical Park* (see Information Sources, page 335).

SPECIAL EVENTS

Family and friends return to Skagway from across the nation for the Norman Rockwell–style scene on the *Fourth of July* (parade, children's races, horseshoe toss, pie eating contest—but no fireworks). Skagway's prolific gardens, publicized nationally as early as 1905, take center stage during the annual *Garden Club Flower Show and Competition* the third weekend in August. In mid-September, hundreds of runners from Alaska and the Lower 48 gather in 10-person teams for Southeast's biggest race, the *Klondike Trail of '98 Road Relay* from Skagway to Whitehorse.

Windfest, the third weekend in March, waves goodbye to winter with a chili cookoff, dances, and similar festivities. The following weekend, Skagway hosts another big sports event, the *Buckwheat Ski Classic* with amateur and professional Nordic ski races at White Pass.

Chapter 9
Off the Main Line

Using the *Aurora* and *LeConte*—the smaller vessels of the Alaska Marine Highway fleet—it is easy to sample some of the fishing towns, vacation retreats, Native villages, and logging communities along the Inside Passage. Away from the bustle of urban centers and tourist crowds, you will have the chance to become acquainted with local residents because people have time to talk with you out in the bush. If you like to fish, hike, canoe, kayak, watch birds, or photograph the wild, you can use the small port as a base to explore the adjacent country. A few of the destinations (Metlakatla, for instance) make excellent day excursions: over in the morning, a quick look around, and back the same day, with a great cruise in the bargain. Or, you can take the ferry to any of the ports and hop a floatplane back. The possibilities are limitless once you make the commitment to diverge from the established path and experience rural Alaska.

All the following communities are accessible via Alaska state ferry as well as scheduled and charter air taxi services. Depending on the destination, ferry service may be available several times a week or once every one or two weeks, so check the schedule in advance. Travel in these villages and small towns is not for the faint of heart or luxury minded but for the adventuresome and self-sufficient. Facilities and services may be limited. Several communities prohibit the sale and serving of alcohol. Check the Lodging Directory, pages 311–32, for available accommodations.

HYDER
Population 100

Way up at the head of the Portland Canal, the 90-mile-long fjord that forms the southern boundary between Southeast Alaska and Canada, lie a tiny community named Hyder and its Canadian neighbor, Stewart. Publicized as the "friendliest ghost town in Alaska," Hyder developed as a supply depot for intermittent mining activities on both sides of the border. Today, the economy depends on tourism. With excellent highway access (from Cassiar Highway 37 in British Columbia) as well as weekly ferry access (from Ketchikan, summer only), Hyder occupies a unique niche in the southern part of the Panhandle.

The neighborly association with Stewart only adds to the uniqueness. Town residents share a Canadian area code (604 instead of 907 like the rest of Alaska) and price their goods in Canadian dollars (but shops and businesses trade in both U.S. and Canadian currencies). Parents may send their children to Canadian schools, billet them out to Ketchikan, the nearest Alaskan community, or school them at home. Some Hyder residents set their clocks to Pacific time; others to Alaska time.

Hyder is the only community in this book that I have not visited, and I hope to correct that. Local residents report a choice of good restaurants and motels, a triplet of bars, five gift shops, a sporting goods store, a library, a museum/information center, and other traveler services. Weary road warriors, they claim, can fuel up on a homecooked meal and the "lowest gas prices for 1,000 miles around." Visitors rave about the mountain and glacier scenery surrounding Hyder. You can drive to the *Salmon Glacier* (20 miles away). During July through September, you are likely to see grizzly and black bears, along with bald eagles and spawning salmon, at *Fish Creek Bridge Viewing Area* (4 miles from Hyder). There are charter fishing boats, mountain bikes, and flightseeing available from Stewart.

Hyder and Stewart coordinate an annual *International Days* celebrating Canada day and Independence Day. The festival begins June 30 and culminates July 4 with a fireworks display. The days between are packed with games, races, food booths, tournaments, dances, and many other events.

The Alaska state ferry *Aurora* currently makes the ten-hour passage between Ketchikan and Hyder/Stewart once a week in summer (the ship actually docks in Stewart). The ferry lays over for a few hours and returns to Ketchikan. There is also scheduled air taxi service from Ketchikan.

METLAKATLA
Population 1,400

The Tsimshian community of Metlakatla is located on the west coast of the Annette Island Indian Reserve. The island, approximately 20 miles long and 12 miles across, is at the southern tip of the Southeast island chain, only 20 miles north of the U.S. and Canadian border. Ketchikan is the nearest large port. The M.V. *Aurora* makes the round trip between Ketchikan and Metlakatla a couple of days per week. The journey takes approximately one and one-half hours each way. The current schedule is such that, at least one day a week, you can leave Ketchikan early in the morning on one run, spend the day in Metlakatla, and catch a second sailing back to Ketchikan the same evening.

Metlakatla was founded by Father William Duncan, a missionary, who led his Tsimshian followers from their former home in British Columbia to establish a model community on this Southeast Alaska island in 1887. The United States government created the Annette Island Indian Reserve in 1891. The community elected not to participate in the Alaska Native Claims Settlement Act of 1971 in favor of retaining its status as a reservation.

Like many other communities in Southeast, Metlakatla is supported by timber and fish. The Annette Hemlock Mill produces cants (squared-off logs with the bark removed) that are later sawn into general construction lumber. Chips are sent to the pulp mill in Ketchikan. Annette Island Packing Company, the community fish-processing plant, operates both a cold storage and cannery during the six-week summer season. The cannery has been in continuous operation since 1890. Many of the salmon come from Metlakatla's four fish traps, the only such traps allowed in the state. On the journey from Ketchikan you may pass one of them: a large, floating assembly of heavy-gauge chicken wire and logs. The salmon are guided into the trap through a series of funneling enclosures. Traps used to be the primary means of harvesting salmon, but the method proved too efficient and the salmon stocks were depleted. The traps were outlawed when Alaska became a state in 1959.

When you exit from the ferry, bear right along Walden Point Road. After a pleasant walk past some stunted trees and muskeg, you will come to the Annette Hemlock Mill and then the cannery (no tours). Continue down the road to the center of town. There is a good camera view of the entire cannery complex from the floatplane dock. Sights around town include an Indian longhouse with a canoe and Tsimshian arts and crafts on display (open weekdays); and the white, twin-steepled William Duncan Memorial Church (not the original, which burned down in 1948). Father Duncan is buried beside the church. His cottage is still standing and available for viewing on weekdays, and weekends by appointment. The missionary lived in the house until his death in 1918.

Metlakatla's four floating fish traps are the only ones allowed in the state.

Metlakatla has a hotel, a grocery store, a small cafe, and several snack bars. There is a grassy bank overlooking the harbor where you can enjoy a picnic while watching the bald eagles.

PRINCE OF WALES ISLAND

Prince of Wales is the largest island in Southeast, measuring 135 miles long by 45 miles wide. The island lies 45 miles west of Ketchikan, an approximate two-and-one-half-hour ride on the *Aurora*. The ferry, which makes the trip several times a week, docks at Hollis, a former gold-mining town and logging camp that is now limited to the ferry terminal, a small float, and a few other services. Prince of Wales has been logged extensively and is undergoing further timber harvest by several Alaska Native corporations, but the island still offers opportunities for travelers. The logging has left the island with more than 1,000 miles of roads—the most extensive road network in Southeast Alaska—which has put some excellent fishing, camping, and kayaking within reach of the family car. But logging is not a gentle or low-profile industry, and it has also left scars.

Sport fishing is excellent on Prince of Wales. Besides the salmon and halibut fishing available off 990 miles of saltwater coast, there are many interior lakes and streams harboring rainbow, steelhead, and cutthroat trout. One of the region's major fly-in fishing lodges, Waterfall Resort, is located on the outer coast of the island (see Remote Inns and Wilderness Lodges, page 302).

In recent years, a massive system of *limestone caves* has been discovered on the north end of the island in the vicinity of El Capitan Peak. Forest Service geologists are still in the process of cataloging the caves, thought to number over 150. The largest, El Capitan, is approximately 600 feet deep—the deepest known cave in the United States. So far only Cavern Lake Cave has been opened to the public; it is accessible via a short trail from the road system. The Forest Service is in the process of constructing a trail to El Capitan Cave, and other caves will be opened as geological and archaeological studies are completed. Contact the Forest Service, Thorne Bay Ranger District Office (907–828–3304) for directions and details.

From Hollis, the road leads westward to connect with a network of old and new logging roads. A turnoff to the south leads to the village of *Hydaburg* (population 405), the principal community of Haida Indians in Southeast. The village was established in 1911–1912 when several Haida villages in the vicinity joined together to form a school. At Hydaburg you will find a wonderful collection of old totem poles, but few visitor facilities.

Craig (population 1,600), 31 miles from Hollis, is situated on a tiny island connected by a short causeway to Prince of Wales. This is a lively community. Loggers and fisherfolk come together to blow off steam at the Craig Inn on Saturday nights. The community was formerly the site of several fish salteries, followed by canneries, and a sizable seine fleet still ties up at the dock. The largest community on Prince of Wales, Craig offers a full range of services: bank, grocery stores, hotels, restaurants, bars, library, and shops. *Alaska Gifts* carries one of the largest selections of Alaska books in Southeast—more than 500 titles.

The nearby community of *Klawock* (population 760), a Tlingit Indian village 24 miles from Hollis, was the site of the first salmon cannery in Alaska in 1878, which operated for fifty-one years. The town has an important collection of totem poles—memorial and mortuary poles that were gathered from abandoned sites farther north on the island, from the village of Tuxekan in particular. The poles are arranged in a park overlooking the town. One of the most striking poles has a 12-foot Killer Whale mounted crosswise atop the figure of Brown Bear. Another unusual pole recalls Raven's efforts to destroy a giant clam that was threatening the people. The clam is shown halfway up the pole. Klawock facili-

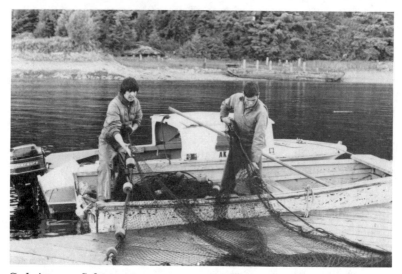

Subsistence fishermen prepare nets at Klawock on Prince of Wales Island.

ties include two comfortable lodges, Fireweed Lodge and Prince of Wales Lodge, with good restaurants and comfortable furnishings.

The road to *Thorne Bay* (population 640) winds northwest from Klawock for 35 miles (59 miles from Hollis) through the interior forest. You will see many signs of logging and wild flowers rimming the road, especially Alaska cotton, fireweed, and bunchberry. Thorne Bay used to be the largest logging camp in Alaska, with a school, church, post office, and shops. Louisiana-Pacific has since packed up most of the logging operation, but the community voted in 1982 to incorporate as a city. There is a grocery and sporting-goods store but few other services. Overnight accommodations consist of bed-and-breakfast lodgings and *McFarland's Floatel,* a floating resort and beachside cabin complex. A short drive out of Thorne Bay takes you to a picnic beach overlooking Clarence Strait; you can sometimes spot cruise ships steaming past in the distance.

Facilities are few up on the north end of Prince of Wales. *Coffman Cove, Whale Pass,* and *Labouchere Bay* are logging camp communities in various stages of evolution. At the extreme northern tip of the island, the fishing villages of *Port Protection* and *Point Baker*—by choice unconnected to and thus unreachable by the island road system—look toward the sea, straining to preserve their privacy and independence.

Except for the stretch between Hollis and Craig/Klawock, the roads on Prince of Wales Island are not paved and some, especially on the north end, are extremely rough. Be sure you have at least one spare tire and ascertain in advance the availability of fuel along your route. As you tour the island, bear in mind that these are logging roads; you have to share the right-of-way with trucks that will not slow down for long. Be prepared to give way.

Taking a car or camper on the ferry from Ketchikan is undoubtedly the most straightforward approach to exploring Prince of Wales, but there are alternatives. You can fly into Klawock and rent a car (there is both wheeled and floatplane service into Klawock from Ketchikan; and floatplane service into Craig, Thorne Bay, and other communities). Or fly one way and ferry the other—the *Prince of Wales Transporter* (907–755–2348) provides shuttle service between the Hollis ferry dock and Craig/Klawock (other locales by special arrangement). Contact the *Prince of Wales Island Chamber of Commerce* (see Information Sources, pages 335–36) for additional information about island communities and services. Also, write for the *Prince of Wales Island Road Guide* from the

Memorial and mortuary poles were brought to Klawock from several abandoned villages on Prince of Wales Island.

Float houses bob in the sunset at Thorne Bay, a former Louisiana-Pacific logging camp.

Forest Supervisor, Tongass National Forest, Federal Building, Ketchikan, Alaska 99901; telephone *(907) 225–3101.* Enclose $3.00.

KAKE
Population 725

The Tlingit community of Kake lies on the northwest corner of Kupreanof Island. Alaska state ferries stop twice a week on a route that includes Petersburg, Sitka, Juneau, and smaller communities; and scheduled air service is available from Juneau, Sitka, and Petersburg. Kake Tribal Corporation, the largest employer in the community, operates logging and cold storage enterprises.

The community has plans to actively enter the visitor trade by renovating and converting a historic cannery building into a guided fishing and hunting lodge. For now, Kake is a handy place to stop for a few hours or overnight if you are touring Southeast by private boat and need to refuel and replenish supplies. There are several stores and restaurants, plus rooms available for overnight or longer stays. Kake offers good fishing for all species of salmon, halibut, and trout, but you will be on your own for these activities.

Kake is the home of Alaska's tallest totem pole (132.5 feet), which was carved by Alaska Indian Arts in Haines for Expo '70 in Osaka, Japan. The pole is anchored with guy wires to the top of a bluff overlooking central Kake. The community has been enjoying something of a cultural renaissance in recent years with the formation of the Keex' Kwaan Dancers, an annual cultural camp, and the revival of many traditional arts and crafts.

ANGOON
Population 705

Angoon is the sole permanent community on 1,709-square-mile Admiralty Island southwest of Juneau. The village straddles a finger of land on the west coast of the island, fronting on a crescent

Kake lies on a gentle curve of beach as did Tlingit villages of old. Aluminum skiffs are drawn up on shore.

of beach on Chatham Strait while turbulent Kootznahoo Inlet rushes past the back door. Angoon remains a stronghold of Tlingit culture within the unspoiled wilderness of Admiralty Island National Monument/Kootznawoo Wilderness, where the villagers co-exist with the island bear and bald eagles as they have for centuries.

Industry came to Angoon in the nineteenth century with the Northwest Trading Company of Portland, Oregon, which built a shore-based whaling station on Killisnoo Island, 3 miles to the south of Angoon. The whale carcasses were processed into oil, bone meal, and fertilizer. Later a herring reduction plant operated on the same site. A second whaling station was established on the southeast tip of Admiralty in 1907. While both ventures were short-lived, the whaling industry brought disaster to the village of Angoon in an incident that is remembered with bitterness today. In 1882, a Tlingit shaman was killed accidentally when a harpoon gun exploded aboard a Northwest Trading Company vessel. The Tlingit community demanded that the trading company compensate for the life of the shaman with a payment of two hundred blankets. When the company refused, the situation escalated and ended with navy vessels coming from Sitka to shell and burn the village houses and canoes. Angoon was rebuilt gradually over the next decade.

The people of Angoon did obtain $90,000 in reparations from the government in 1973. In 1982, one hundred years after the shelling, a memorial potlatch was held to commemorate the unfortunate event and to dedicate three new totem poles, the first steps in what villagers hope will be a major restoration of the community housefronts to a semblance of their 1882 appearance.

Today Angoon's economy is based primarily upon fishing, especially hand-trolling. Many of the rhythms of the old life-style are still apparent in this isolated community. Subsistence fishing takes precedence in August and September when villagers move up Kootznahoo Inlet into Mitchell Bay to set their beach seines and take the salmon the state allows them to catch for personal use.

With the regular service provided by the state ferry system—usually the *LeConte,* which arrives some three times a week on the run between Juneau and Sitka—Angoon is slowly and carefully entering the tourist trade. The attractions are primarily the outdoor recreational opportunities available in and around Angoon and the access the community provides to the vast Kootznawoo Wilderness. The concentration of wildlife on Admiralty Island is phenomenal. Admiralty has the highest brown bear population

The water boils past the dock on turbulent Kootznahoo Inlet in Angoon.

in Southeast (the Tlingit name for Admiralty, Kootznahoo, is translated to mean "bear fort," or "fortress of the bears"). Estimates suggest one brown bear for every square mile. An average of two eagle nesting trees per mile along the 678 miles of shoreline gives Admiralty Island the highest known concentration of bald eagles on the continent. Humpback whales are commonly seen in Mitchell Bay at the upper reaches of Kootznahoo Inlet.

Angoon is the terminus for the Cross-Admiralty Canoe Route from Mole Harbor on Seymour Canal on the eastern shore of the island. The 32-mile route bisects the island via a series of midland lakes and short portages, with Forest Service cabins strategically placed along the way. Allow six to ten days for a leisurely trip. Consult Margaret Piggott's *Discover Southeast Alaska with Pack and Paddle* (The Mountaineers) for a thorough description of this route. and write for the Forest Service brochure and map, *Admiralty Island National Monument/Kootznawoo Wilderness Canoe Route*. Alaska Discovery offers guided canoe and camping trips on the Cross-Admiralty route. Write *Alaska Discovery, 5449 Shaune Road, Suite 4, Juneau, Alaska 99801;* telephone *(907) 780–6226.*

Angoon is well prepared to accommodate visitors. The water-

Three stone faces and a salmon mark a grave near the Angoon ferry terminal, where ferries stop several times a week.

front *Favorite Bay Inn Bed & Breakfast,* near the boat harbor and floatplane docks, offers personable lodging in a 1930s-era home that once served as a general store. The inn rents kayaks and canoes for local exploration. The *Kootznahoo Lodge* has rooms for daily rentals or longer and a restaurant. The lodge overlooks the old floatplane dock on Kootznahoo Inlet. Small boats are usually moored there, too. At any hour, there always seems to be somebody bringing in a load of salmon, halibut, octopus, or other bounty from the sea. If you walk out on the dock and look down into the clear water, you will see some beautiful examples of *metridium,* a large, white sea anemone that clings to the pilings. Groceries and other services are available in the village. A fifteen-minute walk along a well-maintained forest path will take you to the cemetery (go up the hill past the Salvation Army building at the north end of town); or you can follow along the shingle beach. You will see Orthodox crosses side by side with cherubic angels and totemic carvings. The beach lends itself to tide pool investigations and a leisurely picnic lunch.

South of the village on Kootznahoo Inlet you will come to the small boat harbor where the commercial fishing boats tie up. The ferry docks at Killisnoo Harbor opposite Killisnoo Island, approximately 3 miles south of Angoon. There is an old graveyard with some impressive carvings above the beach to the right of the dock (as you face the water). One has three faces and a salmon carved in low relief. Killisnoo Island has several summer cabins and *Whalers Cove Lodge,* a sport-fishing lodge with restaurant and private cabins on the beach.

HOONAH
Population 800

Hoonah is one of three communities on Chicagof Island that can be reached by Alaska state ferry. Hoonah, the largest Tlingit settlement in Southeast, lies on the northeast corner of the island

Government frame houses were constructed after a fire destroyed the old village of Hoonah.

in Icy Strait, just 20 miles from Glacier Bay. In fact, Hoonah legends indicate that their people migrated from Glacier Bay to the present site long ago. Like so many traditional Indian villages that were located near the resources of the sea, Hoonah became a cannery center in the early part of the century. Hoonah Cold Storage continues to be an economic force in the community, but logging is now the primary industry. Huna Totem Corporation, formed under the Alaska Native Claims Settlement Act of 1971, is logging the surrounding lands and exporting timber to Japan.

Hoonah has something to offer visitors looking for an out-of-the-way experience. Lodging is available at the *Hoonah Lodge* and at bed-and-breakfast lodgings, and there is a choice of restaurants. The town is only three hours by ferry from Juneau. The ferry docks about a mile northwest of the town center. As you stroll up the dirt road toward town, you will pass identical wooden frame houses in weathered pastels. The structures were put up under a government housing program after a fire devastated the old village in 1944. Canoes, totem poles, and many valuable pieces of art were destroyed as well. Newer housing developments are on the south side of town. You will pass Thompson Dock, where *Hoonah Cold Storage* buys and processes salmon, halibut, and crab. The cold storage has operated on this site for at least twenty years. You are welcome to look around if they are not too busy. (Stop in at the office first and ask permission.) You can buy fresh fish from the cold storage, too.

Opposite Thompson Dock on the uphill side you will see the *L. Kane Store,* which has been in business since 1893. The storefront is decorated with colorful Eagle and Raven designs. The store carries everything from rubber boots to frozen chocolate eclairs. The Hoonah city offices next door can provide you with any information you need. Farther south the George Hall Jr. Memorial Boat Harbor provides docking, shower, and laundry facilities.

Proceeding north past the ferry terminal, you will pass a graveyard on the right side of the road with old Orthodox crosses and at least one large carved totem among the berry bushes and evergreens. In approximately 2 miles you will come to the old Hoonah Packing cannery that processed salmon until 1944. The complex of buildings is used by Excursion Inlet Packing Co. to outfit its seine fleet. The fleet goes out to seine for salmon in early July. The big seiners, with names like *Gypsy Queen, Mary Joanne,* and *Karen Jean,* are a wonderful sight.

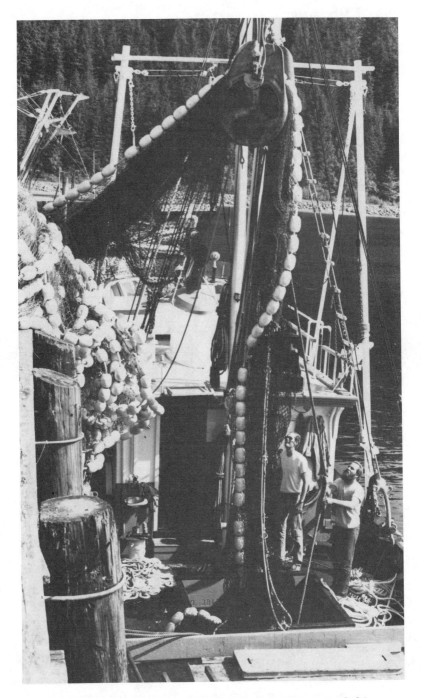

Seine fishermen hoist the net aboard for the start of the fishing season in Hoonah.

TENAKEE SPRINGS
Population 105

Tenakee Inlet, which cleaves Chichagof Island from the north-east shore, was once the site of both crab and salmon canneries. The hamlet of Tenakee Springs, at the north shore of the inlet, developed as a winter retreat for fishermen and prospectors who had discovered that hot sulfur springs bubble out of the earth there at temperatures of 106 to 108 degrees.

By 1900, small, handhewn cabins had sprouted along the beach. Today Tenakee Springs provides a relaxed alternative life-style for approximately one hundred southeasterners who flee the confines of city life for this haven of genteel rusticity. Some full-time residents are retirement age, while others are raising families and working the land. Many homeowners live in Juneau and use Tenakee for a weekend and vacation retreat.

Tenakee Springs offers a relaxed and alternative life-style. Life centers around the hot sulfur bath.

From shipboard—Alaska state ferries make the eight-hour trip from Juneau a couple times a week—Tenakee appears as a long row of dollhouses on stilts along the water. The cabins are arranged along a dirt and gravel path that reaches nearly 8 miles in either direction from the center of town, but most fall within a 2-mile stretch. No vehicles are allowed in the community except an oil truck and a fire truck, although there is an increasing preponderance—some say an alarming preponderance—of three- and four-wheel ATVs (all-terrain vehicles).

The atmosphere in Tenakee is one of studied neglect. Overalls and comfortable surroundings set the tone and no one is too keen on development. Tenakee has electricity and telephones but no city water or sewer system. Some cabins have indoor plumbing, but there are many outhouses stationed over the tide. A walk on the path in either direction yields many arresting images for the camera or canvas: rusted oil drums perched outside each cabin on special wooden platforms, old-fashioned wringer washing machines out on the porch, luxurious flower and vegetable gardens, piles of crab pots, handhewn and notched log cabins, and various contraptions for hauling things from the ferry or floatplane dock or buckets of water from the creek or cold spring.

Tenakee is not without commercial enterprise. *Snyder Mercantile,* at the entrance to the ferry dock, carries all necessary provisions, including marine fuels (hours vary). Sometimes you can buy fresh Tenakee-grown vegetables and day-old eggs. There is a library, post office, school, and city hall. The *Blue Moon Cafe* gives you a burger and super fries, if Rosie feels like cooking. You can even get a therapeutic massage.

More important than any of these is the *bathhouse,* which is the focal point of Tenakee. The painted concrete bathhouse at the end of the ferry dock opposite Synder Mercantile was built to enclose the principal spring in 1940. The water flows into the natural rock bath at the rate of seven gallons per minute. Bath hours are posted: men from 2:00 to 6:00 P.M. and 10:00 P.M. to 9:00 A.M.; women 6:00 to 10:00 P.M. and 9:00 A.M. to 2:00 P.M. These hours are strictly adhered to; mixed bathing is but a wishful dream on the part of the more free-thinking visitors. Life in Tenakee revolves around the bath. It is customary to bathe at least once every day and often twice. Women bring the children and bathe them, too; sometimes they bring the laundry as well. There is an outer dressing room (with a stove for winter use) with hooks for your clothes and benches where you can lie down and cool off when you emerge from the bath. A short flight of steps leads down to an inner door, opening onto the steamy interior of the bath.

The bath itself is a small, deep, rectangular pool. A concrete floor surrounds the bath and channels the overflow to the outside of the bathhouse. The rules are the same as in a Japanese bath; no soap in the water and wash yourself *before* getting in to soak. You start by sitting on the concrete floor. Pick up one of the plastic jugs you will see lying around (currently old Wesson Oil bottles). Dip the jug in the bath and pour the hot water over your body. After you have scrubbed, shampooed, and rinsed via the jug, lower yourself gingerly into the bath for a good soak. (Be sure to remove your silver jewelry before bathing because the water will turn it black.) Before you leave Tenakee, a small donation to the bathhouse fund at Snyder Mercantile is appropriate to help with the upkeep.

Other recreational activities in Tenakee include walking up and down the path; fishing for crab, salmon, and halibut and consuming same; picking salmonberries, raspberries, and thimbleber-

A stroll along the Tenakee path leads past hand-notched cabins and luxurious gardens.

ries; cooking; watching bald eagles and humpback whales cavort off the front deck; and reading an armload of trashy novels brought for the purpose. Tenakee is a form of therapy.

A devastating fire in summer 1993 destroyed several cabins and the waterside Tenakee Inn. As of this writing, the owners of the inn have not decided whether or not to rebuild their visitor accommodations. However, *Snyder Mercantile* rents Tenakee-style rental cabins with cooking facilities at very reasonable prices (especially the big one, which has a fireplace and sleeps six). Reservations are essential during summer and the fall hunting season. The most recent addition to the Tenakee options, the *Tenakee Hot Springs Lodge*, offers homestyle meals and guided sport-fishing and wildlife-viewing packages.

PELICAN
Population 265

The ferry pulls into this small fishing and fish processing town on Lisianski Inlet, on the northwest corner of Chichagof Island, about twice a month on a special run from Juneau—less frequently in winter. If the schedule is suitable, you can make a fun (and very long) day of it by catching the ferry out in the morning for the trip to Pelican, looking around during the two-hour stopover, and returning to Juneau. Or, you can take the ferry out and fly back. The ferry trip takes approximately seven hours in each direction.

Pelican hums during the fishing season with the comings and goings of the commercial fleet and the activity of Pelican Cold Storage, which processes salmon, halibut, crab, herring, black cod, and other species. A company store, cafe, and even a steambath line the wide wooden boardwalk that serves as a street. Locals speak of two institutions in Pelican, both female: Rose Miller of *Rose's Bar and Grill,* where fisherfolk gather to let off steam (stories about wild Fourth of July celebrations at Rose's are legion); and Betty Clausen, who runs the small but effective *Pelican Library,* which provides a warm island of sanity amid the chaotic swirl of cold-storage life.

Pelican is not an old community; it dates from the 1930s when a fish buyer, Kalle Raatikainen, established a fish processing operation and named the settlement after his fish-packing boat. Accommodations include bed-and-breakfast rooms in town, and *Lisianski Lodge* 2 miles up the inlet.

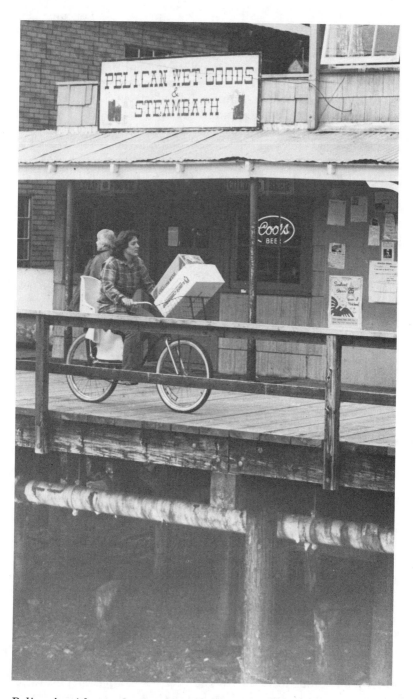

Pelican's wide wooden boardwalk is an expressway for every sort of two- and three-wheeled vehicle. (Scott Foster)

GLACIER BAY NATIONAL PARK AND PRESERVE

Sixteen separate glaciers flow out of the Saint Elias Mountains into the two arms of Glacier Bay. Those privileged to look upon the ice-locked wilderness of the upper bay, described by the great naturalist John Muir as "icy wildness unspeakably pure and sublime," journey back to a time when the present Southeast rain forests were not yet established, and the simplest form of vegetation strove for a tentative hold on the denuded land. In addition to viewing the fantastic glaciers and icebergs of Glacier Bay, visitors often see wildlife. Humpback and orca whales frequent the area. Brown bear may be spotted along the shore and mountain goats on the cliffs high above. Some 200 species of bird have been recorded within the park.

The park headquarters is at Bartlett Cove, at the entrance to the bay. The facilities there include a dock, fifty-five-room lodge with restaurant and lounge, campground, and visitors' center (located upstairs in the lodge) with excellent exhibits illustrating the natural and human history of Glacier Bay. Park naturalists present evening programs at the lodge, guide hikes on a trail through the rain forest at Bartlett Cove, and provide commentary on commercial tour vessels cruising the bay. A nine-and-a-half-hour day cruise into the west arm of Glacier Bay departs daily from Bartlett Cove dock.

There are many different ways to experience the splendor of Glacier Bay during the May through September visitor season. Most (but not all) of the luxury cruise ships include a day of Glacier Bay cruising on their regular Inside Passage itinerary. A couple of companies offer overnight cruises into Glacier Bay on smaller vessels, which give you more time in the park. Alaska Sightseeing/Cruise West (907–586–6300; 800–426–7702) offers a two-night cruise into Glacier Bay from Juneau aboard the fifty-eight-passenger *Spirit of Glacier Bay*. You depart from Juneau in the afternoon, enjoy a nice supper, and wake up the next morning in front of Margerie and Grand Pacific glaciers in the west arm of the bay. You spend the next day cruising both arms of the bay and lingering along the bird colonies of Marble Islands. Passengers have the opportunity to disembark at Bartlett Cove to hike the forest trail and visit the park headquarters at Glacier Bay Lodge before the ship sails for Juneau. Glacier Bay Tours and Cruises (907–463–5510; 800–451–5952) offers two-night cruises from the

Sixteen separate glaciers flow from the mountains into the twin arms of Glacier Bay. (Alaska Division of Tourism)

park entrance at Bartlett Cove aboard the *Executive Explorer* and *Wilderness Explorer*. Local charter operators also offer day and overnight excursions in the area. Alaska state ferries do not travel into the bay.

Then there's the option of taking your own boat into Glacier Bay. For the past several years the Park Service has limited the number of motorized vessels, including cruise ships, entering the bay in order to minimize the disturbance to the humpback whales that feed there in summer. If you wish to take your own boat into the bay during the June 1 to August 31 permit period, you need to write or call ahead for a free seven-day vessel permit. You can request a permit up to sixty days in advance. Write *Glacier Bay National Park and Preserve, P.O. Box 140, Gustavus, Alaska 99826;* or telephone the backcountry and boater permit number, (907) 697–2268. You also can radio Barlett Cove (KWM 20 Bartlett Cove) on VHF Channel 16 when you are in the area to see if a permit is available.

You can even kayak through Glacier Bay with one of the kayak and camping packages (including day trips from Bartlett Cove) offered by *Alaska Discovery (5449 Shaune Road, Suite 4, Juneau, Alaska 99801; telephone 907–780–6226)*. For kayak rentals in

Glacier Bay, contact *Glacier Bay Sea Kayaks, P.O. Box 26, Gustavus, Alaska 99826;* telephone *(907) 697–2257.*

You can fly into the area by air taxi or scheduled jet service on Alaska Airlines (summer only). The airport is located in the rural community of Gustavus, 9 miles by road from Bartlett Cove. Local air services provide flightseeing over Glacier Bay from Gustavus or Bartlett Cove. There is no road access into Glacier Bay or Gustavus from other Southeast communities—you must arrive by boat or plane.

For details concerning sightseeing, camping, fishing, boating, kayaking, and other aspects of the park, contact *Glacier Bay National Park and Preserve, P.O. Box 140, Gustavus, Alaska 99826;* telephone *(907) 697–2230.* Those interested in backcountry camping should be sure and inquire about the availability of fuel.

GUSTAVUS
Population 260

Gustavus is a small, rural, year-round community whose residents enjoy a slower-paced lifestyle that is the envy of their friends in more urban areas of Southeast. In fact several Juneau residents have built weekend or summer cabins in Gustavus and go there to unwind in the better weather that Gustavus usually enjoys. The flat terrain, bordered by the clear water of Icy Strait and surrounded by mountain vistas, makes gardening a treat; in fact Gustavus provided meat and garden produce for nearby canneries in the early part of the century. Strawberries, both wild and cultivated, are something of a Gustavus specialty.

Although Gustavus serves as the gateway and support community to Glacier Bay National Park, the community also deserves consideration as a destination in its own right. Gustavus offers an increasingly wide range of accommodations, topped by some renowned country inns, and a long list of local charter services for salmon and halibut fishing and whale watching trips in Icy Strait. (A local smokehouse, *Salmon River Smokehouse,* sells smoked halibut and salmon and will also provide custom smoking and packing of your fish.) Other services include a grocery store, a cafe, a hardware and building supply store, car rental, and galleries featuring the works of local artists. Several of the inns and lodges provide Gustavus-style bicycles (simple to operate, don't go too fast) for their guests.

An ideal visit to Gustavus might include the day cruise up the

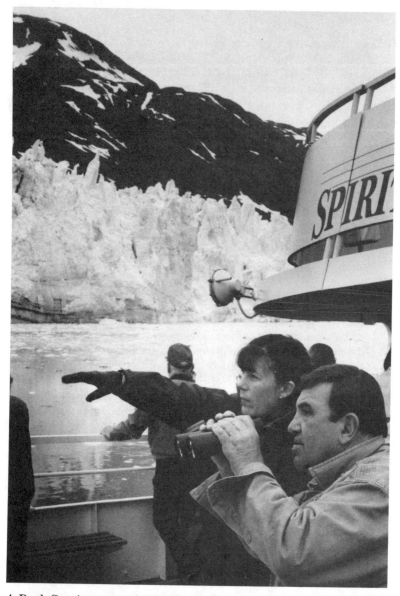

A Park Service naturalist unravels some of the mysteries of Glacier Bay aboard Alaska Sightseeing vessel Spirit of Glacier Bay. *A variety of cruise ships visit the area John Muir described as "icy wildness unspeakably pure and sublime."*

ales Island (but not on the road system). Waterfall has been
ilt out of what was one of the largest canneries in Southeast
aska. Twenty-six cabins have been transformed from cannery
rkers' housing into luxurious guest quarters, each with full
th, wet bar, and refrigerator. There are also newly built condo-
niums. Family-style meals served in the former mess hall capi-
ize on the abundant local seafood. (Two-hundred-pound halibut
ve been caught off the dock.)

Primarily a fishing resort, Waterfall offers first-class fishing
salmon, halibut, and steelhead. You can also hike to the water-
l (1.5 miles on a cedar boardwalk), watch big-screen TV, play
iards, and photograph old cannery buildings. A small store car-
s fishing gear, groceries, and a modest collection of Native arti-
ts.

On the opposite coast of Prince of Wales Island, Sid and Cathy
k operate *Boardwalk Wilderness Lodge* in a sheltered cove
r Thorne Bay. Guests stay in a handhewn log lodge with a hot
and pursue river and saltwater fishing and crabbing.

Northwest of Prince of Wales Island, the mass of Chichagof
Baranof islands forms a triangular barrier against the out-
coast. Near the slender southern tip of Baranof Island lies the
ing village of Port Alexander, a community of approximately
independent-spirited souls, accessed by private boat or float-
e from Sitka or Petersburg. Longtime residents Paul and
le Young offer a small *Rainforest Retreat* in this coastal par-
e of old-growth rainforest, muskeg meadows, and intertidal
hes. The accommodations consist of a modern, spacious cabin
picture windows overlooking bay and mountains, plus addi-
l facilities in the main house. The Youngs invite you to share
daily activities or explore on your own, and they prepare
healthy meals a day, with emphasis on whole grains and
nal garden produce. This is not a fishing lodge or a high-ser-
facility, but a place to relax and enjoy an authentic and spec-
arly scenic corner of Southeast Alaska.

lan Veys looked at a lot of waterfront property in Southeast
ka before acquiring the land for *Pybus Point Lodge.* Situated
old cannery site on Pybus Bay, on the southeast tip of Admi-
Island, the low-key lodge looks out to no other signs of
an intrusion: only mountains, water, islands, and trees. The
ties include a main log lodge with kitchen, dining room, and
room warmed by a huge, custom-designed wood stove, plus
ine-finished, two-bedroom cabins with private baths and in-
ual wood stoves.

though primarily a guided fishing and hunting lodge, Veys

bay from Bartlett Cove, a half-day of fishing and/or whale watching, some excellent meals, and several hours of walking or pedal-
ing along the level roads to work them off. Contact the *Gustavus
Visitors Association* (see Information Sources, pages 335–36) for a
map and brochure of local services and visitor opportunities. All
the major lodging establishments can arrange charter excursions,
including the day cruise up Glacier Bay; and *Puffin Travel*
(907–697–2260), a local travel bureau, coordinates travel arrangements for Gustavus/Glacier Bay and the entire northern Panhandle. The available accommodations in Gustavus range from
full-package inns to cabin rentals and bed-and-breakfast lodgings,
plus the *Glacier Bay Lodge* at Bartlett Cove (see Lodging Directory, pages 311–32, for a full listing). The latter includes a few
dormitory rooms for those seeing Glacier Bay on a minimum bud-
get. At the other end of the scale, the celebrated country inns
pamper visitors with fluffy comforters and private baths plus a
parade of culinary treats from the garden and sea.

One of Alaska's most celebrated kitchens is at the *Gustavus
Inn,* which has been operated by various members of the Lesh
family since the mid-1960s. When I first visited the inn in 1969,
Jack and Sally Lesh were running the old homestead, raising a
family, reporting the weather, driving the school bus, operating
the single telephone in the community, and preparing the finest
meals in Southeast Alaska for a grateful and loyal clientele, some
of whom would fly over from Juneau on a summer evening solely
for the pleasure of sitting at Sally's table. The family lived in the
big farmhouse, and a Quonset hut at the rear provided quarters
for summer guests and the occasional winter road crew. The old
house overflowed with warmth, only part of which was attributable to the big oil stove in the kitchen.

Much has changed in the intervening years—David and JoAnn
Lesh (the second generation) now operate the inn; rooms have
been refurbished and others added; the Quonset hut is gone. But
the kitchen is still renowned throughout Alaska for the produce
picked from the inn's own extensive gardens, the fresh-caught
salmon/halibut/crab, the homebaked breads and wild-berry
desserts, the tried-and-true family recipes. Meals are still served
family style, giving you an opportunity to get acquainted with
your neighbors and hosts. And the old homestead still overflows
with warmth.

The *Glacier Bay Country Inn,* a newer hostelry, stands secluded on 160 peaceful acres of trees, fields, and gardens, a mile
off the main road. The proprietors, Annie and Al Unrein, have
taken care with the pleasant rooms and are doing their part to en-

The country inns of Gustavus are renowned for bountiful meals of home-grown produce and local seafood. The celebrated Gustavus Inn is a former homestead.

hance the community's culinary reputation. The dining room looks out to mountains, trees and wild flowers, and passing bald eagles. An equally tranquil scene surrounds the cozy, five-room *Annie Mae Lodge,* the latest addition to the roster of inns. The front deck of the natural wood lodge looks out to fields and wildflowers surrounding the banks of the Good River.

REMOTE INNS AND WILDERNESS LODGES

In addition to the communities available to the visitor via the Alaska Marine Highway System, there are several remote lodges that *require a floatplane or private boat for access.* They are not reachable by cruise ship, ferry, or road. While an expensive proposition—as much as several hundred dollars per person per day—these secluded inns offer the traveler a uniquely Alaskan experience. Situated on freshwater lakes or saltwater shores, the

wilderness resorts offer outstanding fishing, explorin raphy together with good food and superlative Alask Rates generally include round-trip floatplane tran meals, lodging, guide service, boats and equipment. I clean, freeze, and package your fish for the trip h closed over the winter; write for details. Here are son

Yes Bay Lodge, a family fishing resort, caters e residents, private boaters, and visitors from afar. I an inlet on the mainland 50 miles northwest of Ket fers guided saltwater and freshwater fishing. Me family style with emphasis on Alaska seafood. Th who operate the lodge, have lived at Yes Bay ye most twenty years. In 1990 the family opened a *Mink Bay Lodge,* 50 miles south of Ketchikan in M tional Monument. This lodge, too, offers excellent saltwater fishing for trout, steelhead, salmon, a lodge can arrange fly-in fishing to nearby lakes an the monument.

The most elaborate resort in the Ketchikan a *Resort,* 62 miles west of Ketchikan on the outer c

Waterfall Resort is located at a former cannery workers' cottages are now luxurious guest quart

Bob and Edith Nelson have been welcoming guests to their Thayer Lake wilderness lodge for more than forty summers.

welcomes a mix of guests, including families with children. Besides the cannery relics, the area offers much to see and enjoy, from abandoned fox farms on nearby islands to sea lion rookeries and waterfalls. In summer, humpback whales frequent the area, and brown bear fish the creeks at the end of the salt chuck. Bald eagles feed off the fish trimmings within easy camera range.

Veys lives year-round at the lodge (he's developed quite a following of Petersburg locals for Thanksgiving and Christmas holidays). A builder by trade, he spends the winters crafting furnishings for the lodge and cabins (for example, a 16-foot table to accommodate all sixteen guests at once) and thinking up improvements (a wheelchair ramp, for example). The kitchen makes good use of the local bounty: fresh crab, shrimp, and fish, fish, fish. You fly in by floatplane from Petersburg.

Thayer Lake Lodge is tucked onto the shore of a freshwater lake in the midst of Admiralty Island National Monument Wilderness. Bob and Edith Nelson of Ketchikan began constructing the lodge in 1947 and have hosted summertime guests there every year but one since 1952. Facilities consist of a comfortable main lodge with two upstairs guest rooms plus two independent lakefront cabins. You choose between the Nelson family's cooking at the lodge or self-service in the cabins.

Cutthroat in 9-mile Thayer Lake are not trophy-sized but are plentiful with spinning gear or fly rod. Thayer Lake Lodge is less strictly a fishing resort, however, than a contemplative wilderness experience. The acres of forest surrounding the lodge have heard few human voices. Canoes and aluminum skiffs are at your disposal for exploring the lake: paddle gently about, investigate muskeg meadows, amble along 6 miles of gentle, maintained forest trails, drop a line into the water, listen to the call of the loons. Then, settle back and enjoy the company of your hosts. After forty summers on the lake, the Nelsons have achieved a singular peace with their primitive wilderness surroundings. Ask Bob to explain the workings of his handmade wooden waterwheel.

Lodge and cabins are comfortably rustic, with handbuilt spruce bunks, rock fireplaces, and full bath facilities. Float trips down Thayer Creek to Chatham Strait are available. Thayer Lake Lodge is reached by floatplane from Juneau or Angoon. There is also a trail from the vicinity of Angoon. Many guests fly into the lodge and top off their wilderness adventure with a guided walk/float trip back to Angoon. There, Luke and Connie Nelson (the second generation) operate a small Thayer Lake Lodge extension for guests who want to take advantage of the superb fishing and wildlife-viewing opportunities of Mitchell Bay. You stay in a cozy self-service cabin on Killisnoo Island with a fireplace and incredible view of water and mountains. The Nelsons also offer guided trips to the Stan Price Bear Sanctuary at Pack Creek.

Elfin Cove, a fishing hamlet with a resident population of around thirty, is located on the northwest corner of Chichagof Island, on Cross Sound. Like Pelican, also on Chichagof, the community is close to the Fairweather fishing grounds on the outside coast. There are two harbors. The outer harbor, with a view of Brady Glacier across Cross Sound, contains the floatplane dock,

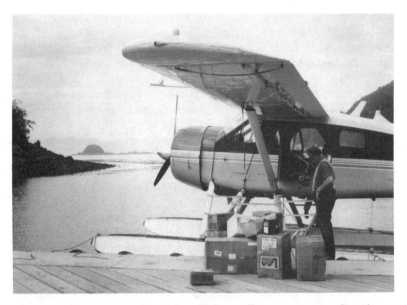

*Floatplanes carry mail and freight as well as passengers into iso-
lated hamlets like Elfin Cove; they depart with boxes of frozen fish
caught by vacationers.*

fuel dock, and the cash buyers who purchase fish from incoming
fishing crews. The inner harbor, connected to the outer by a narrow channel called The Gut, is edged with a wooden boardwalk
lined with tiny cabins and, increasingly, larger vacation homes.
Fishing and pleasure boats can tie up at either of two protected
floats. On summer nights the inner harbor fills with fishing boats,
sailboats, and private cruisers from Southeast ports and elsewhere. Access is by private boat or floatplane only—Wings of
Alaska makes one scheduled flight daily from Juneau in summer.

With singular salmon and halibut fishing only minutes away,
Elfin Cove has developed into a major fly-in sport-fishing center.
Four substantial fishing lodges and a couple of smaller outfits operate out of the community. They are largely self-contained;
guests fly in on day one and out on day five or day six and have
little contact with the rest of the community in between. Their
meals are provided at their respective lodges (whose dining rooms
are not open to the general public).

The major fishing lodges are: *Elfin Cove Lodge,* which overlooks the floatplane dock and Brady Glacier; *Tanaku Lodge,* situated across the outer harbor from the community; *Cross Sound*

Lodge; and *Cove Lodge.* The latter offers accommodations on a bed-and-breakfast basis as well as the full fishing package. Otherwise, lodging in Elfin Cove is limited to a couple of B and Bs and cabin rentals and some not-very-appealing rooms above the Elf Inn restaurant.

Elfin Cove contains a small grocery store, liquor store, laundromat, sport-fishing shop, variety store, and self-service library. Meals are available at the Elf Inn. Folks start banging on the door early in the morning for pancakes and homemade cinnamon rolls, and the steady stream of people continues until the last burger and enormous helping of real fries has been consumed at night. There are no skiff rentals at Elfin Cove, but you can arrange for day-fishing or sightseeing charters.

Around the corner to the west from Elfin Cove, Lisianski Inlet knifes into the mass of Chichagof Island. The boardwalk fishing village of Pelican lies within the protected waters of the inlet. Two miles from town, a fifty-year-old log cabin homestead overlooks the beach. Paul Corbin (a commercial fisherman) and Gail Corbin (the Pelican magistrate), bought the four-acre homestead from the second owner and opened the doors some years later as *Lisianski Lodge.* The facilities include a few rooms upstairs in the spruce-

Boardwalk buildings overlook the inner harbor of tiny Elfin Cove on Chichagof Island.

A fifty-year-old beachfront cabin offers visitors a taste of home-steading at Lisianski Lodge near Pelican. (Sarah Eppenbach)

log cabin, a separate guest cabin with kitchen and private bath, and an interesting assortment of skiffs and other watercraft.

You have the option of chartering aboard the *Demijohn,* Paul's 53-foot ketch outfitted for fishing and sightseeing, or signing up for a "personalized Alaskan safari" on the *Goodtime Charley,* a 26-foot C-Dory operated by the Corbins' son, Denny. You eat Gail's home cooking family style in front of the window, where you can keep an eye out for passing sea otters and humpback whales.

There's nothing at all fancy about Lisianski Lodge. Staying there might be described as an "Alaskan homestead vacation" —

you sort of fit in with what's going on (berry picking, fish smoking, picking wild goose-tongue down by the creek). Like hiking? Wild flowers? Photography? Gail loves an excuse to go bushwhacking through the muskegs and forests behind the lodge and across the inlet. The Corbins will take you salmon or halibut fishing, beach-combing, or wildlife watching. If you're lucky they may even take you on an expedition to White Sulphur Hot Springs on the outer coast.

Hosts Sherrie and Randall Brewington share their Alaska bush lifestyle with a very limited number of guests (two to four) at *Chilkat Wilderness Lodge* at the northern end of the Panhandle, approximately 50 miles from Haines. Situated at the headwaters of the Chilkat River, within the Chilkat Bald Eagle Preserve, the lodge and guest cabin share the backcountry with moose, grizzly bears, mountain goats, wolves, and plenty of bald eagles. You reach the lodge by charter boat or plane.

Randy serves as your guide for wildlife viewing, hiking, canoe-ing, or fishing for coho, Dolly Varden, and cutthroat trout. Sherrie prepares hearty meals served family style in the lodge. High-country backpacking trips are available also. The lodge operates year-round.

Southeast Alaska Lodging Directory

This Lodging Directory has been compiled from listings provided by the visitors bureaus of Southeast Alaska as well as other sources and does not necessarily reflect the personal recommendations of the author.

Key to Column Headings

$ Summer rates, ranging from the least expensive room with one person to the most expensive double room with two persons. Taxes may be additional. Many establishments offer reduced rates in other seasons. Write or call for current prices.

YR   Open year-round
RST   Restaurant
PB   Private baths
PH   Telephone in room
WH   Wheelchair access (inquire about specific facilities)
NS   Non-smoking rooms available

HAINES

Hotels/Motels

	UNITS	$	YR	RST	PB	PH	WH	NS
Captain's Choice Motel	39	$82–$97	x		x	x	x	
Eagle's Nest Motel	9	$60–$80	x		x	x	x	
Ft. Seward Condos	4	$75	x		x			

Captain's Choice Motel
P.O. Box 392
Haines, AK 99827
(907) 766–3111
(800) 247–7153
(800) 478–2345 in AK, YT, BC

Eagle's Nest Motel
P.O. Box 250
Haines, AK 99827
(907) 766–2891
(800) 354–6009

Ft. Seward Condos
P.O. Box 75
Haines, AK 99827
(907) 766–2425

	UNITS	$	YR	RST	PB	PH	WH	NS
Ft. Seward Lodge	10	$40–$55	x	x	x		x	x
P.O. Box 307								
Haines, AK 99827								
(907) 766–2009								
Hotel Hälsingland	60	$75–$85		x	x	x		
P.O. Box 1589								
Haines, AK 99827								
(907) 766–2000								
(800) 542–6363								
(800) 478–2525 in AK, YT, BC								
Mountain View Motel	9	$59–$74	x		x		x	
P.O. Box 62								
Haines, AK 99827								
(907) 766–2900								
(800) 478–2902 in AK, YT, BC								
Thunderbird Motel	20	$60–$80	x		x	x	x	x
P.O. Box 589								
Haines, AK 99827								
(907) 766–2131								
(800) 327–2556								

Bed and Breakfasts

Cathedral Peaks B & B
7.5 Mi. Haines Hwy.
P.O. Box 381
Haines, AK 99827
(907) 766–2763
(907) 766–2634 in winter

Chilkat Eagle B & B
Fort Seward
P.O. Box 387
Haines, AK 99827
(907) 766–2763

Chilkat Valley Inn B & B
8.5 Mi. Haines Hwy.
P.O. Box 861
Haines, AK 99827
(907) 766–3331

Ft. Seward Bed & Breakfast
Fort Seward
P.O. Box 5
Haines, AK 99827
(907) 766–2856

Officers' Inn Bed & Breakfast
Fort Seward
P.O. Box 1589
Haines, AK 99827
(907) 766–2000
(800) 542–6363
(800) 478–2525 in AK, YT, BC

The River House B & B
P.O. Box 1009
Haines, AK 99827
(907) 766–2060

Summer Inn Bed & Breakfast
247 Second Ave.
P.O. Box 1198
Haines, AK 99827
(907) 766–2970

Hostels

**Bear Creek Camp and
Youth Hostel**
P.O. Box 1158
Haines, AK 99827
(907) 766–2259

JUNEAU

Hotels/Motels

	UNITS	$	YR	RST	PB	PH	WH	NS
Alaskan Hotel & Bar 167 S. Franklin St. Juneau, AK 99801 (907) 586–1000	40	$45–$73	x		x	x		
Best Western Country Lane Inn 9300 Glacier Hwy. Juneau, AK 99801 (907) 789–5005 (800) 528–1234	52	$95–$120	x		x	x	x	x

	UNITS	$	YR	RST	PB	PH	WH	NS
Breakwater Inn 1711 Glacier Ave. Juneau, AK 99801 (907) 586–6303 (800) 544–2250	41	$75–$85	x	x	x	x	x	x
Driftwood Lodge 435 W. Willoughby Ave. Juneau, AK 99801 (907) 586–2280 (800) 544–2239	63	$55–$95	x		x	x	x	x
Inn at the Waterfront 455 S. Franklin St. Juneau, AK 99801 (907) 586–2050	21	$42–$59	x	x	x	x		x
Juneau Airport Travelodge 9200 Glacier Hwy. Juneau, AK 99801 (907) 789–9700 (800) 255–3050	86	$105–$115	x	x	x	x	x	x
The Prospector Hotel 375 Whittier St. Juneau 99801 (907) 586–3737	58	$90–$125	x	x	x	x	x	x
Silverbow Inn 120 Second St. Juneau, AK 99801 (907) 586–4146	7	$99–$109	x	x	x	x		x
Super 8 Motel 2295 Trout St. Juneau, AK 99801 (907) 789–4858 (800) 800–8000	75	$79–$122	x		x	x	x	x
Westmark Baranof 127 N. Franklin St. Juneau, AK 99801 (907) 586–2660 (800) 544–0970	194	$59–$124	x	x	x	x	x	x

	UNITS	$	YR	RST	PB	PH	WH	NS
Westmark–Juneau	105	$88–$152	x	x	x	x	x	x

51 W. Egan Dr.
Juneau, AK 99801
(907) 586–6900
(800) 544–0970

Lodges

	UNITS	$	YR	RST	PB	PH	WH	NS
Aldersheim Lodge	9	$20–$60	x				x	x

P.O. Box 210447
Auke Bay, AK 99821
(907) 789–5952
(907) 780–4778

Bed and Breakfasts

A Channel View With A Room
1775 Dimond Dr.
Juneau, AK 99801
(907) 586–1734

A Cozy Log Bed & Breakfast
8668 Dudley St.
Juneau, AK 99801
(907) 789–2582

Bed and Breakfast Inn–Juneau
1801 Old Glacier Hwy.
Juneau, AK 99801
(907 463–5855

Blueberry Lodge on the Tidelands
9436 N. Douglas Hwy.
Juneau, AK 99801
(907) 463–5886

Cashen Quarters Bed & Breakfast
315 Gold St.
Juneau, AK 99801
(907) 586–9863

Crondahls Bed & Breakfast
626 Fifth St.
Juneau, AK 99801
(907) 586–1464

Dawson's Bed and Breakfast
1941 Glacier Highway
Juneau, AK 99801
(907) 586–9708

Eagle's Nest Bed & Breakfast
P.O. Box 20537
Juneau, AK 99802
(907) 586–6378

Evergreen Bed & Breakfast
643 Main St.
Juneau, AK 99801
(907) 586–3917

Grandma's Feather Bed
9300 Glacier Hwy.
Juneau, AK 99801
(907) 789–5566

Island Getaway
4440 Columbia Blvd.
Juneau, AK 99801
(907) 789–0702

Jan's View Bed & Breakfast
P.O. Box 32254
Juneau, AK 99803
(907) 463–5897

The Lost Chord Bed & Breakfast
2200 Fritz Cove Rd.
Juneau, AK 99801
(907) 789–7296

Pearson's Pond Luxury Inn
4541 Sawa Circle
Juneau, AK 99801
(907) 789–3772

Point Lena Bed & Breakfast
P.O. Box 211526
Auke Bay, AK 99821
(907) 789–9843

Pot Belly Bed & Breakfast
5115 N. Douglas Hwy.
Juneau, AK 99802
(907) 586–1279

Sepel Hollow Bed & Breakfast
10901 Mendenhall Loop Rd.
Juneau, AK 99801
(907) 789–5220

Sutton Place Bed & Breakfast
205 Seward St.
Juneau, AK 99801
(907) 463–3232

Windsock Inn Bed & Breakfast
P.O. Box 240223
Douglas, AK 99824
(907) 364–2431

Hostels

Juneau International Hostel
614 Harris St.
Juneau, AK 99801
(907) 586–9559

KETCHIKAN

Hotels/Motels

	UNITS	$	YR	RST	PB	PH	WH	NS
Best Western Landing 3434 Tongass Ave. Ketchikan, AK 99901 (907) 225–5166 (800) 428–8304	76	$89–$102	x	x	x	x	x	x
Gilmore Hotel 326 Front St. Ketchikan, AK 99901 (907) 225–9423	40	$64–$88	x	x	x	x		x
Ingersoll Hotel 303 Mission St. Ketchikan, AK 99901 (907) 225–2124 (800) 478–2124 in AK	58	$79–$89	x		x	x		x

	UNITS	$	YR	RST	PB	PH	WH	NS
New York Hotel & Cafe	8	$79	x		x	x		x
207 Stedman St.								
P.O. Box 9112								
Ketchikan, AK 99901								
(907) 225–0246								

	UNITS	$	YR	RST	PB	PH	WH	NS
Super 8 Motel	82	$79–$102	x		x	x	x	x
2151 Sea Level Dr.								
Ketchikan, AK 99901								
(907) 225–9088								
(800) 800–8000								

	UNITS	$	YR	RST	PB	PH	WH	NS
Westmark Cape Fox Lodge	72	$140–$158	x	x	x	x	x	x
800 Venetia Way								
Ketchikan, AK 99901								
(907) 225–8001								
(800) 544–0970								

Lodges/Resorts

	UNITS	$	YR	RST	PB	PH	WH	NS
Alaskan Home Fishing Lodge	5	$55–$95	x	x	x	x		x
11380 Alderwood St. N.								
Ketchikan, AK 99901								
(907) 225–6919								
(800) 876–0925								
(Fishing packages available;								
meals for guests only)								

	UNITS	$	YR	RST	PB	PH	WH	NS
Salmon Falls Resort	52	$115–$147		x	x	x	x	x
16707 N. Tongass Hwy.								
P.O. Box 5700								
Ketchikan, AK 99901								
(907) 225–2752								
(Fishing packages available)								

Bed and Breakfasts

C–Flee Beachfront Hideaway
16295 N. Tongass Hwy.
Ketchikan, AK 99901
(907) 225–9460

Classic Stop Bed and Breakfast
P.O. Box 5863
Ketchikan, AK 99901
(907) 225–1120

D & W Bed & Breakfast
412 D–1 Loop Rd. N.
Ketchikan, AK 99901
(907) 225–3273
(800) 551–8654

The Great Alaska Cedar Works
1527 Pond Reef Rd.
Ketchikan, AK 99901
(907) 247–8287

The Heckman House
445 Front St.
Ketchikan, AK 99901
(907) 225–6357

Ketchikan Bed and Breakfast/
Ketchikan Bed and Breakfast Association
P.O. Box 5015
Ketchikan, AK 99901
(907) 225–8550

Main Street Bed and Breakfast
P.O. Box 7473
Ketchikan, AK 99901
(907) 225–8484

North Tongass Bed and Breakfast
P.O. Box 879
Ward Cove, AK 99928
(907) 247–0879

Park Avenue Suites
11380 Alderwood St. N.
Ketchikan, AK 99901
(800) 876–0925
(800) 478–6919 in AK

Sarajustine's Bed and Breakfast
P.O. Box 9532
Ketchikan, AK 99901
(907) 225–6567

Water Street Bed & Breakfast
1508 Water St., Middle
P.O. Box 5015
Ketchikan, AK 99901
(907) 225–8550

Hostels

Ketchikan Youth Hostel
400 Main St.
P.O. Box 8515
Ketchikan, AK 99901
(907) 225–3319

PETERSBURG

Hotels/Motels

	UNITS	$	YR	RST	PB	PH	WH	NS
Beachcomber Inn 3.8 Mi. Mitkof Hwy. P.O. Box 570 Petersburg, AK 99833 (907) 772–3888	8	$50–$65	x	x	x			
Narrows Inn 1 Mi. Mitkof Hwy. P.O. Box 1048 Petersburg, AK 99833 (907) 772–4288	25	$55–$85		x	x	x		
Scandia House 110 N. Nordic Dr. P.O. Box 689 Petersburg, AK 99833 (907) 772–4281	24	$50–$83	x		x	x		
Tides Inn 307 N. First St. P.O. Box 1048 Petersburg, AK 99833 (907) 772–4288	48	$70–$100	x		x	x	x	

Lodges

	UNITS	$	YR	RST	PB	PH	WH	NS
Green Rocks Lodge 7.5 Mi. Mitkof Highway P.O. Box 110 Petersburg, AK 99833 (907) 772–4744 (Includes fishing package)	3	$140	o	o	o	o	o	x

Bed and Breakfasts

Broom Hus Bed & Breakfast
P.O. Box 427
Petersburg, AK 99833
(907) 772–3459

Gypsy Bed & Breakfast
P.O. Box 793
Petersburg, AK 99833
(907) 772–4531

Jewel's By the Sea Bed & Breakfast
806 S. Nordic Dr.
P.O. Box 1662
Petersburg, AK 99833
(907) 772–3620

Sing Lee Bed & Breakfast
15 Sing Lee Alley
P.O. Box 1625
Petersburg, AK 99833
(907) 772–4700

Water's Edge Bed & Breakfast
P.O. Box 1201
Petersburg, AK 99833
(907) 772–3736

SITKA

Hotels/Motels

	UNITS	$	YR	RST	PB	PH	WH	NS
Potlatch Motel 713 Katlian St. Sitka, AK 99835 (907) 747–8611	32	$70–$78	x	x	x	x	x	x
Sitka Hotel 118 Lincoln St. Sitka, AK 99835 (907) 747–3288	55	$54–$60	x	x	x			
Super 8 Motel 404 Sawmill Creek Blvd. Sitka, AK 99835 (907) 747–8804; (800) 800–8000	35	$73–$90	x		x	x	x	x

	UNITS	$	YR	RST	PB	PH	WH	NS
Westmark Shee Atika 330 Seward St. Sitka, AK 99835 (907) 747–6241	96	$115–$128	x	x	x	x	x	x

Lodges

	UNITS	$	YR	RST	PB	PH	WH	NS
Baranof Sportsman's Vacations 325 Seward St. Sitka, AK 99835 (907) 747–4937 (Sleeps 10)	—	$160			x		x	
Burgess Bauder's Lighthouse P.O. Box 277 Sitka, AK 99835 (907) 747–3056 (Sleeps 8)	—	$125	x		x	x		
Siginaka Lodge/ Wild Strawberry Inn 724 Siginaka Way P.O. Box 2300 Sitka, AK 99835 (907) 747–8883 (800) 770–2628	8	$55–$75	x		x	x	x	x
Wind Song Charters 1715 A Edgecumbe Dr. Sitka, AK 99835 (907) 747–3675 (Sleeps 6)	—	$150			x			x

Bed and Breakfasts

A&B Bed and Breakfast
2305 Halibut Point Rd.
Sitka, AK 99835
(907) 747–8778

Abner's Bed and Breakfast
200 Seward St.
Sitka, AK 99835
(907) 747–8779

Alaska Ocean View B & B
1101 Edgecumbe Dr.
Sitka, AK 99835
(907) 747–8310

Annahootz Bed and Breakfast
P.O. Box 2870
Sitka, AK 99835
(907) 747–6498

Aurora Borealis Inn
P.O. Box 556
Sitka, AK 99835
(907) 747–1076

Bed Inn 518
518 Monastery St.
Sitka, AK 99835
(907) 747–3305

Biorka Bed and Breakfast
611 Biorka St.
Sitka, AK 99835
(907) 747–3111

Brownies Bed and Breakfast
2038 Halibut Point Rd.
Sitka, AK 99835
(907) 747–5402

The Bunkhouse
3302 Halibut Point Rd.
Sitka, AK 99835
(907) 747–8796

Candy's Bed and Breakfast
P.O. Box 2967
Sitka, AK 99835
(907) 747–8213

Creek's Edge Guest House
P.O. Box 2941
Sitka, AK 99835
(907) 747–6484

Hannah's Bed and Breakfast
504 Monastery St.
Sitka, AK 99835
(907) 747–8309

Helga's Bed and Breakfast
2821 Halibut Point Rd.
Sitka, AK 99835
(907) 747–5497

Jamestown Bed and Breakfast
117 Jamestown Dr.
Sitka, AK 99835
(907) 747–5643

Karras Bed and Breakfast
230 Kogwanton St.
Sitka, AK 99835
(907) 747–3978

Mountain View B & B
P.O. Box 119
Sitka, AK 99835
(907) 747–8966

The New Archangel House
204 New Archangel St.
Sitka, AK 99835
(907) 747–8583

Otter Cove Bed and Breakfast
P.O. Box 66
Sitka, AK 99835
(907) 747–8160

Puffin Bed and Breakfast
506 Verstovia St.
Sitka, AK 99835
(907) 747–3912

Seaview Bed and Breakfast
203 Harbor Dr.
Sitka, AK 99835
(907) 747–3908/8020

Sitka House Bed and Breakfast
325 Seward St.
Sitka, AK 99835
(907) 747–4937

Hostels

Youth Hostel
303 Kimshan St.
Sitka, AK 99835
(907) 747–8356

Other

Sheldon Jackson College Summer Housing
801 Lincoln St.
Sitka, AK 99835
(907) 747–5220
(Dormitory rooms)

SKAGWAY

Hotels/Motels

	UNITS	$	YR	RST	PB	PH	WH	NS
Gold Rush Lodge Sixth and Alaska P.O. Box 514 Skagway, AK 99840 (907) 983–2831	12	$65–$85	x		x	x		x
Golden North Hotel Third and Broadway P.O. Box 343 Skagway, AK 99840 (907) 983–2451	32	$60–$85	x	x	x	x	x	x
Portland House Fifth and State P.O. Box 393 Skagway, AK 99840 (907) 983–2493	9	$30–$45		x				
Sgt. Preston's Lodge Sixth and State P.O. Box 538 Skagway, AK 99840 (907) 983–2521	23	$55–$90	x		x	x		

	UNITS	$	YR	RST	PB	PH	WH	NS
Westmark Inn	220	$79–$132		x	x	x	x	x
Third and Spring								
P.O. Box 515								
Skagway, AK 99840								
(907) 983–6000								
(800) 544–0970								
Wind Valley Lodge	29	$53–$69			x	x	x	x
22nd and State								
P.O. Box 354								
Skagway, AK 99840								
(907) 983–2236								

Bed and Breakfasts

Gramma's Bed & Breakfast
Seventh and State
P.O. Box 315
Skagway, AK 99840
(907) 983–2312

Skagway Inn
Seventh and Broadway
P.O. Box 500
Skagway, AK 99840
(907) 983–2289

Hostels

Skagway Home Hostel
Third between State and Main
P.O. Box 231
Skagway, AK 99840
(907) 983–2131

WRANGELL

Hotels/Motels

	UNITS	$	YR	RST	PB	PH	WH	NS
Harding's Old Sourdough Lodge	18	$55	x	x	x		x	x
1104 Peninsula Ave.								
P.O. Box 1062								
Wrangell, AK 99929								
(907) 874–3613								

	UNITS	$	YR	RST	PB	PH	WH	NS
The Roadhouse Lodge	10	$50–$60	x	x	x	x		x
The Stikine Inn	34	$55–$75	x	x	x	x	x	x
Thunderbird Hotel	8	$55	x	x	x	x	x	

The Roadhouse Lodge
4 Mi. Zimovia Hwy.
P.O. Box 1199
Wrangell, AK 99929
(907) 874–2335

The Stikine Inn
107 Front St.
P.O. Box 990
Wrangell, AK 99929
(907) 874–3388

Thunderbird Hotel
223 Front St.
P.O. Box 110
Wrangell, AK 99929
(907) 874–3322

Bed and Breakfasts

Clarke Bed and Breakfast
732 Case Ave.
P.O. Box 1020
Wrangell 99929
(907) 874–2125/3863

D & D's Bed and Breakfast
120 3rd St.
P.O. Box 972
Wrangell, AK 99929
(907) 874–3970

Harbor House
Shakes St.
P.O. Box 2027
Wrangell, AK 99929
(907) 874–2277

Rooney's Roost Bed and Breakfast
206 McKinnon St.
P.O. Box 552
Wrangell, AK 99929
(907) 874–2026/3622

OFF THE MAIN LINE

ANGOON

Favorite Bay Inn Bed & Breakfast
P.O. Box 101
Angoon, AK 99820
(907) 788–3104
(800) 423–3123

Kootznahoo Lodge
P.O. Box 134
Angoon, AK 99820
(907) 788–3501

Thayer Lake Lodge/Angoon
P.O. Box 211614
Auke Bay, AK 99821
(907) 789–5646
(907) 225–3343

Whalers Cove Sportfishing Lodge
P.O. Box 101
Angoon, AK 99820
(907) 788–3123
(800) 423–3123

ELFIN COVE
(Also see Wilderness/
Fly-In Fishing Lodges)

Bixby's B&B
P.O. Box 13
Elfin Cove, AK 99825
(907) 239–2255
Winter: P.O. Box 240941
          Douglas, AK 99824
          (907) 364–2181

The Cove Lodge
P.O. Box 33160
Juneau, AK 99803-3160
(907) 239–2221
(907) 790–2626
(800) 382–3847

The Elf Inn
P.O. Box 22
Elfin Cove, AK 99825
(907) 239–2204

Shearwater Lodging and Charters
P.O. Box 57
Elfin Cove, AK 99825
(907) 239–2223

HOONAH

Hoonah Lodge
P.O. Box 320
Hoonah, AK 99829
(907) 945–3636

Hubbard's Bed and Breakfast
709 Huna Court
P.O. Box 205
Hoonah, AK 99829
(907) 945–3414

Tina's Room Rentals
P.O. Box 234
Hoonah, AK 99829
(907) 945–3442

HYDER

Grand View Inn
27 Hyder Ave.
Hyder, AK 99923
(604) 636–9174

Sealaska Inn
Premier and Nevada Sts.
Hyder, AK 99923
(604) 636–2486

KAKE

New Town Inn
P.O. Box 222
Kake, AK 99820
(907) 785–3472

Nuggett Inn
P.O. Box 516
Kake, AK 99830
(907) 785–6469

METLAKATLA

Metlakatla Hotel and Suites
P.O. Box 670
Metlakatla, AK 99926
(907) 886–3456

PELICAN
(Also see Wilderness/Fly-In Fishing Lodges)

Rose's Bar and Grill
P.O. Box 754
Pelican, AK 99832
(907) 735–2265

PRINCE OF WALES ISLAND
(Also see Wilderness/Fly-In Fishing Lodges)

Bucareli Bay Bed and Breakfast
P.O. Box 473
Craig, AK 99921
(907) 826–2951

Columbine Inn
P.O. Box 155
Klawock, AK 99825
(907) 755–2287

Fireweed Lodge
P.O. Box 116
Klawock, AK 99825
(907) 755–2930

Haida–Way Lodge
P.O. Box 90
Craig, AK 99921
(907) 826–3268

Klawock Bay Inn
P.O. Box 137
Klawock, AK 99825
(907) 755–2929

Log Cabin Resort and R.V. Park
P.O. Box 54
Klawock, AK 99925
(907) 755–2205
(800) 544–2205

McFarland's Floatel
P.O. Box 19149
Thorne Bay, AK 99919
(907) 828–3335

Prince of Wales Lodge
P.O. Box 72
Klawock, AK 99925
(907) 755–2227

Ruth Ann's Motel
P.O. Box 145
Craig, AK 99921
(907) 826–3378

Southeast Retreat
P.O. Box 476
Thorne Bay, AK 99919
(907) 755–2994

Tenakee Springs

Snyder Mercantile
P.O. Box 505
Tenakee Springs, AK 99841
(907) 736-2205

Tenakee Hot Springs Lodge
P.O. Box 3
Tenakee Springs, AK 99841
(907) 736-2400/2245
(Fishing packages available)

Glacier Bay/Gustavus

Country Inns

These establishments operate on the American Plan: Daily rates include lodging and three full meals.

Annie Mae Lodge
P.O. Box 80
Gustavus, AK 99826
(907) 697-2346

Glacier Bay Country Inn
P.O. Box 5
Gustavus, AK 99826
(907) 697-2288
Winter: P.O. Box 2557
           St. George, UT 84771
           (801) 673-8480

Gustavus Inn
P.O. Box 60
Gustavus, AK 99826
(907) 697-2254
Winter: 7920 Outlook
           Prairie Village, KS 66208
           (913) 649-5220

Lodges

Alaska Seair Adventures
P.O. Box 299
Gustavus, AK 99826
(907) 697-2215

Fairweather Lodge and Adventures
P.O. Box 148
Gustavus, AK 99826
(907) 697-2334

Glacier Bay Lodge
76 Egan Dr., Suite 130
Juneau, AK 99801
(907) 463-5510
(800) 451-5952
Winter: 520 Pike St., Suite 1610
           Seattle, WA 98101
           (800) 451-5952

Bed and Breakfasts

A Puffin's Bed and Breakfast
P.O. Box 3
Gustavus, AK 99826
(907) 697-2260
(800) 478-2258

Good Riverbed & Breakfast
P.O. Box 37
Gustavus, AK 99826
(907) 607-2241

Salmon River Cabins
P.O. Box 13
Gustavus, AK 99826
(907) 697-2245

Tri Bed & Breakfast
P.O. Box 214
Gustavus, AK 99826
(907) 697-2425

Whalesong Lodge
P.O. Box 5
Gustavus, AK 99826
(907) 697–2288
Winter: P.O. Box 2557
      St. George, UT 84771
      (801) 673–8480

WILDERNESS/ FLY-IN FISHING LODGES

Most wilderness and fly-in sport-fishing lodges offer multiday packages that include lodging, all meals, equipment, and guided fishing or other activities. When comparing rates, check whether or not the package includes round-trip floatplane transportation, and how many full days of guided fishing or other activities are included. The sample rates listed below are based on double occupancy. Most lodges offer a selection of packages—write for details and current prices.

ADMIRALTY ISLAND

Pybus Point Lodge
1873 Shell Simmons Rd.
Juneau, AK 99801
(907) 790–4866
$1,800 per person 3 days/3 nights

Thayer Lake Lodge
P.O. Box 211614
Auke Bay, AK 99821
(907) 789–5646; 225–3343
$150 per person per night (full meals)
$105 per cabin per night (housekeeping rate; cook your own meals)

CHICHAGOF ISLAND: ELFIN COVE

The Cove Lodge
P.O. Box 33160
Juneau, AK 99803-3160
(907) 239–2221; 790–2626
(800) 382–3847
$1,950 per person 6 nights/5 days
(Bed & breakfast rate: $70–$90/day)

Cross Sound Lodge
P.O. Box 85
Elfin Cove, AK 99825
(800) 323–5346
$2,400 per person 5 nights/6 days
Winter: 15917 NE Union Rd.,
      Suite 115
      Ridgefield, WA 98642

Eagle Charters
P.O. Box 69
Elfin Cove, AK 99825
(907) 239–2244
$2,200 per person 5 nights/6 days
Winter: 4200 NE 60th St.
      Vancouver,WA 98661

Elfin Cove Lodge
P.O. Box 44
Elfin Cove, AK 99825
(907) 239–2212; (800) 422–2824
$2,392 per person 4 nights/4 days
Winter: P.O. Box 4007
      Renton, WA 98057
      (206) 813–0600

Tanaku Lodge
P.O. Box 49
Elfin Cove, AK 99825
(907) 239–2205
$2,195 per person 5 nights/6 days
Winter: 1060 Old Salem Rd., N.E.
      Albany, OR 97321
      (503) 928–4868

CHICHAGOF ISLAND: PELICAN

Lisianski Lodge
P.O. Box 776
Pelican, AK 99832
(907) 735–2266
$110–$130 per person per day (includes lodging and three meals; guided fishing and other activites extra)

HAINES VICINITY

Chilkat Wilderness Lodge
P.O. Box 881
Haines, AK 99827
(907) 766–2665/2349
$200 per person per day
$510 per person 2 nights/3 days

KETCHIKAN VICINITY

Yes Bay Lodge/Mink Bay Lodge
P.O. Box 8660
Ketchikan, AK 99901
(907) 225–3875
(800) 999–0784
$1,790 per person 4 nights/3 days

PRINCE OF WALES ISLAND

Boardwalk Wilderness Lodge
P.O. Box 6440
Ketchikan, AK 99901
(907) 828–3918
(800) 327–9382
$2,075 per person 3 nights/4 days

Sportsman's Cove Lodge
P.O. Box 2486
Olympia, WA 98507-2486
(206) 956–3333
(800) 962–7889
$1,299 per person 2 nights/3 days

Waterfall Resort
P.O. Box 6440
Ketchikan 99901
(907) 225–9461
(800) 544–5125
$2,275 per person 3 nights/4 days

SITKA VICINITY

Rainforest Retreat
P.O. Box 8005
Port Alexander, AK 99836
(907) 568–2229
$80 per person per day
(includes meals and lodging; reduced rates for families and extended stays)

Annual Celebrations, Festivals, and Special Events

JANUARY
· **Alcan 200 Snow Machine Race**, Haines.

FEBRUARY
· **Festival of the North**, Ketchikan. Month-long arts, music, and drama festival.
· **Tent City Winter Festival**, Wrangell (First weekend in February). Food and craft fair and contests celebrating gold rush days.
· **Devil's Thumb Days**, Petersburg. Winter carnival.
· **Winterfest**, Juneau. Outdoor events and family activities.

MARCH
· **First City Folk Festival**, Ketchikan (two days). Acoustic and folk music by local musicians and guest artists.
· **Coffman Cove Salmon Derby** (March through July).

APRIL
· **Prince of Wales Island Trade Show**, Craig (two days). Local merchants demonstrating wares and services; food booths and prizes.
· **Craig/Klawock Salmon Derby** (April through June).

· **Thorne Bay Salmon Derby** (April through July).
· **Alaska Folk Festival**, Juneau. Week-long series of free concerts and workshops with Alaska folk musicians.
· **Alaska State Community Theatre Festival**, Haines (odd-numbered years). Juried theater productions from Alaskan communities.
· **Windfest, Skagway** (third weekend in April). Dances, chili cook-off, other festivities.
· **Buckwheat Ski Classic**, Skagway. Amateur and professional Nordic ski races.

MAY
· **Mayfest.** Month-long schedule of special events and activities taking place throughout Southeast Alaska.
· **King Salmon Derby**, Ketchikan (Memorial Day weekend and two following weekends).
· **King Salmon Derby**, Wrangell.
· **Little Norway Festival**, Petersburg (third weekend of May). Folk dances, contests, Norwegian food celebrating Norwegian Independence Day.
· **Salmon Derby,** Petersburg (Memorial Day weekend).
· **Sitka Salmon Derby** (continues in June).

· **Juneau Jazz & Classics Festival.** Ten-day schedule of performances and workshops by visiting national artists.

JUNE

· **Sitka Summer Music Festival,** Sitka (three weeks). Chamber music performances by visiting national artists.

· **Sitka Symposium on Human Values and the Written Word,** Sitka. Guest writers and lecturers.

· **All-Alaska Logging Championships,** Sitka (last weekend of June).

· **International Days,** Hyder (June 30–July 4). Joint Independence Day celebration with Stewart, British Columbia.

JULY

· **Independence Day celebrations,** communities throughout Southeast Alaska.

· **Logging Carnival,** Ketchikan (July 4). Competitive logging events.

· **Prince of Wales Island Fair and Logging Show,** Thorne Bay (late July).

· **Loggers' Rodeo,** Wrangell (July 4). Competitive logging events.

· **Dalton Trail Days,** Haines (July 1–4). Joint celebration with Haines Junction.

AUGUST

· **Blueberry Festival,** Ketchikan. Summer street fair.

· **Great Alaska Sportfishing Championship,** Ketchikan. One-day fish-off among disk jockeys from the Lower 48.

· **Golden North Salmon Derby,** Juneau (three days).

· **Southeast Alaska State Fair,** Haines (second or third week of August). Five-day regional fair with exhibits and events.

· **Master Anglers Tournament,** Haines.

· **Garden Club Flower Show and Competition,** Skagway (third weekend in August).

SEPTEMBER

· **Klondike Trail of '98 Road Relay,** Skagway. Ten-person relay teams running from Skagway to Whitehorse.

OCTOBER

· **Octoberfest,** Petersburg. Arts and crafts fair.

· **Alaska Day Festival,** Sitka (around October 18). Five-day celebration of Alaska Purchase, featuring costume ball, parade, reenactment of transfer ceremonies.

NOVEMBER

· **Winter Arts Faire,** Ketchikan (Saturday after Thanksgiving).

· **Holiday Fest,** Sitka (November through January). Various holiday festivities including Russian Christmas and Starring.

· **Juneau Public Market** (Thanksgiving weekend). Mega arts, crafts, and merchandising fair.

DECEMBER

· **Annual Art Walk and Wearable Art Show,** Ketchikan.

· **Gallery Walk,** Juneau. Evening gallery showcase and Christmas festivities.

Information Sources

GENERAL

Alaska Bed & Breakfast
  Association
369 South Franklin St.
Suite 200
Juneau, AK 99801
·(907) 586–2959

Alaska Department of Fish and
  Game
Public Communications Section
P.O. Box 25526
Juneau, AK 99802-5526
(907) 465–4112

Alaska Marine Highway System
Reservations and Information
P.O. Box 25535
Juneau, AK 99802-5535
(907) 465–3941 or (800) 642–0066
From WA: (800) 585–8445
From Canada: (800) 665–6414
TDD/VOICE: (800) 764–3779

Bellingham
Terminal: (206) 676–8445
Recorded schedule information:
(206) 676–0212

Haines
Terminal: (907) 766–2111/2112
Recorded schedule information:
(907) 766–2113

Juneau
Terminal: (907) 789–7453
Recorded schedule information:
(907) 465–3940

Ketchikan
Terminal: (907) 225–6182/6183
Recorded schedule information:
(907) 225-6181

Petersburg
Terminal: (907) 772–3855/3856
Recorded schedule information:
(907) 772–3855

Prince Rupert, British Columbia
Terminal: (604) 627–1744/1745
Recorded schedule information:
(604) 627–1744/1745

Sitka
Terminal: (907) 747–8737
Recorded schedule information:
(907) 747–3300

Skagway
Terminal: (907) 983–2941/
  2942/2943
Recorded schedule information:
(907) 983–2229

Wrangell
Terminal: (907) 874–2021
Recorded schedule information:
(907) 874–3711

Alaska Pass
P.O. Box 351
Vashon, WA 98070-0351
(206) 463–6550 or (800) 248–7598

Alaska State Division of Tourism
P.O. Box 110801
Juneau, AK 99811-0801
(907) 465–2010

Southeast Alaska Tourism Council
P.O. Box 20710
Juneau, AK 99802-0710
(907) 586–4777

U.S. Forest Service
(Tongass National Forest and
cabin information)
Centennial Hall
101 Egan Drive
Juneau, AK 99801
(907) 586–8751

White Pass & Yukon Route
P.O. Box 435
Skagway, AK 99840
(907) 983–2217 or (800) 343–7373
From Northwest Canada: (800)
478–7373

LOCAL VISITORS' BUREAUS

Gustavus Visitors Association
P.O. Box 167
Gustavus, AK 99826
(907) 697–2358/2260

Haines Visitors' Bureau
P.O. Box 518
Haines, AK 99827
(907) 766–2234 or (800) 458–3579

Hyder Community Association
P.O. Box 149
Hyder, AK 99923
(604) 636–9148

Juneau Convention and
  Visitors' Bureau
134 Third Street
Juneau, AK 99801
(907) 586–2201

Ketchikan Visitors' Bureau
131 Front Street
Ketchikan, AK 99901
(907) 225–6166 or (800) 770–2200

Petersburg Visitor Center
P.O. Box 649
Petersburg, AK 99833
(907) 772–3646

Prince of Wales Chamber of
  Commerce
P.O. Box 497
Craig, AK 99921
(907) 826–3870

Prince Rupert Convention and
  Visitors' Bureau
P.O. Box 669
Prince Rupert, BC
Canada V8J 3Sl
(604) 624–5637

Sitka Convention and Visitors'
  Bureau
P.O. Box 1226
Sitka, AK 99835
(907) 747–5940

Skagway Convention and
  Visitors' Bureau
P.O. Box 415
Skagway, AK 99840
(907) 983–2854

Wrangell Chamber of Commerce/
  Visitors' Bureau
P.O. Box 49
Wrangell, AK 99929
(907) 874–3901

NATIONAL PARKS

Admiralty National
Monument/Kootznawoo
  Wilderness
8461 Old Dairy Road
Juneau, AK 99801
(907) 586–8790

Glacier Bay National Park
  and Preserve
P.O. Box 140
Gustavus, AK 99826
(907) 697–2230

Klondike Gold Rush National
  Historical Park
P.O. Box 517
Skagway, AK 99840
(907) 983–2921

Misty Fiords National Monument
3031 Tongass Avenue
Ketchikan, AK 99901
(907) 225–2148

Sitka National Historical Park
P.O. Box 738
Sitka, AK 99835
(907) 747–6281

Suggested Reading

PLANNING YOUR TRIP

The Milepost: All-the-North Travel Guide. Anchorage/Seattle: Alaska Northwest Books [annual].

Miller, Mike and Marilyn. *Camping Alaska and Canada's Yukon.* Old Saybrook, CT: The Globe Pequot Press, 1989.

Searby, Ellen. *Alaska's Inside Passage Traveler.* Occidental: Windham Bay Press [annual].

HISTORY

De Armond, R. N., ed. *Early Visitors to Southeastern Alaska: Nine Accounts.* Anchorage: Alaska Northwest Publishing Company, 1978.

Muir, John. *Travels in Alaska.* Boston: Houghton Mifflin Company, 1979.

NATIVE ART AND CULTURE

Garfield, Viola E., and Forrest, Lynn A. *The Wolf and the Raven: Totem Poles of Southeastern Alaska,* 2nd ed. Seattle and London: University of Washington Press, 1961.

Holm, Bill. *Northwest Coast Indian Art: An Analysis of Form.* Seattle and London: University of Washington Press, 1965.

Stewart, Hilary. *Indian Fishing: Early Methods on the Northwest Coast.* Seattle and London: University of Washington Press, 1977.

Stewart, Hilary. *Looking at Indian Art of the Northwest Coast.* Seattle and London: University of Washington Press, 1979.

THE OUTDOORS

Armstrong, Robert H. *Guide to the Birds of Alaska* (revised edition). Anchorage/Seattle: Alaska Northwest Books, 1990.

Connor, Cathy, and Daniel O'Haire. *Roadside Geology of Alaska.* Missoula, MT: Mountain Press Publishing Company, 1988.

O'Claire, Rita, with Robert Armstrong and Richard Carstensen. *The Nature of Southeast Alaska: A Guide to Plants, Animals, and Habitats.* Anchorage/Seattle: Alaska Northwest Books, 1992.

Piggott, Margaret H. *Discover Southeast Alaska with Pack and Paddle.* Seattle: The Mountaineers, 1990.

Washburne, Randel. *The Coastal Kayaker: Kayak Camping on the Alaska and B.C. Coast.* Old Saybrook, CT: The Globe Pequot Press, 1983.

White, Helen A., ed. *The Alaska-Yukon Wild Flowers Guide.* Anchorage: Alaska Northwest Publishing Company, 1974.

COMMERCIAL FISHING

Caldwell, Francis E. *Pacific Troller: Life on the Northwest Fishing Grounds.* Anchorage: Alaska Northwest Publishing Company, 1978.

Upton, Joe. *Alaska Blues: A Fisherman's Journal.* Anchorage: Alaska Northwest Publishing Company, 1977.

Index

About the Author

Sarah Eppenbach moved to Juneau from her native California in 1971. She has written about Alaska and other places for such publications as *Alaska Airlines Magazine*, *Travel & Leisure*, and *Travel–Holiday*. She is the author of the text portion of *Southeast Alaska*, a contemporary portrait of the Inside Passage by photographer Nancy Simmerman (Graphic Arts Center Publishing Company). In *Alaska's Southeast: Touring the Inside Passage* she shares her interest in the people, history, and landscape of the part of Alaska she knows the best.